SHAKESPEARE ANI

EARLY MODERN LITERATURE IN HISTORY

General Editor: Cedric C. Brown
Professor of English and Head of Department, University of Reading

Within the period 1520–1740 this series discusses many kinds of
writing, both within and outside the established canon. The
volumes may employ different theoretical perspectives, but they
share an historical awareness and an interest in seeing their texts
in lively negotiation with their own and successive cultures.

Titles include:

Anna R. Beer
SIR WALTER RALEGH AND HIS READERS IN THE
SEVENTEENTH CENTURY: Speaking to the People

Cedric C. Brown and Arthur F. Marotti (*editors*)
TEXTS AND CULTURAL CHANGE IN EARLY MODERN
ENGLAND

Ronald Knowles (*editor*)
SHAKESPEARE AND CARNIVAL: After Bakhtin

James Loxley
ROYALISM AND POETRY IN THE ENGLISH CIVIL WARS:
The Drawn Sword

Mark Thornton Burnett
MASTERS AND SERVANTS IN ENGLISH RENAISSANCE
DRAMA AND CULTURE: Authority and Obedience

The series Early Modern Literature in History is published
in association with the Renaissance Texts Research Centre
at the University of Reading.

Shakespeare and Carnival

After Bakhtin

Edited by

Ronald Knowles

First published in Great Britain 1998 by
MACMILLAN PRESS LTD
Houndmills, Basingstoke, Hampshire RG21 6XS and London
Companies and representatives throughout the world

A catalogue record for this book is available from the British Library.

ISBN 0–333–71141–6 hardcover
ISBN 0–333–71142–4 paperback

 First published in the United States of America 1998 by
ST. MARTIN'S PRESS, INC.,
Scholarly and Reference Division,
175 Fifth Avenue, New York, N.Y. 10010

ISBN 0–312–21277–1

Library of Congress Cataloging-in-Publication Data
Shakespeare and carnival : after Bakhtin / edited by Ronald Knowles.
p.   cm. — (Early modern literature in history)
Includes bibliographical references (p.   ) and index.
Contents: A short report and not otherwise / Stephen Longstaffe —
Carnival and death in Romeo and Juliet / Ronald Knowles — The
carnivalesque in A midsummer night's dream / David Wiles —
Shakespeare's battle of carnival and Lent / François Laroque —
Facing Puritanism / Kristen Poole — The evacuation of Falstaff (The
merry wives of Windsor) / Jonathan Hall —Towards a theory of play
and the carnivalesque in Hamlet / Phyllis Gorfain — Shakespeare's
carnival and the sacred, Measure for measure and The winter's tale /
Anthony Gash — Swimming on bladders : the dialogics of reformation
in Shakespeare & Fletcher's Henry VIII / Gordon McMullan.
ISBN 0–312–21277–1
1. Shakespeare, William, 1564–1616—Knowledge—Manners and
customs.   2. Carnival in literature.   3. Literature and history–
–England—History—16th century.   4. Literature and history–
–England—History—17th century.   5. Bakhtin, M. M. (Mikhail
Mikhaïlovich), 1895–1975.   I. Knowles, Ronald, 1940–
II. Series.
PR3069.C37S53 1998
822.3'3—dc21   97–32204
                                                              CIP

This book is printed on paper suitable for recycling and made from fully managed and sustained forest
sources.

10   9   8   7   6   5   4   3   2   1
07   06   05   04   03   02   01   00   99   98

Printed and bound in Great Britain by Antony Rowe Ltd, Chippenham, Wiltshire

Contents

Contents

Acknowledgements

The editors of the following journals are thanked for permission to republish here: *Shakespeare Survey* for Ronald Knowles's essay which originally appeared as 'Carnival and Death in *Romeo and Juliet*: a Bakhtinian Reading'; *Shakespeare Quarterly* for Kristen Poole's essay which first appeared as a longer version entitled, 'Saints Alive! Falstaff, Martin Marprelate and the Staging of Puritanism'; *Hamlet Studies* for Phyllis Gorfain's 'Towards a Theory of Play and the Carnivalesque in *Hamlet*'. D.S. Brewer are thanked for permission to reproduce passages from David Wiles' *Shakespeare's Almanac: A Midsummer Night's Dream, Marriage and the Elizabethan Calendar* (1993). Permission to reproduce a detail from Bruegel's 'The Triumph of Death' is by courtesy of the Museo Prado, Madrid; the Bibliothèque publique et universitaire, Geneva, is thanked for permission to publish an illustration from 'Danse aux aveugles' (Ms. fr. 182, f. 198r).

The editor would like to thank Cheryl Foote for her word-processing skills, alacrity and patience.

Notes on Contributors

Anthony Gash lectures in the School of English and American Studies at the University of East Anglia, where he is Chair of the Drama Sector and, in 1993, founded the MA programme in Theatre Directing. He has also been a visiting lecturer at the Royal Academy of Dramatic Art. Publications include: *Word and Image in the Theatre* (1988); 'Carnival against Lent: the Ambivalence of Medieval Drama', in David Aers (ed.), *Medieval Literature, Criticism, Ideology and History* (1986); 'Carnival and the Poetics of Reversal', in Julian Hilton (ed.), *New Directions in Theatre* (1993). He is currently writing *The Substance of Shadows: Shakespeare's Dialogue with Plato* for Routledge.

Phyllis Gorfain is Professor of English and Chair of the Women's Studies Programme at Oberlin College in Oberlin, Ohio. She has written several articles on topics combining folklore studies and Shakespeare, with an emphasis on play, riddles and ritual. She is also a folklorist who has done fieldwork in Africa and written articles on folklore and ethnographic topics among the Mbeere of central Kenya. Her current work centres on issues of gender and metaphor, textual questions, ritual and performance in *Measure for Measure* and *Much Ado About Nothing*.

Jonathan Hall is an Honorary Research Fellow at the Bakhtin Centre, University of Sheffield. His research interests include the theories of the Bakhtin school in relation to psychoanalysis, discourse and power, and the history or histories of subject formation. These interests are developed in his book: *Anxious Pleasures: Shakespearean Comedy and the Nation State* (1995) and a number of articles. He has lectured widely in the field of comparative literature, literary and cultural theory, and film, and has organized and participated in numerous conferences. He is currently working on a book on literature and psychosis within the process of modernization in Western culture.

Ronald Knowles, the editor of this volume, is Senior Lecturer in English at the University of Reading. He has written widely on

Harold Pinter, and is Associate Editor in Britain of *The Pinter Review: Annual Essays*. Recent books include *1 & 2 Henry IV*. 'The Critics Debate' (1992); *Understanding Harold Pinter* (1995); *Gulliver's Travels. The Politics of Satire* (1996). He is currently editing *2 Henry VI* for the Arden Shakespeare.

François Laroque is Professor of English Renaissance Studies at the University of Sorbonne Nouvelle (Paris III). He is the author of *Shakespeare's Festive World* (1991) and *Court, Crowd and Playhouse* (1993). Recently, he has edited a *History of English Literature, 1550–1996* (1997) and Marlowe's *Doctor Faustus* (1997).

Stephen Longstaffe lectures in English literature at the University College of St. Martin, Lancaster. He has published articles on Marlowe, Shakespeare's histories and Elizabethan drama. He is currently writing a book-length study of the politics of the English history play.

Gordon McMullan is a lecturer in English at King's College, London. His publications include *The Politics of Unease in the Plays of John Fletcher* (1994), and a collection of essays, *The Politics of Tragicomedy: Shakespeare and After* (1992), edited with Jonathan Hope. He has a further collection of essays, *Renaissance Configurations: Voices/Bodies/Spaces, 1580–1690* (1998), and is currently completing a new edition of Shakespeare and Fletcher's *Henry VIII* for the Arden Shakespeare.

Kristen Poole is an assistant professor in the English Department at the University of Delaware. She has published articles in *Shakespeare Quarterley* and *Studies in English Literature*. She is currently working on a book project entitled *Deforming Reformation: The Grotesque Puritan and Social Transformation in Early Modern England*.

David Wiles is a Reader in Drama at Royal Holloway College, University of London. His publications include *The Early Plays of Robin Hood* (1981), *Shakespeare's Clown: Actor and Text in the Elizabethan Playhouse* (1987) and *Shakespeare's Almanac: A Midsummer Night's Dream, Marriage and the Elizabethan Calendar* (1993). He also writes on classical theatre and his most recent work is *Tragedy in Athens: Performance Space and Theatrical Meaning* (1997).

1

Introduction

Ronald Knowles

This book, the first devoted to Shakespeare and Mikhail Bakhtin's ideas of the carnivalesque, derives from the Reading Literature and History Conference of 1995. Within the large structure of that conference, contributors were invited to submit papers to a separate wing entitled 'Shakespeare, Carnival and Society'. Included here are essays by Anthony Gash, Ronald Knowles, François Laroque, Stephen Longstaffe and Gordon McMullan which derive ultimately from that event. Others, some of whom were unable to attend the conference, were later commissioned to contribute to the project. The essays by Jonathan Hall, Kristen Poole, Phyllis Gorfain and David Wiles add considerably to the diversity and depth of the volume as a whole.

Within the topic 'Shakespeare, Carnival and Society', contributors to the conference and the book were encouraged to take any approach they wished. This is now reflected in the range of the collection, which varies from such topics as a Bakhtinian reinterpretation (Knowles) and calendrical iconology (Laroque) to a reinvestigation of the religious and philosophical roots of Bakhtin's thought (Gash) and a critique of Bakhtin's methodology (Wiles). The collection offers an assessment of the interpretative possibilities of the carnivalesque in Shakespeare 'after Bakhtin's' celebrated study *Rabelais and His World*[1] and indicates the further critical and theoretical directions which may be developed by scholars and students alike (see Gorfain on carnival and modern theories of play). At the same time, according with the identity of the series of books in which it appears, this collection offers several ways of historicizing, or re-historicizing Bakhtinian theory.

Although, as might be expected in a volume on the carnivalesque, there is a concentration in this collection on the plays of the 1590s, both comedies and English histories, it also extends its deliberations to tragedy – Knowles writes on death in *Romeo and Juliet*, and Gorfain on play and metacommunication in *Hamlet* – and to some late plays – *The Winter's Tale* and the Shakespeare/Fletcher collaboration, *Henry VIII*. Bakhtin's ideas, also, are located in many different ways, with regard to the cultural traditions of Shakespearean theatre and to the ideological and political contexts of Bakhtinian thought. Yet within the range of playtexts and argumentative standpoints represented in these essays, some strong lines of continuity have emerged. It is not surprising, perhaps, that several essays touch on popular festive practices or interrogate how Bakhtin's ideas translate to the player–audience exchanges of live theatre; more surprising is a repeated concern with the almost satiric representation of Puritanism and Reformation, so that we have a series of grotesque comic bodies from Cade, through Falstaff (bulking large in the middle of the volume) to Wolsey. Some convergences suggest that, in the great awareness of political and cultural discourses in late twentieth-century scholarly writing, the ideas of Bakhtin can still elicit major re-evaluative lines of enquiry in the study of Shakespeare.

Space does not permit here an extensive overview of Bakhtin's work, and many of his key concepts are examined, in any case, in the essays themselves. Since the postwar rediscovery of Bakhtin in Russia and his eventual fame in the West, there are now many studies, both introductory and specialist, including a biography.[2] This sketch is provided for the reader who is interested in Shakespeare and festive culture but is new to the Russian thinker; while the reader already familiar with Bakhtin's work can turn directly to the essays themselves, each of which may be read independently and is self-contained.

Mikhail Mikhailovich Bakhtin was born in 1895 and died in 1975. The son of a bank manager, he grew up in Vilnius and then Odessa, eventually gaining a degree in classics and philology at the University of Petrograd in 1918. As a schoolteacher in Nevel in western Russia, Bakhtin managed to evade the harsh realities of civil war in the capital. In 1924 he moved back to Leningrad after a formative intellectual period in Vitebsk, where he shaped his early ideas along with the thought of such figures as Valentin Voloshinov and Pavel Medvedev. Poor health and poor Marxism made employment difficult and the latter led to his arrest in 1929 for alleged association with underground members of the Russian Orthodox Church. He was sentenced to internal exile in

Kazakhstan. Nevertheless, Bakhtin continued thinking and writing. Obscurity as a teacher in the Mordovia State Teachers College in Saransk probably saved him from Stalin's purges. Rediscovery during the 1950s reversed Bakhtin's situation and he is now well known, because of the heterogeneity of his work, to theorists of literature, anthropologists, linguists and cultural historians generally. Bakhtin was a great believer in the pluralism of thought and culture, and what he called 'unfinalizability' – the open-endedness of things – as if all forms of life were part of a huge, ongoing 'dialogue', another key concept. In contrast to the systematizers he disliked, such as the Russian Formalists, Marxists and followers of Saussurean linguistics, this may seem attractive, but it makes schematic reduction of his ideas rather difficult, not to say risky. However, Bakhtin's career may be divided into five periods.[3] From 1919 to 1924 Bakhtin was concerned with the interrelationship of ethics, cognition and aesthetics but in terms of acts not words, as he wished to avoid the autotelic formalism of his contemporaries. In the second period, 1924 to 1930, he worked on *Problems of Dostoevsky's Creative Art*, which was later revised and published in English as *Problems of Dostoevsky's Poetics*.[4] Here Bakhtin confirmed the primacy of the written or spoken *utterance* of dialogic discourse over that of the synchronic system of Saussurean linguistics. The dialogic discourse of Dostoevsky's polyphonic novel is contrasted with Tolstoyan monologism. Dostoevsky's dialogues were open-ended, characters were allowed equal utterance in their own right as against the monological author as the all-controlling spokesman of unilateral authority and truth. To use Morson and Emerson's term, Bakhtin's creation of a 'prosaics' through study of Dostoevsky led, in the 1930s, the third period, to a series of extensive essays on the novel, which were put together eventually as *The Dialogic Imagination*.[5] Most important was the concept of the 'chronotope' (*chronos*, time; *topos*, place), the interrelatedness of space and time in 'Forms of Time and of the Chronotope in the Novel', from Greek romance to Rabelais.

Fourthly, having considered Dostoevsky's representation of the city as deriving from a carnivalesque sense of life,[6] and having pondered on the Rabelaisian chronotope,[7] Bakhtin worked on a large-scale work, which he intended to submit for a doctorate and which was published in the west as *Rabelais and His World*. Ostensibly Bakhtin's project was to reveal the origins of *Gargantua and Pantagruel* in the popular culture of medieval and Renaissance carnival. The dialogism of Dostoevsky was related to the heteroglossia of the marketplace and town square in the chronotope of carnival.[8] Heteroglossia is the English word for a Russian term that Bakhtin coined – *raznorecie*, literally 'multispeechedness'.[9] For Bakhtin the reality of language lay not in the abstract norms of theoretical linguistics but out there, in the endless multiplicity and richness of actual speech, of dialect and idiolect, of slang and swearing, of trade and profession, of the street and the dining room, of court and country, of past and present, of both literature and life, all subject to the everchanging contexts of society and history from the slogan of the day to the expression of an epoch. Furthermore, there is speech within speech, as if every single utterance, spoken or written, echoed its past contexts, situations and meanings – the historical dynamics of connotation in constant struggle with the opposing force of monologism, as Bakhtin witnessed in the USSR under Stalin. Carnival opposes all that is Stalinist: the dialogical voice of unofficial culture in the people resisted the theological monologism of the Catholic Church (and tyrannical communism); the grotesque body was celebrated, not condemned as sinful (or sanitized by canons of Soviet realism); collective laughter in broad daylight defeats eschatological terror (and laughter as sinful in Russia);[10] vitalist primitivism replaces the ascetic and life-denying culture of celibate prelacy. The utopian freedom of permanent becoming transcends the prison house of dogma and Gulag of dissent.[11]

The chief studies of Bakhtin's fifth period are found in *Speech Genres and Other Late Essays*,[12] which offer a recapitulation after a reappraisal of the early work. As the title suggests, they reaffirm the centrality of the social and historical ramifications of utterance.

Rabelais and His World is a huge work and, as its critics point out, it suffers from repetition within and between most of the lengthy chapters on laughter, language, festive forms, banquet imagery, the grotesque body and its 'material lower stratum'. However, the substantial Introduction offers a valuable survey of all that follows, and Bakhtin's chief ideas are brought out there before fuller elaboration. At the heart of Bakhtin's idea of carnival are the antinomies of life and death, or rather the resolution of any such antinomy in the cyclic renewal of life which subsumes death into the larger constant of regenerative becoming made manifest in the seasons and human gestation. (Dialogism is the fecund impregnation of language, monologism a cadaver.)

Hence the importance of the festive feast or banquet linking natural harvest and bodily sustenance in the organic cycle of time. Carnival always celebrates renewal. One often quoted passage says so much that it is timely to reproduce it here. It is where Bakhtin develops the concepts of 'degradation' and 'grotesque realism':

Degradation and debasement of the higher do not have a formal and relative character in grotesque realism. 'Upward' and 'downward' have here an absolute and strictly topographical meaning. 'Downward' is earth, 'upward' is heaven. Earth is an element that devours, swallows up (the grave, the womb) and at the same time an element of birth, of renascence (the maternal breasts). Such is the meaning of 'upward' and 'downward' in their cosmic aspect, while in their purely bodily aspect, which is not clearly distinct from the cosmic, the upper part is the face or the head and the lower part is the genital organs, the belly, and the buttocks. These absolute topographical connotations are used by grotesque realism, including medieval parody. Degradation here means coming down to earth, the contact with earth as an element that swallows up and gives birth at the same time. To degrade is to bury, to sow, and to kill simultaneously, in order to bring forth something more and better. To degrade also means to concern oneself with the lower stratum of the body, the life of the belly and the reproductive organs; it therefore relates to acts of defecation and copulation, conception, pregnancy, and birth. Degradation digs a bodily grave for a new birth; it has not only a destructive, negative aspect, but also a regenerating one. To degrade an object does not imply merely hurling it into the void of nonexistence, into absolute destruction, but to hurl it down to the reproductive lower stratum, the zone in which conception and a new birth take place. Grotesque realism knows no other lower level; it is the fruitful earth and the womb. It is always conceiving.

(p. 21)

Grotesque realism celebrates the grotesque body occluded by the aesthetics of neoclassical beauty, the body with genitals and orifices, a body of organic processes rather than the self-contained body of proportional beauty. Think of the contrast between the sweaty bodies of a living carnival crowd as against the single, static marble statue elevated by a pedestal.

Carnival turns the world upside down. Hierarchies are reversed and suspended. Clothes are worn back to front. Comic crownings and uncrownings take place. Fools become kings, lords of misrule preside, boy bishops are elected, and so on. Bawdy is the outspoken language of the lower body, and sacred parody dethrones the hieratic. Carnival folk-laughter is egalitarian, and derision, not death, is the great leveller.

It is not difficult to criticize Bakhtin's views. The utopian and idealized representation of the *volk* is apparent. The binary division into official/unnofficial, low/high, dialogic/monologic echoes the principles of structuralism which Bakhtin was sceptical of and resisted. There is evidence to show that various levels of medieval society took part in carnival.[13] Violence was endemic to carnival, but it is largely overlooked by Bakhtin.[14] For all the historical materials adduced Bakhtin never stops to examine closely one particular carnival, as Le Roy Ladurie was to do in his equally famous *Carnival at Romans* (1981). Richard M. Berrong has devoted a whole book to Bakhtin's view of Rabelais.[15] Generally speaking he shows that what Bakhtin says is largely true of *Pantagruel* but much less so of *Gargantua*, where the carnivalesque elements are largely silenced as Rabelais tempered the low as he moved from a popular to a more refined humanist taste. Though Bakhtin does not ignore Rabelais' humanism, he considerably plays down the Erasmian tradition of learned wit as part of Renaissance humanist culture.[16] (See Anthony Gash's essay.)

These are not petty cavils, but Bakhtin's work on carnival remains for many reasons a powerful, exuberant and challenging work which continually attracts new readers. However one feels about the view of Rabelais, Bakhtin's writing on parody and the medieval world would be invaluable in itself. Further, his lifelong fascination with the Menippean or Lucianic mode of writing which reappears in *Rabelais and His World* has arguably done more than any other writing to redirect literary scholars and cultural historians to a neglected field of study. Again, throughout the book Bakhtin makes apparent the wide-ranging ramifications of carnival, the carnivalesque and carnivalization in the whole of western history, from the actual carnivals of the medieval world to the attenuated forms that survive in capitalist society.[17]

Bakhtin, it should be said, did not create the study of festivity and carnival. In English literary studies particularly such figures as Northrop Frye and C.L. Barber have been hugely influential since the 1950s.[18] But both offered a fundamentally conservative approach, whereas Bakhtin's radical analysis brings out the deeply ideological significance of such phenomena in a way that has been claimed by Marxist, anarchist and humanist.[19] Yet such pigeon-holes seem so confining. When I first picked up *Rabelais and His World* and read the chapter on laughter it took me back many years to my first experience of hearing Carl Orff's *Carmina Burana* – the joyful discovery of a whole new vibrant world. More pointedly, Bakhtin's insistence on the cultural ambivalence and perseverance of carnival images began a reconsideration of Shakespeare which consequently stimulated the idea for this volume.

Shakespeare is mentioned in passing many times in *Rabelais and His World*. Only once does Bakhtin stop and make further comment, but most suggestively:

> The analysis we have applied to Rabelais would also help us to discover the essential carnival element in the organization of Shakespeare's drama. This does not merely concern the secondary, clownish motives of his plays. The logic of crownings and uncrownings, in direct or in indirect form, organizes the serious elements also. And first of all this 'belief in the possibility of a complete exit from the present order of this life' determines Shakespeare's fearless, sober (yet not cynical) realism and absence of dogmatism. This pathos of radical changes and renewals is the essence of Shakespeare's world consciousness. It made him see the great epoch-making changes taking place around him and yet recognize their limitations.
>
> Shakespeare's drama has many outward carnivalesque aspects: images of the material bodily lower stratum, of ambivalent obscenities, and of popular banquet scenes.
>
> (p. 275)

In the Dostoevsky book Bakhtin names Shakespeare as one of the sources of a carnivalized vision of life along with such figures as Boccaccio, Rabelais and Cervantes. He elaborates, but with a particular emphasis:

> We are speaking here not of the influence of individual themes, ideas, or images, but rather of the deeper influence of *a carnival sense of the world itself*, that is, the influence of the very *forms* for visualizing the world and man, and that truly *godlike freedom* in

approaching them which is manifest not in the individual
thoughts, images, and external devices of construction, but in
these writers' work as a *whole*.

(pp. 157–8)

Earlier, in discussion of Dostoevsky as creator of the polyphonic
novel, Bakhtin acknowledges his contemporary A.V. Lunacharsky's
comparable view and quotes extensively his supporting view of
Shakespeare as a predecessor in this respect, '"Shakespeare is polyphonic to the extreme"'. To an extent Bakhtin agrees: 'Lunacharsky
is correct in the sense that certain elements, embryonic rudiments,
early buddings of polyphony can indeed be detected in the dramas
of Shakespeare' (p. 33). This is immediately qualified: 'but to speak
of a fully formed and deliberate polyphonic quality in
Shakespeare's dramas is in our opinion simply impossible.' And
then he gives his reasons:

> First, drama is by its very nature alien to genuine polyphony;
> drama may be multi-levelled, but it cannot contain *multiple worlds*;
> it permits only one, and not several, systems of management.
>   Secondly, if one can speak at all of a plurality of fully valid
> voices in Shakespeare, then it would only apply to the entire
> body of his work and not to individual plays. In essence each
> play contains only one fully valid voice, the voice of the hero,
> while polyphony presumes a plurality of fully valid voices
> within the limits of a single work – for only then may polyphonic
> principles be applied to the construction of the whole.
>   Thirdly, the voices in Shakespeare are not points of view on
> the world to the degree they are in Dostoevsky; Shakespearean
> characters are not ideologists in the full sense of the word.

(p. 34)

So it appears that Shakespeare is carnivalesque, but not polyphonic. Yet both concepts are linked by Bakhtin's overarching idea
of dialogism which parallels his other term, heteroglossia. From an
empirical point of view it would be quite impossible to find any
Shakespearean play with just 'one fully valid voice', the hero's, or
otherwise – think of the problems this would create with a work
like *1 Henry IV*. But the larger issue is raised by Bakhtin's first
objection: that drama in its very nature cannot be polyphonic. The
oddest thing of all is that the opposite seems self-evident.[20] This is a

well-known bias in Bakhtin's thinking, which at times can be rather inconsistent. Bakhtin's admiration for the dialogized prose of the Dostoevskian novel sometimes led him to extreme positions. He believed that the multi-voiced aspect of truly dialogized discourse is actually lessened by the act of speaking: 'loud and living intonation excessively monologizes discourse and cannot do justice to the other person's voice present in it' (*Dostoevsky*, p. 198). This will depend, surely, on the play and the actor, and can hardly be a *necessary* principle. An apt remark of Falstaff's comes to mind: 'I have a whole school of tongues in this belly of mine' (*2 Henry VI* 4.3.18) – some of which are re-examined by Kristen Poole in this volume. Bakhtin offers a generalization: 'In drama the world must be made from a single piece. Any weakening of this monolithic quality leads to a weakening of dramatic effect. The characters come together dialogically in the unified field of vision of author, director, and audience, against the clearly defined background of a single-tiered world' (p. 17). If everything is reversed then you have a statement which would be most appropriate for the *Henry IV*s.

It is commonly considered that when talking of drama Bakhtin principally has classical tragedy in mind, for example in his early 1920s essay 'Author and Hero in Aesthetic Activity', where the hero is seen as the bearer of the dramatist's tragic view of life, weighed down by the monologism of fate and form, as in Aristotle's account in the *Poetics*.[21] He saw the heroes of Racine in a comparable way: 'Racine's hero is all objective existence, stable and fixed, like plastic sculpture' (*Dostoevsky*, p. 51). Yet in a brief aside he can refer to such playwrights as Hauptmann and Ibsen and 'the whole of Naturalist drama' as becoming 'novelized',[22] presumably in contrast to the dominant conventions of 'The Well Made Play', as Marvin Carlson speculates.[23] To take a Brechtian view one could argue that Bakhtin's ideas on drama are in part formed in reaction to the eighteenth- and nineteenth-century elevation of Greek tragedy by German aesthetics to a monolith of official culture. The revision and clarification of Bakhtin's views are indicated in a footnote he added to *The Dialogic Imagination* (p. 405, n. 62). Considering that 'Dramatic dialogue is determined by a collision between individuals who exist within the limits of a single world and a single unitary language', he adds, 'We are speaking, to be sure, of pure classical dramas as expressing the ideal extreme of the genre. Contemporary realistic social drama may, of course, be heteroglot and multi-languaged.' It seems quite extraordinary that Bakhtin rarely mentions that most polyphonic of all modern dramatists, his compatriot Anton Chekhov, upon whose death he delivered a commemorative address.[24]

Monologism characterizes the literature sponsored by a hierarchic society, but forms of comedy within that society, from Aristophanes to the Tudor interludes, foster what Bakhtin calls in *The Dialogic Imagination* 'the internal dialogic essence of language itself' (p. 405). Even within something as monologistic as the medieval mystery cycles dramatizing the grounds of salvation in a biblical story, the carnivalesque dialogized voice is heard.[25] When emergent capitalism shakes the old hierarchies, the prescriptive ethics and aesthetics of neoclassical decorum, which demarcate the chronotopes of class, voice and humour, begin to break down and new hybrids emerge both in drama and prose, including Shakespeare's plays. In a late article entitled 'Response to a Question from the *Novy Mir* Editorial Staff' Bakhtin fully reinstated Shakespeare. As Ilkka Joki puts it:

> here he is willing to admit that Shakespeare was Rabelais' equal, if not his superior, in the transmission of dialogized heteroglossia based on the demotic. In his article Bakhtin draws attention to the 'semantic treasures' 'hidden in the language' of Shakespeare, above all 'in the strata of the popular language that before Shakespeare's time had not entered literature, in the diverse genres and forms of speech communication in ... primary carnival forms ... that were shaped through millenia ...'[26]

It is to be deeply regretted that Bakhtin did not write one of his lengthy essays on Shakespeare, perhaps pursuing his arresting remark that 'after Shakespeare, everything in drama becomes trivial'.[27] But from another point of view, Bakhtin knew that in the life of art 'the work and the world represented in it enter the real world and enrich it, and the real world enters the work and its world as part of the process of its creation, as well as part of its subsequent life, in a continual renewing of the work through the creative perception of listeners and readers'.[28] In the hope of carnivalesque affirmation and renewal this volume offers Shakespeare 'after' Bakhtin.

NOTES

1. Bloomington: Indiana University Press, 1984. Page references are to
    this edition (translated by Hélène Iswolsky and originally published
    by the Massachusetts Institute of Technology, 1968).
2. For a biographical survey of the life and work, to which all Bakhtin
    scholars are indebted, see Katerina Clark and Michael Holquist,
    Mikhail Bakhtin (Cambridge, Mass., and London: Harvard University
    Press, 1984). Simon Dentith, *Bakhtinian Thought. An Introductory
    Reader* (London and New York: Routledge, 1995) does an excellent
    job. Michael Holquist's *Dialogism. Bakhtin and His World* (London
    and New York: Routledge, 1990) is an authoritative account.
    K. Hirschkop and D. Shepherd (eds.) offer collected essays on *Bakhtin
    and Cultural Theory* (Manchester: Manchester University Press, 1989).
    Mikhail Bakhtin. Creation of a Prosaics (Stanford: Stanford University
    Press, 1990) by Gary Saul Morson and Caryl Emerson is the most
    extensive study to date and includes a 30-page index which makes it
    very convenient to follow up Bakhtin's various ideas. But Morson
    and Emerson's qualified presentation of carnival, however, has led to
    some debate, see n.18 below.
3. This account is indebted to Morson and Emerson, pp. 64–77.
4. The authoritative translation is by Caryl Emerson (Minneapolis and
    London: University of Minnesota Press, 1984). This is Bakhtin's
    revised version of 1963. The original Russian edition was published
    in 1929. Cited hereafter as *Dostoevsky*.
5. Austin: University of Texas Press, 1981. In addition to the chrono-
    tope essay, 'Epic and Novel', 'From the Prehistory of Novelistic
    Discourse', and 'Discourse in the Novel' are included.
6. See especially pp. 160–1.
7. 'The Folkloric Bases of the Rabelaisian Chronotope', *The Dialogic
    Imagination*, pp. 206–24.
8. See Viacheslav V. Ivanov, 'The Dominant of Bakhtin's Philosophy:
    Dialogue and Carnival', in David Shepherd (ed.), *Bakhtin, Carnival
    and Other Subjects* (*Critical Studies* vol. 3, no. 2–vol. 4, no. 1/2.
    Amsterdam and Atlanta, GA: Rodopi, 1993), pp. 3–12.
9. See Dentith, *Bakhtinian Thought*, p. 35.
10. Considerable insight on this subject is provided by Sergei
    S. Averintsev, 'Bakhtin and the Russian Attitude to Laughter', in
    Bakhtin, Carnival and Other Subjects (see n. 8), pp. 13–19.
11. See Michael Gardiner, 'Bakhtin's Carnival: Utopia as Critique', in
    Bakhtin, Carnival and Other Subjects (see n. 8), pp. 20–47.
12. Austin: University of Texas Press, 1986. For Bakhtin's individual
    essays and their collection and publication in Russian and English,
    see Morson and Emerson, pp. xvii–xx.
13. See Berrong, n. 15 below, pp. 1–17.
14. See Peter Stallybrass and Allon White, *The Politics and Poetics of
    Transgression* (London: Methuen, 1986), Introduction pp. 1–26, which
    has an excellent discussion of the strengths and weaknesses of the

Bakhtinian carnivalesque, with extensive bibliographical reference to literary theory, social anthropology and cultural studies.

15. Richard M. Berrong, *Rabelais and Bakhtin. Popular Culture in 'Gargantua and Pantagruel'* (Lincoln and London: University of Nebraska Press, 1986).

16. D.W. Jefferson's seminal article still remains useful, see '*Tristram Shandy* and the Tradition of Learned Wit', *Essays in Criticism* I (1951), pp. 225–48.

17. See Ronald Knowles, 'Bunburying with Bakhtin: a Carnivalesque Reading of *The Importance of Being Earnest'*, *Essays in Poetics* 20 (1995), pp. 170–81.

18. A very helpful detailed overview of the influence of Frye and Barber is provided by Wayne A. Rebhorn, 'After Frye: A review-article on the interpretation of Shakespearean comedy and romance', *Texas Studies in Language and Literature* vol. 24, no. 4 (1979), pp. 553–82. This may be supplemented and brought up to date by consulting Annabel Patterson's account – 'Bottoms Up: Festive Theory', in *Shakespeare and the Popular Voice* (Oxford: Blackwell, 1989), pp. 57–70.

19. See Anthony Wall and Clive Thomson, 'Cleaning Up Bakhtin's Carnival Act', *Diacritics* 23 (1993), pp. 47–70.

20. As Marvin Carlson agrees, see 'Theater and Dialogism', in Janelle G. Reinelt and Joseph R. Roach, *Critical Theory and Performance* (Ann Arbor: The University of Michigan Press, 1992), pp. 313–23.

21. See *Art and Answerability. Early Philosophical Essays by M.M. Bakhtin*, edited by Michael Holquist and Vadim Liapunov (Austin: University of Texas Press, 1990), p. 226.

22. *The Dialogic Imagination*, p. 5.

23. See n. 19, p. 19.

24. Clark and Holquist, *Mikhail Bakhtin*, p. 42.

25. *Rabelais*, p. 15. See Anthony Gash, 'Carnival against Lent: The Ambivalence of Medieval Drama', in David Aers (ed.), *Medieval Literature: Criticism, Ideology, and History* (New York: St. Martin's Press, 1986), pp. 74–98: Kristina Simeonova, 'The Aesthetic Function of the Carnivalesque in Medieval English Drama', in *Bakhtin, Carnival and Other Subjects* (see n. 8), pp. 70–9.

26. The *Novy Mir* article is found in *Speech Genres*. Ilkka Joki's major contribution to and development of a Bakhtinian interpretation of theatre is *Mamet, Bakhtin, and the Dramatic. The Demotic as a Variable of Addressivity* (Åbo: Åbo Akademi University Press, 1993). My introduction is indebted to his discussion, pp. 58–66. A general study that has become recognized as a seminal work is Michael Bristol's *Carnival and Theater: Plebeian Culture and the Structure of Authority in Renaissance England* (New York and London: Methuen, 1985).

27. *Speech Genres*, p. 171, n. 11.

28. *The Dialogic Imagination*, p. 254.

2

'A short report and not otherwise': Jack Cade in 2 *Henry VI*

Stephen Longstaffe

Thomas Hobbes was no Bakhtinian. In *Leviathan* he asserts that 'during the time men live without a common Power to keep them all in awe, they are in that condition which is called Warre', as 'the nature of war, consisteth not in actuall fighting'. In terms strangely reminiscent in places of Bakhtin's carnival, he defines this liminal time thus:

> when men live without other security, than what their own strength, and their own invention shall furnish them withall ... there is no place for Industry and consequently no Culture of the Earth, no Navigation ... no commodious Building ... no Knowledge of the face of the Earth; no account of Time; no Arts; no Letters; no Society; and which is worst of all, continuall feare, and danger of violent death; And the life of man, solitary, poore, nasty, brutish, and short.[1]

Where Hobbes sees 'no' culture, or even society, without a centripetal power ('awe'), Bakhtin, writing from a centripetal regime, finds in a carnival without 'awe' a 'second life of the people'. He theorizes language itself as inescapably contestatory, continually constituted through interaction between different kinds of utterance, each aware of its other and in an implicit dialogue with it, through his concepts of dialogism and social heteroglossia. I will argue that Bakhtinian concepts can be employed to enable a reading of the 'Jack Cade' scenes of Shakespeare's 2 *Henry VI*, which addresses their articulation of social criticism, their use of grotesque laughter, their stagings of danger and their possible closure.[2] Drama in Bakhtin's writings is often a negative example of the monological, either demonstrating a lack of the dialogic qualities he identifies as characteristic of the modern novel, or as carnival's Other.[3] Undaunted, recent critics take issue with his sometimes sweeping dismissals of drama, paradoxically providing the theoretical groundwork for re-reading drama on Bakhtinian lines. Tzvetan Todorov points out that the dialogic qualities Bakhtin confidently assigns to the novel are actually 'properties of discourse' rather than of a particular genre, and concludes that Bakhtin's description of the novel genre (and thus of genre in general) is 'not very coherent, and ultimately irrational'.[4] Graham Pechey suggests that the 'actor-narrators' of Brecht's epic theatre dialogize speech and gesture, and that the Brechtian epic's dialogic critique of illusionism 'jogs the memory of drama as to bring about a return to the carnivalesque'. He further suggests that drama 'is perhaps not so much monological in essence as *monologized* by being read as "literature" rather than theatre'.[5] Robert Cunliffe questions Bakhtin's assumption that drama positions its audience as passive voyeurs, spectators at a monologic performance rather than dialogic participants. He concludes that 'the great advantage of Bakhtin' is his refusal, when considering the carnivalesque, to analyse drama solely on the level of the world represented on stage: 'he analyses drama as a "lived situation" and not as a read text, and ... he is particularly attentive to the body, to space, and to non-cognitive processes of "decoding" events.'[6] Ilkka Joki's study of David Mamet focuses more closely on the dialogicality of the represented world in drama, stressing that even within this world whilst 'we cannot reduce dialogicality to a mere exchange of utterances ... dialogue and conversational discourse are obviously major elements in dialogicality.'[7] In other words, Cunliffe and Pechey suggest that Bakhtin may be used to read the action of performance, Joki the performed action, in so far as they can be considered separately.[8]

Bakhtin's work on the comic has already been productively deployed to read early modern drama. Manfred Pfister credits Bakhtin with challenging the dominant post-Aristotelian view of the comic in which laughter is punitive, 'one of society's ways of affirming its norms and stabilizing the consensus on which it is founded', with a comic 'celebrating transgression and the levelling and inversions wrought on established hierarchies'.[9] For Pfister, the pioneering work of Frye, Barber and Weimann on comic transgression and inversion does not recognize, as Bakhtin's conception of carnival and the carnivalesque does, its political, even revolutionary, aspects. This conception has been powerfully dismissed for its nostalgia, its idealization and its insistence on 'the immaculate innocence of laughter'.[10] But Michael Gardiner argues that Bakhtin's carnival is a 'critical Utopia' rather than a 'blueprint Utopia'.[11] It is not an image of a future ideal society; rather, it is critically oriented towards the present and a '"making strange" of hegemonic genres, ideologies, and symbols'; its nonsense elements recognize the impossibility of conceptualizing a revolutionary alternative in the present situation. In Jonathan Dollimore's terms, it presupposes but does not ratify 'real life'.[12] Understood in this sense, it is a useful starting point for a consideration of the Cade scenes' transgressive comic-critical agenda and actions.

With their emphasis on festivity, parody and ideological as well as physical conflict, these scenes are clearly amenable to a Bakhtinian reading.[13] But even though the West's discovery of Bakhtin has contributed to a profound shift in the way critics write about early modern festivity, rebellion and inversion, much recent writing on 2 *Henry VI*, whilst registering the presence of heteroglossia and the carnivalesque in these scenes, reaches the same conclusions as 'pre-Bakhtinian' (or 'Hobbesist') critics of the play. For earlier critics, these discursive and physical challenges were clearly placed as 'disorder'.[14] For E.M.W. Tillyard in 1944, the rising had three functions: 'to forward York's plot, to extend the scope of the action to all sections of the community, and to offer the impious spectacle of the proper order reversed.'[15] Tillyard's brief statement set the agenda for most criticism of the rising for thirty-odd years, and his first two points still meet with general agreement, though a significant number of critics dissent from the view that the Cade scenes merely present an 'impious spectacle'. To borrow Barber's terminology, whilst recent critics are more positive than earlier generations about at least some of the 'release' elements in these scenes, it is common to insist that they move towards a monological 'clarification' of the ridiculous danger of empowered commoners. At best, some elements, such as the social criticism voiced, are allowed a certain power to resist this clarification.

The essential question to address is suggestively formulated in Bakhtin's development of the term 'parodic stylization'. He points out that in this kind of representation, 'the intentions of the representing discourse are at odds with the intentions of the represented discourse', the aim being 'to destroy the represented language'. In the context of *2 Henry VI*, the rising's festive and levelling operations are shown in order to discredit them. But Bakhtin warns that for parodic stylization to 'be authentic and productive' rather than 'gross and superficial' it 'must re-create the parodied language as an authentic whole, giving it its due as a language possessing its own internal logic and one capable of revealing its own world inextricably bound up with the parodied language.'[16] Parody functions within, and by its nature has to faithfully represent, heteroglossia, for the object of the parody 'becomes the arena of conflict between two voices ... [which are] ... not only detached and distanced, they are hostilely counterposed.'[17] Gary Saul Morson points out that for a parody to succeed it must not only 'target' an 'original utterance' to which it is antithetical, but that 'the fact that it is intended by its author to have a higher semantic authority than the original must be clear.'[18] A modified version of this concept, 'ventriloquism', has recently (and influentially) been deployed in Annabel Patterson's work on Shakespeare. Just as in parodic stylization an 'authentic whole' must be presented, in ventriloquizing 'the ventriloquist must himself utter, in order to refute them, ethical and pathetic claims whose force may linger beyond his powers of persuasion.'[19] Ventriloquism is an apt term in this context; its literal meaning is 'belly talk', and *Coriolanus* demonstrates effectively how understanding belly talk is a function of the listener's position in relation to (for example) the politics of scarcity and dispossession. Indeed, 'ventriloquism' in this context is an arresting example of a Bakhtinian internally dialogized sign: it signifies speech that seems to come from the seat of reason, the head, but also comes from the seat of appetite, the belly.

Attempting parodic stylization, of course, does not ensure that the parodied utterance is clearly put in its place through the parodic utterance, just as the success of the 'refutation' posited by Patterson must be rigorously assessed. Recent writers, however, tend to agree that in the Cade scenes the parodic stylization of historical commons action is a success, for two main reasons. The parvenu players, and their writer, are often seen to distance themselves from the rising (and therefore from the contemporary social protest it evokes) through emphasizing its destructiveness, with the implication that Cade and the others would have been seen by a metropolitan audience as a threat, and thus their actions and agenda repudiated. Much of the destruction caused or proposed, after all, is in London.[20] So Shakespeare's portrayal of Cade, Richard Wilson argues, not only represents Shakespeare's own 'revulsion from the *vox populi* and the stinking breath he insists goes with it', but also a calculated bid for exemption from a ban on playing in force in 1592.[21]

The other element contributing to the success of these scenes as parodic stylization is mockery. Richard Helgerson sees Cade himself as a particular target: 'Cade's appearance, his social pretension, his manner of speaking, his reforming ideas, his arbitrary brutality are all made to seem ridiculous. Even his followers mock him.'[22] Phyllis Rackin characterizes this process as a dynamic interaction between emphasizing threat and ridiculing it: 'dissident sentiments are first evoked, then discredited and demonised as sources of anxiety, and finally defused in comic ridicule and brutal comic violence.'[23] The audience stops laughing with, and starts laughing at, the Kentishmen.[24] The nature of this laughter is most clearly articulated by Paola Pugliatti. When Shakespeare wrote these scenes, she asserts, 'the kind of laughter that came to his mind was not the liberating and festive laughter of the carnival tradition; it was the grim, bitter, moralistic laughter that comes from the grotesque, a laughter that proclaims some kind of disease.'[25]

It might be objected that stressing the rising's illogicality plays down its parodic logic. Ellen Caldwell and Ronald Knowles both point out, using different examples, that Cade's command that the pissing conduit run with wine parodies traditional accession celebrations, and that his displaying of enemies' heads upon poles was practised by the Tudors and their predecessors.[26] Others, wishing to rescue the rising's timely articulation of social grievances from this mocking dismissal, present Cade's followers, or other unseen commoners, as 'commons-sensical' social critics. Elsewhere in the play, Annabel Patterson argues, are acceptable models for redressing abuses, as the play distinguishes 'between authoritative and specious mediation of popular goals and grievances' in its structuring around a contrast between Cade, who 'fails every test for the popular spokesman', and Salisbury.[27] Michael Hattaway contrasts Cade's radicalism, 'informed by conservatism and megalomania', with the 'alternative and populist vantage point' offered by other participants in the rising.[28] Michael Bristol, contrariwise, insists that the grievances retain their power in any circumstances, and that however much criticism identifies Cade as 'a pathetic, ludicrous and potentially vicious aberration ... the speeches of Cade and his followers constitute a powerful political and discursive indiscretion. The feelings of the characters are those of class resentment, bitterness, and a specific sense of historical inequity and injustice.'[29] Thomas Cartelli likewise detects 'a politically astute reckoning with a long list of social grievances whose inarticulate and violent expression does not invalidate their demand for resolution.'[30]

Recent critical work thus differs from the mid-century orthodoxy more in its perception of the work text or staging has to do to make the rising's reforming agenda dangerously ridiculous than in its conclusions. That contemporaries were aware of the ways texts performed such work is suggested by Sir Edmund Tilney's annotations to the manuscript of the unproduced *Sir Thomas More*. Though its textual history is complicated, it is clear that *More* remained unproduced at least partly because of its staging of Londoners rioting against the abuses of resident aliens. The play's first two acts, which deal with the 1517 'Ill May Day' riots, and their (unhistorical) quelling by the magistrate More, prompted Tilney to instruct the writers to 'leave out the insurrection wholly with the cause thereof and begin with Sir Thomas More at the mayor's sessions with a report after of his good service done ... a short report and not otherwise at your own perils.'[31] These annotations suggest that, at least during periods of especial tension, the staging of carnivalesque commons violence without adequate framing was unacceptable. Tilney's prohibition recognizes that showing More's 'good service' means a staging of the riot he allegedly stopped. The proposed solution is to report rather than stage the riot, but even then Tilney clarifies the nature of this report: it has to be 'short' *and* framed by stagings of other examples of More's 'good service'. The play, if altered according to Tilney's instructions, would open showing More acting at sessions to oppose the Lord Mayor's unjust sentence on a purse lifter, report his containment of the riot (or, as Tilney calls it, the 'insurrection'), and then show either his merciful intervention by proxy once the rioters are on the scaffold, or his playing a trick on Erasmus. Tilney's reaction is even more telling bearing in mind that when revising the play for submission to him, a clown role was created quite possibly specifically 'to discredit the actions of the rebels'.[32] His proposed alterations are clearly intended to make these scenes more monological, and provide an 'authoritative' framing perspective on the grievances ventriloquized. There is no reason to suppose that there was the same animus towards nobility or gentry in the audience of 2 *Henry VI* as Tilney feared there might be towards aliens in an audience for *More*. But, on the other hand, Tilney's intervention also suggests that we should be wary of assuming that merely showing Cade's violent actions would frighten an audience into repudiating his politics, or that his illogical speech and actions could be trusted to appear simply ridiculous.[33]

I would like to investigate further the Cade scenes by imagining how the play may be more dialogical in performance than has been allowed. The dialogism of performance, and especially the possibility of a provocative disjunction between actor and role, is currently a fruitful topic of enquiry in early modern literary studies. Gender criticism especially finds the transvestite actor a productive site for investigation. In their writings on history plays, Richard Helgerson and Phyllis Rackin point out that the spectacle of commoners playing nobles is another potentially disruptive disjunction.[34] This is pithily expressed in Helgerson's mock-paradox at the beginning of his discussion of 2 *Henry VI*: 'No one below the rank of earl appears on stage in the opening scene of *The Contention*. No one above the rank of joiner appeared on stage in the opening scene of *The Contention*. Both these statements are true.'[35] I will investigate a third (and relatively neglected) disjunction: the presence of the clown – as both 'character' and 'performer' – in the early plays of the London theatres. The consensual dating of 2 *Henry VI* to the early 1590s suggests that Cade may have been played by the clown Will Kemp.[36] David Wiles, in *Shakespeare's Clown*, analyses Kemp's persona, as represented in his account of his morris dance to Norwich in *Kemp's Nine Days' Wonder*, and in the roles he is likely to have played. Kemp does not present himself as a gentleman; though others refer to him as 'Master Kemp' he calls himself Will Kemp. He casts himself as to some extent as a 'traditional Lord of Misrule' on his progress towards Norwich.[37] Perhaps most significantly for my purposes, he refers to Thomas Deloney as 'Chronicler of the memorable liues of the 6. yeomen of the west, Jack of Newbery, the Gentle craft, & such like honest men: omitted by Stow, Hollinshead, Grafton, Hal, froysart, & the rest of those wel deseruing writers.'[38] *Jack of Newberie* (*c.* 1597) is dedicated to 'all famous Cloth-Workers in England', and presents itself as a 'pleasant and delectable Historie' which has 'raised out of the dust of forgetfulness a most famous and worthy man', John Winchcombe, a wealthy clothier in the reign of Henry VIII. As for the trade itself, 'Among all manuall Arts vsed in this Land, none is more famous for desert, or more beneficiall to the Commonwealth, than is the most necessary Art of Clothing.'[39] The first thing an audience hears about Cade, of course, is that he is a clothworker.[40]

Notwithstanding what Kemp's public relationship with the artisans of the past and their place in the chronicles may have been, a hitherto unnoticed contemporary reference in *2 Henry VI* makes it easier to imagine a clowning performance of Cade marked by dialogism. In the Folio text of *2 Henry VI*, Cade says on his entrance not only that his father is a Mortimer, and his mother a Plantagenet, but also that his wife 'came of the Lacies'. This is a topical reference to the attempts of Albrecht Laski, a Polish nobleman, to provide himself with an English ancestry in the previous decade.[41] He arrived in the country at the end of April 1583, and was received with honour by the Queen, who lent him Winchester House in Southwark to live in, and got up tournaments in his honour.[42] He was soon taken up by the court. In June, after attending the wedding of Lord Norris's daughter, he went up the Thames to Oxford on the royal barge with Sir Philip Sidney and Giordano Bruno, where he was received with fireworks and feasting, saw some plays and attended disputations on astrology.[43] 'After living in great splendour and contracting many debts', Laski left the country for Prague on 22 September, the day after Sidney's wedding, accompanied by John Dee.[44] During his stay, Laski , who was interested in the occult and had corresponded with Dee from the continent, asked Dee to investigate his links to the ancient house of Lacy. Dee's famous library contained materials on the Lacy lands in Ireland, and before long his angelic conversations assured him that Laski was going to achieve the religious union of Christians, Muslims and Jews.[45] In return for this information, Laski gave him an entrée into the court of Rudolf II.

Dee was not the only person Laski asked about his forebears. He also approached John Ferne, a young Lincolnshire lawyer, already the author of a manuscript on gentility. Ferne later considered himself so damaged by his association with Laski that in 1586 he published the genealogy he had constructed for him, showing that the Lacy line had died out two centuries before, and that its lands had passed to the crown.[46] *The Blazon of Gentrie* contains both this genealogy (*Lacyes Nobilitie*), and a heraldic tract called *The Glory of Generositie*. The openings of both books refer to Laski, 'the man,

whose greatnesse and worthiness you say, is recorded in the histories of his nation: yet his behaviour towards us, declared none of
these', according to *Lacyes Nobilitie*, while the *Glory of Generositie*
sees print 'in that I might notifie to the worlde, my integrytye and
direct behaviour unjustlye sclaundered, in the deduction of some
broken, and uncertain lynes or genalogies of **Lacies**, sometimes
Earles of **Lyncolne**, drawne by me, at the request of an honorable
personage.'[47] Clearly Ferne had been accused of concocting a false
Lacy genealogy for Laski.

So in mentioning the Lacies as if they support his claim Cade jux-
taposes his parody of York's genealogy (York's father was a
Plantagenet, his mother a Mortimer) with a reference to the preten-
sions to English nobility of an impecunious Polish noble recently
dwelling on the South Bank (200 yards, in fact, from the site of the
Rose, erected less than a year after Ferne's book came out, and where
2 Henry VI is usually thought to have been first performed). It is
commonplace to assume that Cade is seriously trying to fool his
followers into thinking he has a genuine claim to the throne. But if he
is seriously trying to do so, why does Cade associate his own fake
genealogy with a recent and presumably well-known example of an
Elizabethan fake genealogy? This undercutting topicality is recupera-
ble to a traditional account of the rising as an in-joke (or even an inn-
joke), a sneer at Cade's inability to construct a halfway believable
claim. But the alternative that I wish to explore is that Cade can be
performed as deliberately signalling at its outset that the rising is
ludic and ludicrous, carnivalesque, aware of its own contradictions,
and that Kemp as a performer could well have dialogically provided a presentation of Cade the character, in which the two senses
of the word 'clown' interacted so as to cast in doubt who was who.

The presentation of Cade lacks some of the more obvious
framing/containment theatrical strategies which could provide a
clear negative perspective on him for an audience. For example, he
is not silenced by his social superiors. He is not papistical. He is not
marked as speaking with a particular accent, though the prose of
most of his speeches is a social marker. The destruction of London
is not only not staged (perhaps a matter of technical possibility) but
lacks 'the kind of detailed commentary on undramatized action
that would have lent a great deal more judgmental fervor to [the]
representation of the episode in question.'[48] However, critics identify other aspects of the Cade scenes as working, more subtly but
just as effectively, to monologize the rising. Cade is often seen to be

isolated, though it is his followers, rather than his social superiors, who provide an authoritative (and mocking) critical perspective on him. Cade defends himself with bravado against his elite opponents, but the mockery of Dick the butcher or Smith the weaver is unanswered, and Cade in secretly criticizing himself even seems to license their perspective. The key staging point in creating this effect is the use of asides, which all modern editions of the play include.

Cade is given two solo asides.[49] The first comes in his first scene. When confronted by Stafford's brother over his descent from the Mortimers with the words 'Jack Cade, the Duke of York hath taught you this', he replies in an aside, 'He lies, for I invented it myself' (4.2.132-3). Cade is clearly keeping this invention from his followers, and therefore seriously trying to persuade them that he has a claim to the throne. In Annabel Patterson's words, he really is 'an impostor aristocrat ... hawking his false claims to the name of Mortimer by way of a romantic fiction, the tale of a noble child stolen from its cradle by a beggarwoman, and now returned to claim its inheritance.'[50] Cade's other solo aside comes at the end of Lord Say's blank verse defence of himself:

Say. Whom have I injured, that ye seek my death?
   These hands are free from guiltless blood-shedding,
   This breast from harbouring foul deceitful thoughts.
   O let me live!
Cade. [*Aside*] I feel remorse in myself with his words; but I'll bridle it: he shall die, an it be but for pleading so well for his life. – Away with him! He has a familiar under his tongue; he speaks not in God's name.

                                                                    (4.7.86–93)

Cade admits here Say's eloquence, his own pity and the unreasonable basis for Say's execution, before publicly passing sentence. For Barbara Hodgdon, this shows that 'the class rebellion reproduces systems of repressive authority in not being able to afford moral distinctions.'[51] This execution for pleading well appears as a private foible, grounded in an envious and conscious wilfulness. Again, this laying bare of his motives is kept from both his opponents and his followers.

There are also two longer passages consensually annotated with asides, both of which do much to suggest relations between Cade and his followers. One comes on his arrival in London.

Cade. So, sirs. Now go some and pull down the Savoy; others to th'
  Inns of Court; down with them all!
Dick. I have a suit unto your lordship.
Cade. Be it a lordship, thou shalt have it for that word.
Dick. Only that the laws of England may come out of your mouth.
Holland. [*Aside*] Mass, 'twill be sore law then, for he was thrust in
  the mouth with a spear, and 'tis not whole yet.
Smith. [*Aside*] Nay, John, it will be stinking law, for his breath stinks
  with eating toasted cheese.
Cade. I have thought upon it, it shall be so. Away, burn all the records
  of the realm; my mouth shall be the parliament of England.
Holland. [*Aside*] Then we are like to have biting statutes, unless his
  teeth be pulled out.
Cade. And henceforward all things shall be in common.

                                                              (4.7.1–15)

Here 'the rebel's demagogic orality is unsympathetically
opposed to the democratic written.'[52] Cade institutes himself as
lawgiver, but if he rules, the law will be sore, stink, bite; his
destruction of the law is privately dismissed by those it ostensibly
seeks to serve.[53] Whether the followers are cowed or mutinous,
they plainly are not speaking to their leader. Neither is he speaking
for them.

Cade the deceiver and the sceptical commons are most
often referred to in connection with Cade's very first scene,
where he sets out his claim to the throne in terms of virtue and
genealogy.

Cade. We John Cade, so termed of our supposed father –
Dick. Or rather of stealing a cade of herrings.
Cade. For our enemies shall fail before us, inspired with the spirit of
  putting down kings and princes – Command silence.
Dick. Silence!
Cade. My father was a Mortimer –
Dick. [*Aside*] He was an honest man, and a good bricklayer.
Cade. My mother a Plantagenet –
Dick. [*Aside*] I knew her well; she was a midwife.
Cade. My wife descended of the Lacies –
Dick. [*Aside*] She was indeed a pedlar's daughter, and sold many
  laces.
Smith [*Aside*] But now of late, not able to travel with her furred
  pack, she washes bucks here at home.

Cade. Therefore am I of an honourable house.

Dick. [*Aside*] Ay, by my faith, the field is honourable; and there was he born under a hedge, for his father had never a house but the cage.

Cade. Valiant I am.

Dick. No question of that: for I have seen him whipped three market-days together.

Cade. I fear neither sword nor fire.

Weaver [*Aside*] He need not fear the sword, for his coat is of proof.

Dick. [*Aside*] But methinks he should stand in fear of fire, being burnt i' th' hand for stealing of sheep.

Cade. Be brave then, for your captain is brave, and vows reformation.

(4.2.26–53)

Cade's claim is a parody of York's, so in presenting his grounds he sets himself up as a potential king like his mentor. Frank Albers points out that by so claiming the throne, 'he adopts and confirms his enemies' inegalitarian mode of distributing and justifying power'.[54] By doing this, Cade at the rising's opening signals that he wants power just for himself, and is using the rising to get it. This megalomania is, however, undercut by his followers' asides, which Michael Hattaway sees as providing important framing material for an audience, as 'Dick the Butcher ... witheringly exposes in his asides the contradictions of Cade's claims', though this comforting scepticism is itself undercut later as Dick joins in wholeheartedly with 'slaughtering' the rising's opponents.[55] Taken as a whole, these four segments are often used explicitly to show that Cade is a hypocrite and/or a deceiver, that he hijacks a respectable redress riot by intimidation or demagoguery, and that his followers, whilst going along with him, mock him, thus indicating the failure of the deception.[56] Even when explicit reference to these asides is not made, critical opinions of, for example, Cade's hypocrisy, clearly depend upon their implications as explored above.

This kind of duplicity, of course, is everywhere in Henry VI's court, where Suffolk and Margaret make particular use of asides clearly unheard by others on-stage, and where the treacherous Machiavel York operates. Tillyard in the 1940s identified the Cade rising as mirroring the disorder within the nation as a whole, and Cade himself as mirroring York. He is, after all, working for York, unlike his followers.[57] Recent criticism follows Tillyard, seeing the rising functioning as both subplot to, and parody of, York's own courtly disorder.[58] York 'literally replaces' Cade, entering as Iden leaves with Cade's body.[59] Phyllis Rackin goes further, seeing Cade both as an agent of York and as mouthing on Shakespeare's behalf a travesty of radical utopianism: 'Cade does not fully or finally speak for himself. As York's pawn and alter ego, he follows a scenario of York's devising, a plot laid out in soliloquy before Cade ever reaches the stage ... As Shakespeare's, he proposes a revolution so radical and so ludicrous that it discredits the just grievances it addresses.'[60] There is a double ventriloquism here; Cade is both York's creation and Shakespeare's. Within the performed action he is to be understood as a pawn in York's game of claiming the throne; but he is also to be understood as part of Shakespeare's project, outside the play, of repudiating the common and clownish. Cade speaks for (is reducible to) Shakespeare, or York.[61] Nothing could be more monologic. Cade is effectively repudiated, silenced not by his superiors, but by his equals, and by the recognition by all that he is a hypocrite using the rising for his own ends. He is mocked; he and his followers are shown as endangering the commons as well as the elite; he is an agent (and thus does not represent anyone other than York and, latterly, himself); he is motivated by hatred, envy and bloodlust.

Several aspects of this composite argument about the performed action are, however, difficult to reconcile to the action of performance if Cade is also Kemp's creature. Audiences would not see, in Kemp/Cade, a 'clown' in the sense of a ridiculous and inferior rustic, but such a clown *played* by a well-known professional clown, also of low social status, but appearing ridiculous because he *intends* to be. The figure Kemp/Cade is thus an internally dialogized one, doubling in one person the two senses of 'clown', just as York's description of Cade dancing a mock-morris places 'him' as both a country 'clown' and the 'clown' later to dance the Nine Days' Wonder. The Lacy reference, in this context, shows that Kemp/Cade is *not* seriously claiming the throne, that Kemp is not submerged in his role as the 'historical' Cade, and that 'he' is signalling a break with York's project to use him as a stalking horse for his own claim. Kemp/Cade not only inverts York's own genealogy, but adds in an obviously fake ancestor of his own.

Is Kemp as clown ridiculing Cade the historical personage?[62] In the terms of Bakhtin's work on parodic stylization, the clown (Kemp) would need to have visibly greater 'semantic authority' than the clown (Cade) for this to be so. On the face of it, semantic authority would seem to belong to the contemporary popular clown rather than the historical despoiler of London. But would it be possible in performance to distinguish 'Cade' from 'Kemp'? There is a significant continuity between the actions and speeches of Cade and clownish characteristics, so much so that Cade seems to be written in part as a clown. Can it be clear at each moment that Kemp is distanced from the distinctly Kemp-like language or behaviour of his 'character'? Notwithstanding the clarity of the Kemp persona outside the theatre, is 'Kemp' in performance a stable enough construct in the first place to be distinguishable from the character he is 'playing'? After all, the clown himself is a dialogic figure, composed of wisdom and folly, vulnerability and violence. If, as Morson suggests, the term parody only applies to 'those double-voiced texts or utterances that clearly indicate which of their conflicting voices is to be regarded as authoritative', can this then be called parody at all?[63] I suggest that the Cade/Kemp figure is closer to what Morson calls 'metaparody', in which 'each voice may be taken to be parodic of the other; readers are invited to entertain each of the resulting contradictory interpretations in potentially endless succession.'[64] In other words, 'Cade' is (as critics have pointed out) a parody of the historical Cade; this parody is then itself parodied by Kemp, and the result is not simply parody but metaparody.[65]

Seeing Kemp/Cade as breaking with York on his first appearance also makes a more Bakhtinian reading of these scenes possible, because reading the rising as primarily signifying something else, whether this be York's ambition or the disorder in the body politic, makes it difficult to see the performed action as carnivalesque. In fact, the scenes do not conform to the usual sense of sub-plot, whose functions they are often seen as performing. The scenes are not interwoven with contrasting court (or rebellion) scenes (they are interrupted only once by other action), and, as S.C. Sen Gupta points out, there is far too little of York in these scenes for them to refer back to his plans or his disorder strongly.[66] Bakhtin's carnival too is emphatically not to be experienced or theorized as a secondary version of something else. While it lasts, carnival is 'the people's second life, organized on the basis of laughter. It is a festive life.'[67] To read the rising as primarily imitating the actions of the 'main plot' is thus to read it as something other than carnivalesque, to recognize its similarity to the court action whilst effacing its difference and otherness, to read a communal, utopian, public, comic, festive process as a version of serious, pragmatic, privatized, aristocratic faction. It is an uncanny restatement of absolutist politics to read the actions of the commons solely as versions of the actions of the nobility, and thereby to set up a frame of binary oppositions which inevitably downgrades the rising. For example, if the 'main plot' features a single scheming noble, then in the 'subplot' Cade must be read as that scheming 'noble'. Much character criticism of Cade, I would suggest, is at least partly based on the necessity to find a sub-plot equivalent to York.

But Kemp/Cade does not have to be read as the isolated and ambitious figure that York is. Again, Bakhtin's carnivalesque suggests another focus. Carnival is not a matter of leader and followers, actor and spectator/commentator. Bakhtin insists that carnival does not know footlights, and is 'not a spectacle seen by the people; they live in it, and everyone participates because its very idea embraces all the people. Whilst carnival lasts, there is no other life outside it.'[68] Carnival's power is diffused amongst all the participants and its speech is 'frank and free, permitting no distance between those who come into contact with each other and liberating from norms of decency and etiquette imposed at other times'.[69] Critics see footlights operating in these scenes, and restraint of speech; but these insights both crucially depend on the presence of asides, for Cade's asides divide him from his followers and his followers' asides show that while they may be with him, an important critical impulse is kept under wraps. A properly Bakhtinian reading cannot accommodate asides.

But it does not have to. Whilst asides are clearly appropriate to the court scenes preceding the rising, Bakhtin's insistence on the place of laughter in 'the second life of the people' offers a way of reading encompassing the mocking contradictions the rising's 'asides' seem to embody. Carnivalesque laughter 'is festive; it is universal in scope; it is directed at all and everyone, including the carnival's participants; it is ambivalent, it is gay, triumphant, and at the same time, mocking, deriding. It asserts and denies, it buries and revives.'[70] A Bakhtinian reading of these scenes does not have to bracket off contradiction and critique to characters' private thoughts; it can function without 'private thoughts' at all. As Jonathan Hall points out, monologic interpretations reconstitute the contradictions of dialogism as the effect of interiority: 'monologism reconstructs the dialogism of signs as tantalizing or haunting evidence of a hidden, secret, and elusive "other" self.'[71] For a reading asserting the success of the parodic stylization in producing a monologic closure, Dick the Butcher and the rest do not *really* believe in Cade; Cade does not *really* believe in himself. The truth lies in their mocking or self-mocking asides, their privileged interiority. Bakhtin, however, insists that, for carnival, mockery is part of public celebration. To draw a distinction in these scenes between the the liberating laughter of carnival and the mocking laughter of the grotesque, as Paola Pugliatti and others have done, is to recuperate Bakhtin's radical theorization of the ambivalence of laughter to a form of binary affirmation or rejection. Rejection of the individual is affirmation of the collective for Bakhtin, for grotesque laughter mocks the individual in the knowledge that the collective will survive (as, of course, all of the Kentish commons, apart from Cade, do). It is worth remembering, too, that Kemp characteristically appeared with a group of 'clowns', and that the carnivalesque spectacle thus is doubled: it looks both like a collective historical action and the kind of clown scene that Kemp appears in.[72]

So for the first scene, imagine Kemp/Cade flanked by Dick and Smith, who address their undercutting comments to an audience, on stage or off, joining Cade's illusion-breaking parody of a claim to the throne with their own parody of supporting such a claim, which effectively establishes 'Cade' as a commoner, and the rising as predicated upon a carnivalesque doubleness, whose keynote is their ability to moralize two meanings in one word. Once this is established, 'Cade' does not have to hide his invented genealogy; in fact it is a token of the nature of the rising, always-already undercutting itself. Cade/Kemp can admit this fabrication publicly to Stafford's brother, whilst asserting that *this* genealogy is his own invention. Cade the character is not York's creature; Kemp the performer is reminding the audience of his early keynote utterance's 'extempore' and self-directed wit. Recognizing that the laws coming from Cade/Kemp's mouth will smell of cheese is just the kind of disrespectful chop logic clowns use publicly, moralizing, as before, two meanings in one word. It is also a carnivalesque appropriation of the law from its existence in writing to one in, not merely a part of the body, but a sore and smelly – in other words, *grotesque* – part of the body. The mouth, of course, is one of the clown's most important resources, as Joseph Hall's attack on clowns in his 1597 *Virgidemiarum* shows:

> … mids the silent rout
> Comes leaping in a selfe-misformed lout,

And laughs, and grins, and frames his Mimick face,
And justles straight into the princes place ...
A goodly grace to sober *Tragick Muse*,
When each base clown his clumbsie fist doth bruise,
And show his teeth in double rotten-row,
For laughter at his selfe-resembled show.[73]

Cade's toasted cheese may even be a specifically Kempian reference. Kemp's clowning is mentioned in *The Pilgrimage to Parnassus*, where Dromo, speaking to a clown, says that 'Clownes have been thrust into playes by head and shoulders, ever since Kempe could make a scurvey face', and advises him that 'if thou canst but drawe thy mouth awrye, laye thy legge over thy staffe, saw a peece of cheese asunder with thy dagger, lape up drinke on the earth, I warrant thee, theile laughe mightilie.'[74] Cade the cheese-eater with bad breath sounds rather like a theatrical clown, if not Kemp himself. For the final 'aside' Cade magnanimously recognizes Say's eloquence before pronouncing sentence publicly on behalf of all on-stage. Pleading well deserves death, for what Say considers a defence is actually exhibit A against him, both in his missing the point of the accusation and the language he employs.

In other words, the speeches of both Cade and his characters can be considered within the carnivalesque context not as primarily denoting an absence of reasonable discourse but skill with a particular kind of utterance picking up and turning the wrong side outward someone else's speech.[75] Cade and his followers are always in dialogue with another's speech, whether in replying to a specific utterance, or addressing a kind of utterance (for example, a proclamation). Their speech is frank and free, there are no footlights between them, and for a while an image of carnival power exists, one with its basis in the contradictions of carnival laughter which, Bakhtin reminds us, is directed at all and everyone, including the carnival's participants.[76]

Bakhtin's conceptions of dialogism and the carnivalesque enable a reading of these scenes which addresses the ways in which their presentation of ridiculous danger may function. Reading these scenes without asides suggests a more carnivalesque performed action, which incorporates the mockery and danger of the rising into a framework of critical release. A dialogic figure, such as Kemp/Cade, complicates the easy assumption that the parodic Cade Shakespeare provided was simply 'transmitted' to an audi-

ence, or that the carnivalesque was simply on display as a speci-
men of documented historical threat. The entry of a character
crying 'Jack Cade' just after Cade has stated it will be death for
anyone not to address him as Lord Mortimer is so ludicrously pat
as to be metadramatic; that he is 'knocked down' before he is killed
suggests a staging for comic effect. Nobles' heads on poles, the
'climax of horror' for Tillyard, is not merely a parody of the aristocratic skulls Thomas Platter saw on London Bridge in 1599.[77] It also
offers the opportunity for gruesome slapstick – getting through
doors, improvised jousting, frightening those in the expensive
seats. Violence and death can be grotesquely funny. Death as a
laughing matter may be horrific for the individual concerned; other
people's deaths need not be so, especially in a London where social
tensions were at their highest for decades and cruel sport a spectacle to rival the theatre. Ultimately it is the presence of commoners
in the audience and others on-stage willing to perform in this way
that enable such a carnivalesque spectacle to be suggested. Whether
such a performance ever took place is unknowable; but Bakhtin's
work, in its valorization of doubleness and conflict, surely performs
a service in making us less sure that it could not have done.

NOTES

1. Thomas Hobbes, *Leviathan*, ed. K. Minogue (London: Dent, 1973),
   p. 64.
2. Though the Cade scenes in Q show signs of reworking into a more
   innocently clownish text, for example losing a great deal of the
   mutual class animus in F, there is no reason to suppose that F was
   immediately reworked along these lines. In thinking about the play in
   performance, therefore, I refer to an edition based on F, which must
   have been the starting point for the actors, rather than use Q, which is
   possibly evidence of what some of them eventually made of it.
3. For example, see *The Dialogic Imagination*, ed. Michael Holquist;
   trans. Caryl Emerson and Michael Holquist (Austin: University of
   Texas Press, 1981), pp. 405–6; *Rabelais and His World*, trans. Hélène
   Iswolsky (Bloomington: Indiana University Press, 1984), p. 7;
   Problems of Dostoevsky's Poetics, ed. and trans. Caryl Emerson, with
   an introduction by Wayne C. Booth (Manchester: Manchester
   University Press, 1984), pp. 33–4.
4. Tzvetan Todorov, *Mikhail Bakhtin: The Dialogical Principle*, trans. Wlad
   Godzich (Manchester: Manchester University Press, 1984), p. 90.
5. Graham Pechey, 'On the Borders of Bakhtin: dialogisation, decolonisation', in Ken Hirschkop and David Shepherd (eds.), *Bakhtin and*

Cultural Theory (Manchester: Manchester University Press, 1989), pp. 60, 61.

6. Cunliffe, p. 67. Jonathan Hall makes a similar point about Bakhtin's theorization of the sign in *Anxious Pleasures: Shakespearean Comedy and the Nation-State* (London: Associated University Presses, 1995), p. 35.

7. Ilkka Joki, *Mamet, Bakhtin and the Dramatic: The Demotic as a Variable of Addressivity* (Åbo: Åbo University Press, 1993), p. 64.

8. These terms are from Thomas Whitaker's *Fields of Play in Modern Drama* (Princeton, NJ: Princeton University Press, 1977), as quoted in T.G. Bishop, *Shakespeare and the Theatre of Wonder* (Cambridge: Cambridge University Press, 1996), p. 178.

9. Manfred Pfister, 'Comic Subversion: A Bakhtinian view of the comic in Shakespeare', *Deutsche Shakespeare-Gesellschaft West Jahrbuch* (1987), pp. 27, 35.

10. Peter Stallybrass and Allon White, *The Politics and Poetics of Transgression* (Methuen: London, 1986), p. 19; Sergei Averintsev, 'Bakhtin and the Russian Attitude to Laughter', in David Shepherd (ed.), *Bakhtin: Carnival and Other Subjects*, p. 17.

11. Michael Gardiner, 'Bakhtin's Carnival: Utopia as critique', in David Shepherd (ed.) *Bakhtin: Carnival and Other Subjects*, p. 22. The term 'critical Utopia' is from Tom Moylan, *Demand the Impossible: Science Fiction and the Utopian Imagination* (London: Methuen, 1986).

12. Jonathan Dollimore, *Sexual Dissidence* (Oxford: Clarendon Press, 1991), p. 85.

13. The festive elements were briefly noted by C.L. Barber in *Shakespeare's Festive Comedy* (Princeton, NJ: Princeton University Press, 1959), p. 13, and more thoroughly in François Laroque, *Shakespeare's Festive World*, trans. Janet Lloyd (Cambridge: Cambridge University Press, 1991), pp. 250–1. See also Peter Stallybrass, '"Drunk with the cup of liberty": Robin Hood, the carnivalesque, and the rhetoric of violence in early modern England', in *The Violence of Representation: Literature and the History of Violence*, ed. Nancy Armstrong and Leonard Tennenhouse (London: Routledge, 1989).

14. The disorder/order binary opposition, Michael Bristol points out, is based on the unspoken assumption that 'the nation-state is the natural and necessary political form emerging from some kind of archaic disorder and consolidating itself against marginal forms of residual feudal anarchy or popular resistance'. See his *Carnival and Theater: Plebeian Culture and the Structure of Authority in Renaissance England* (London: Methuen, 1985), p. 199. A representative example of the common 'pre-Bakhtinian' position is Geoffrey Bullough, *Narrative and Dramatic Sources of Shakespeare III* (London: Routledge and Kegan Paul, 1960), pp. 95–7. For a discussion of the agenda of earlier criticism, see Richard Wilson, *Will Power* (London: Harvester Wheatsheaf, 1993), pp. 22–7. A notable exception to the tendency to assume Shakespeare hated commoners is provided by J. Palmer, who remarks that it is 'strange that those who find in Cade's barbarity an

indication of Shakespeare's horror of the mob should neglect to find in the barbarity of Queen Margaret or of my lords Clifford and York an indication of his horror of the nobility', in *Comic Characters of Shakespeare* (1945), reprinted in *Political and Comic Characters of Shakespeare* (London: Macmillan, 1961), pp. 318–19.

15. E.M.W. Tillyard, *Shakespeare's History Plays* (London: Chatto and Windus, 1944; reprinted London: Pelican, 1988), p. 189.
16. *The Dialogic Imagination*, pp. 363–4.
17. *Problems of Dostoevsky's Poetics*, p. 160.
18. Gary Saul Morson, 'Parody, History, and Metaparody', in *Rethinking Bakhtin: Extensions and Challenges*, ed. Gary Saul Morson and Caryl Emerson (Evanston, Ill: Northwestern University Press, 1989), p. 67.
19. Annabel Patterson, *Shakespeare and the Popular Voice* (Oxford: Basil Blackwell, 1989), p. 42.
20. Phyllis Rackin, *Stages of History* (London: Routledge, 1990), p. 214.
21. Wilson, p. 28; see also Richard Helgerson, *Forms of Nationhood* (Chicago: Chicago University Press, 1992), p. 213.
22. Helgerson, p. 212. See also Wilson, p. 29, and Stephen Greenblatt, *Learning to Curse: Essays in Early Modern Culture* (London: Routledge, 1990), p. 123.
23. Rackin, pp. 219–20.
24. Manfred Pfister sees this shift as linked to the 'fundamental contradiction' that in the promised Utopia, 'Jack Cade shall be king ... and even aims at dynastic legitimacy!' in 'Comic subversion', p. 36. See also Ellen Caldwell, 'Jack Cade and Shakespeare's *Henry VI, Part 2'*, *Studies in Philology* XCII:1 (1995), p. 50.
25. Paola Pugliatti, *Shakespeare the Historian* (London: Macmillan, 1996), p. 170.
26. Caldwell, pp. 54, 59, and Ronald Knowles, 'The Farce of History: Miracle, combat, and rebellion in *2 Henry VI'*, *The Yearbook of English Studies* 21 (1991), p. 185.
27. Patterson, pp. 50, 48. See also Pugliatti, p. 164.
28. Michael Hattaway (ed.), *The Second Part of King Henry VI* (Cambridge: Cambridge University Press, 1991), p. 40. All quotations are from this edition.
29. Bristol, p. 89. See also Caldwell, p. 51.
30. Thomas Cartelli, 'Jack Cade in the garden: Class consciousness and class conflict in *2 Henry VI'*, in *Enclosure Acts: Sexuality, Property and Culture in Early Modern England* ed. Richard Burt and John Michael Archer (Ithaca, NY: Cornell Univeristy Press, 1994), p. 58.
31. Antony Munday et al., *Sir Thomas More*, ed. Vittorio Gabrieli and Georgio Melchiori (Manchester: Manchester University Press, 1990), p. 17.
32. Munday et al., *Sir Thomas More*, p. 27; though if Kemp had already played Cade in the manner explored below, and was, as David Wiles suggests, the prospective clown in *More*, Tilney, alerted to the unsettling potential of the Cade scenes in performance, may have been influenced by them to censor the later play.

33. Louis Montrose points out, as have many others, that London's city fathers, in their letters to Burghley or the Privy Council, 'claim that theatrical images of vice always compel imitation, never aversion', in *The Purpose of Playing: Shakespeare and the Cultural Politics of the Elizabethan Theatre* (London: University of Chicago Press, 1996), p. 49.
34. See the chapters 'Staging exclusion', in Helgerson and 'Historical Kings/Theatrical Clowns', in Rackin.
35. Helgerson, p. 204.
36. Knowles, p. 181.
37. David Wiles, *Shakespeare's Clown: Actor and text in the Elizabethan playhouse* (Cambridge: Cambridge University Press, 1987), pp. 24–8. Richard Helgerson emphasizes much more the way Kemp's progress departs from recognized customary and holiday traditions, p. 229.
38. *Kemp's nine days' wonder*, introductory notes by J.P. Feather (London: Johnson Reprint Corporation, 1972), D3v.
39. *Jack of Newberie*, in *The Works of Thomas Deloney*, ed. Francis Oscar Mann (Oxford: Clarendon Press, 1912), pp. 2, 3.
40. For discussion of Deloney and the Elizabethan cloth industry, see Laura Stevenson, *Praise and Paradox: Merchants and Craftsmen in Elizabethan Popular Literature* (Cambridge: Cambridge University Press, 1984). Richard Wilson discusses the disruptiveness of London clothworkers and the implications for Shakespeare's Cade, pp. 31–44. Ronald Knowles offers the counter-Deloney example of John of Leiden, a tailor (p. 176).
41. A fuller version of the story is in my 'Jack Cade and the Lacies', forthcoming in *Shakespeare Quarterly*.
42. John Bossy, *Giordano Bruno and the Embassy Affair* (London: Vintage, 1992) p. 22.
43. J. Nichols (ed.), *The Progresses, and Public Processions, of Queen Elizabeth*, Vol. II (London: J. Nichols, 1788), pp. 204–6.
44. *CSP Venetian* 8, p. 92; Katherine Duncan-Jones, *Sir Philip Sidney: Courtier Poet* (London: Hamish Hamilton, 1991), p. 250.
45. *The Autobiographical Tracts of Dr John Dee*, in *Remains Historical and Literary Connected with the Palatine Counties of Lancaster and Chester* (Manchester: Charles Simms, for the Chetham Society, 1851), p. 29; Nicholas Clulee, *John Dee's Natural Philosophy: Between Science and Religion* (London: Routledge, 1988), pp. 197–9.
46. John Ferne, *Lacyes Nobilitie*, in *The Blazon of Gentrie* (London: John Windet, 1586), p. 129.
47. Ferne, *Lacyes Noblitie*, p. 5; *The Glory of Generositie*, in Ferne, *The Blazon of Gentrie*, A2v.
48. Cartelli, p. 57, who also points out (p. 55) that many of the elite characters are shown to have a strong animus against 'the abject people', and are thus shown to be partial as commentators. Michael Hattaway, in his 1991 edition of 2 *Henry VI*, points out that there is also 'no speech proclaiming that obedience to authority was enjoined upon men by St Paul, as there is in *Sir Thomas More*', p. 28.

49. For definitions of different kinds of asides, see Bernard Beckerman, *Shakespeare at the Globe 1599–1609* (New York: Macmillan, 1962), pp. 186-92.
50. Patterson, p. 49.
51. Barbara Hodgdon, *The End Crowns All: Closure and Contradiction in Shakespeare's History* (Princeton, NJ: Princeton University Press, 1991), p. 259.
52. Simon Shepherd, *Marlowe and the Politics of the Elizabethan Theatre* (Brighton: Harvester Press, 1986), p. 33.
53. Hattaway, p. 26; Pugliatti, p. 171.
54. Frank Albers, 'Utopia, Reality and Representation: the case of Jack Cade', *Shakespeare Jahrbuch* 127 (1991), p. 78; see also William Hawley, *Critical Hermeneutics and Shakespeare's History Plays* (New York: Peter Lang, 1992), p. 41.
55. Michael Hattaway, 'Rebellion, Class Consciousness, and Shakespeare's 2 *Henry VI*', *Cahiers Élisabéthains* 33 (1988), p. 18; see also Pugliatti, p. 170.
56. For one of the most extreme formulations of this position, see Derek Cohen, *The Politics of Shakespeare* (London: Macmillan, 1993), p. 60.
57. Even seeing Cade as a Misrule Lord reinforces his links with York, who is then the person who 'licenses' him.
58. See especially David Riggs, *Shakespeare's Heroical Histories* (Cambridge, Mass.: Harvard University Press), 1971, pp. 124–5.
59. Hodgdon, p. 259.
60. Rackin, p. 219.
61. This common critical position is perhaps at its most extreme in Sandra Billington's brief discussion of the play, in which Cade is discussed almost entirely in terms of what he reveals about York, in her *Mock Kings in Medieval Society and Renaissance Drama* (Oxford: Clarendon Press, 1991), pp. 143–4.
62. Knowles, p. 183.
63. Morson, p. 81.
64. Ibid.
65. Morson points out that one metaparodic genre is the rhetorical paradox, the praise of something essentially unpraiseworthy, and cites Erasmus' *Praise of Folly* as one of its most complex examples. Another is the 'meta-utopia', 'dialogues between utopia and the parody of utopia'. There are significant affinities between both genres and the Cade scenes.
66. Sen Gupta is worth quoting at length as a counter to the consensus on Cade as York's creature: 'Jack Cade is the most interesting figure in the play, but the space – almost a whole act – given to his adventures is excessive, if we regard York as the protagonist. It is true that York has had something to do with the Kentish rising, but the connexion is so thin that when he returns from Ireland, he does not mention Cade in his soliloquies, and when he gives out that one of the reasons for which he has not disbanded the army is that he wanted to fight the rebel Cade (5.1), no one contradicts the hypocritical plea, though earlier (4.1) Sir Humphrey Stafford's brother told Cade that all his pretences were taught by the Duke. It seems that by

the time Jack Cade has gained his full stature as a dramatic character, his connexion with the Duke of York's designs on the throne has been forgotten'. See *Shakespeare's Historical Plays* (Oxford: Oxford University Press, 1964), p. 70.

67. *Rabelais*, p. 8.
68. *Rabelais*, p. 7. The virtually continuous nature of the rising may again point to Kemp. David Wiles points out that the roles he identifies as Kemp's 'seem to be structured in order to allow him to rehearse his own sections of the play independently' and that 'contact with the main plot remains tangential', pp. 106, 102.
69. *Rabelais*, p. 10.
70. *Rabelais*, pp. 11–12.
71. Jonathan Hall, 'Unachievable Monologism and the Production of the Monster', in *Bakhtin: Carnival and other subjects*, p. 104.
72. Wiles, p. 106.
73. Joseph Hall, *Virgidemiarum II*, Liber 1, Satire 3, quoted in Christopher Sutcliffe, 'Kempe and Armin: the management of change', *Theatre Notebook* 50:3 (1996), p. 126.
74. *The Return to Parnassus*, ed. J.B. Leishman (London, 1949), pp. 129–30, quoted in Sutcliffe, p. 127. Q states that Cade on his entry to Iden's land 'lies down picking of herbs and eating them', perhaps a piece of comic business similar to lapping up drink from the earth.
75. This kind of language-use is a central part of Bakhtin's theorization of heteroglossia: 'As a living, socio-ideological concrete thing, as heteroglot opinion, language, for the individual consciousness, lies on the borderline between oneself and the other. The word in language is half someone else's. It becomes "one's own" only when the speaker populates it with his own intention, his own accent, when he appropriates the word, adapting it to his own semantic and expressive intention. Prior to this moment of appropriation, / the word does not exist in a neutral and impersonal language (it is not, after all, out of a dictionary that the speaker gets his words!), but rather it exists in other people's mouths, in other people's contexts, serving other people's intentions: it is from there that one must take the word, and make it one's own. And not all words for just anyone submit equally easily to this appropriation, to this seizure and transformation into private property: many words stubbornly resist, others remain alien, sound foreign in the mouth of the one who appropriated them and who now speaks them; they cannot be assimilated into his context and fall out of it; it is as if they put themselves in quotation marks against the will of the speaker' (*The Dialogic Imagination*, pp. 293–4).
76. Though there is not space to explore the issue here, Q has many features suggesting a more 'clownish' performance than F: an increase in the number of sexual references, comic confusion over whether Say is speaking French, Dutch or Italian, Cade on first-name terms with his 'followers', and the arming of the equivalents of Bevis and Holland with a 'long staffe' each rather than a sword.
77. Thomas Cartelli, *Marlowe, Shakespeare, and the Economy of Theatrical Experience* (Philadelphia: Pennsylvania University Press, 1991), p. 51.

3

Carnival and Death in
Romeo and Juliet

Ronald Knowles

As the title *Rabelais and His World* indicates, Bakhtin is primarily concerned with medieval culture, but he does offer many fascinating asides on the carnivalesque in the early modern world, and in Shakespeare particularly. 'Shakespeare's drama', he writes, 'has many outward carnivalesque aspects: images of the material body lower stratum, of ambivalent obscenities, and of popular banquet scenes.' He also suggests that 'the analysis we have applied to Rabelais would also help us to discover the essential carnival element in the organization of Shakespeare's drama. This does not merely concern the secondary clownish motives of his plays. The logic of crownings and uncrownings, in direct or indirect form, organises the serious elements also' (p. 275).

In this essay I shall argue that Shakespeare's inheritance of carnival or festive culture finds expression in *Romeo and Juliet* by means of the three Bakhtinian categories indicated above: the body, bawdy and the banquet.[1] I shall argue that the complex figure of Juliet's nurse can be seen beyond her obvious comic realism as representing something much larger, the Bakhtinian 'grotesque body' as well as 'mock' Fortune. Secondly, Capulet's 'old accustom'd feast' (1.2.20),[2] though not a public carnival, has carnivalesque elements, along with the highly structured comedy of the servants and musicians, generally. Thirdly, there are the many instances of proverbs and bawdy wit in the play. Together these three elements contribute to much of the comedy, but this comedy has a profound cultural ambivalence. The issue is ultimately not so much Carnival versus Lent, as life versus death. For Bakhtin the triumph of life is always expressed by the laughter of the people.

In most discussions of *Romeo and Juliet* Shakespeare's most radical carnivalesque innovation usually goes unacknowledged. In drama, romantic love was commonly the subject of comedy. Shakespeare challenges the worlds of myth and legend which conventionally provided tragic heroes and heroines by introducing the first romantic tragedy. Critics have indeed always recognized the preponderance of comic materials in *Romeo and Juliet* though nearly all modern productions severely cut the carefully placed comic scenes of Act 4. A carnivalesque critique of Petrarchan love in the play is found in several forms, but perhaps most tellingly in the technique of burlesque juxtaposition in scenic structure. The subjective world of idealized love is seen to resist the social world of festival and to succumb to 'star-cross'd' fate in spite of all the ministrations of an earthly Fortune which is benignly represented in the domesticated and naturalized figure of Juliet's nurse. The tragedy of Romeo and Juliet will always remain the fulcrum, but the cultural dimensions of the play reach back to the collectivity of joyous carnival on the one hand, and on the other look forward to what Bakhtin calls 'the interior infinite' (p. 44), the capitalist culture of individualism which developed out of the Middle Ages.

For Bakhtin the ideology which carnival challenged derived from the dogma of Catholicism. In *Romeo and Juliet* the ideology of romantic love is conjoined with that of the death cult of the second half of the fifteenth century which persisted into the Renaissance, particularly in painting, illustrations and emblems linking love, festivity and death, as we shall see.

Three associated ideas underpin Bakhtin's theory of carnival culture: 'the material bodily principle', 'the concept of grotesque realism' and 'the collective ancestral body' (pp. 18–19). The occasion of carnival itself makes apparent the relationship of the materialist principle with the pattern of the cyclical year in which the ecclesiastical is naturalized by seasons, in contrast to the eschatological rigours of linear time, from creation to doomsday. All these ideas are implied in the Nurse's speech in her first appearance on stage (1.3.2ff).

Juliet's nurse is a metamorphosis of Bakhtin's material bodily principle. Lower-class comic garrulity, taken from a hint in the source, always runs the risk of critical condescension – perhaps nowhere more so than in Coleridge's reference to the Nurse's 'uncultivated understanding'[3] – but the discernible carnivalesque pattern of the Nurse's references transcend critic, character and caricature. The boy-actor or actress of the Nurse should appear aged. Shakespeare made the disparity in age between Juliet and the Nurse even greater than in his source by lowering Juliet's age from 16 to 13 while following the original reference to the Nurse as an 'ancient dame'.[4] Her senility is indicated by her relative toothlessness, 'I have but four' (l.13) she says, and her physical appearance should be consonant with this.

The Nurse's first words in response to Lady Capulet's 'where's my daughter' (l.1), 'Now by my maidenhead at twelve year old/I bade her come' (ll.2–3) ironically parallel her with Juliet, who will also lose her maidenhead at thirteen in the course of the play. Youth, puberty, virginity and the onset of sexual life are evoked as part of a pattern of natural human growth. The religious imprecation 'God forbid' (l.4) follows the endearments 'What, lamb. What, ladybird' (l.3), thus aligning human and divine affection and concern in terms of the natural world. Following her first query concerning 'Lammas-tide' (l.15) the Nurse embarks on what has become known as 'the Nurse's speech', which includes two more references to 'Lammas Eve' (ll.17, 21), Juliet's birthday. These are the only references to this festival in Shakespeare's works. This, again, aligns the religious with the natural; Lammas, or loaf-mass day, with old age and birth. Lammas day is the first of August, a harvest festival at which loaves of bread made from the first ripe corn were consecrated. Harvest is often found as a metaphor or analogy for death (for example 'all flesh is grass', *Isaiah* 40.6), but here death is transformed into life in the provision of sustaining food. Ominously, Juliet is to be cut down by death before Lammas eve, pre-empting the natural harvest of her body in the fructification of marriage. Juliet is paralleled with the Nurse's daughter: 'Susan and she – God rest all Christian souls –/Were of an age' (ll.18–19). The phrase 'Well, Susan is with God' (l.19) is free from regret or sadness, and the recollection of the earthquake in the same context as Susan's death and Juliet's weaning suggests again both death and birth, disaster and generation, as natural occurrences, just as 'Shake! quoth the dovehouse' (l.33) converts danger and death to laughter and life. (The weaning is important for the iconography of the Nurse as Fortune and will be returned to shortly.) The established pattern of the naturalization of the religious, a carnivalesque inversion, is extended in the juxtaposition of 'by th' rood' (l.36), 'God be with his soul' (l.39) and 'by my holidame' (l.43) with the Nurse's recollection of her husband picking up Juliet after an accident:

> 'Yea', quoth he, 'dost thou fall upon thy face?
> Thou wilt fall backward when thou has more wit,
> Wilt thou not, Jule?'

> (ll.41–3)

A dead man is brought to life in comic anticipation of young Juliet eventually fulfilling her sexual nature, a cyclic continuity of life emphasized by the Nurse's hyperbolic vindication of the triumph of nature over time.

> The pretty wretch left crying and said 'Ay' ...
> I warrant, and I should live a thousand years
> I never should forget it.

> (ll.44, 46–7)

Remembered as a toddler, Juliet is then anticipated as a bride: 'And I might live to see thee married once' (l.61). After Lady Capulet's literary conceit on 'the volume of young Paris' face' (l.81) concluding 'By having him, making yourself no less' (l.95), the Nurse roundly adds 'No less, nay bigger. Women grow by men' (l.95), thereby completing the cyclic pattern of her speech with yet further generation. This sense of cyclic generation is continued within a festive setting when old Capulet exchanges reminiscences with his cousin at the revels, looking on the young masquers, recalling their youthful masking, weddings and birth (1.5.16–40). But as we shall see, this carnivalesque dance of life is haunted by the late medieval dance of death.

In the Nurse and Juliet we have in emergent realism a splitting of the image of the grotesque body. Bakhtin remarks that 'in the seventeenth century some forms of the grotesque began to degenerate into static "character" presentation and narrow "genrism"' (p. 52). In earlier culture the images of the 'real grotesque ... present simultaneously the two poles of becoming: that which is receding and dying, and that which is being born; they show two bodies in one.' Elsewhere Bakhtin points out terracotta figures from antiquity, of 'senile pregnant nags ... laughing ... it is pregnant death, a death that gives birth' (p. 25). As an example of an image of the duality of the body surviving but only as 'a pale reflection of its former dual nature' Bakhtin cites the suckling of a child (p. 322), and refers to Eckermann's *Conversations with Goethe* in which the German poet speculates that in a lost painting called 'The Weaning of a Child', then attributed to Correggio, 'the sacred becomes all-human' (p. 252). Unfortunately, in his consideration of *Romeo and Juliet*, this carnival inversion of Goethe's views did not extend to the Nurse and Mercutio, for 'these two figures, and what surrounds them, come in only as farcical interludes, and must be as unbearable to the minds of the lovers on the stage as they are to us'.[5] Carnival laughter, central to Bakhtin's theory, annoys Goethe as merely 'farcical interludes', but Shakespeare's mixture of comedy and tragedy may be seen as an insistent festive laughter resisting the prescriptions of neoclassicism, though to some extent compromising with genre by giving a certain kind of comedy to the lower orders. The Nurse's laughter echoes a whole culture, not simply a character from below stairs. In Bakhtin's terms, Rabelais, Cervantes and Shakespeare embodied the Renaissance conception of laughter in its 'deep philosophical meaning', affording 'one of the essential forms of truth concerning the world', when 'the world is seen anew, no less (and perhaps more) profoundly than when seen from the serious standpoint' (p. 66). In the Nurse's speech and laughter life-affirming joyousness subsumes the metaphysics of religion and death, banishes fear, and celebrates the regenerative cycle of organic being – the essence of carnival.

As the Nurse represents a certain kind of love and life which is contrasted in the play with romantic love and death, so at a conscious level, probably taking a few hints from Chaucer, Shakespeare seems to have contrasted malign fate with the Nurse as benign fortune. The Nurse, like Friar Laurence, has several functions within the play beyond the limitations of naturalist character furthering plot. In his ramified presentation Shakespeare includes both pragmatic carnivalesque and human limitation. Howard R. Patch's *The Goddess Fortuna in Medieval Literature*[6] still remains one of the best sources of information on the subject and the following references are indebted to this study. In one of the seminal works of western culture, Boethius's *The Consolation of Philosophy*, Fortune as nurse says, in Chaucer's translation, 'Whan than nature brought the foorth out of thi modir wombe, I resceyved the nakid and nedy of alle thyngs, and I norissched the with my richesses'.[7] In Renaissance iconography Fortune is consequently depicted with the right breast exposed and bearing a cornucopia.[8] Changeable Fortune laughs and cries; we have heard the

Nurse laughing and she later weeps.[9] Perhaps the most common attributes of Fortune are her fickleness and the idea of her as a strumpet. 'O Fortune, Fortune! All men call thee fickle', Juliet cries; and later in the same scene the Nurse declares, 'Romeo's a dishclout to him' (3.5.219), fickly transferring her allegiance to Paris. Earlier the Nurse approaches Romeo seeking 'some confidence', upon which Mercutio exclaims 'A bawd! A bawd! A bawd!' (2.4.126, 128). To add physical emphasis to this symbolic incrustation on realist character, Shakespeare has Juliet insist, impatient of the Nurse's return from Romeo, 'O, she is lame' (2.5.4). This echoes a detail of Chaucer's depiction of Fortune in *The Book of the Duchess*, 'she goth upryght and yet she halt'.[10] Shakespeare's suggestion is in direct contrast to the source in Brooke, where at one point the Nurse rushes home 'with spedy pace'.[11] This is made into a rather blatant joke immediately after by Juliet, who responds to the Nurse's 'Hie you to the cell' with 'Hie to high fortune! Honest Nurse, farewell' (2.5.78–9). In contrast to the comedy of the Nurse and Fortune's hobbling, Fate and death will strike with tragic haste.

However, it is in the evocation of the nurse weaning Juliet that Shakespeare most finely balances traditional iconography and dramatic character:

> When it did taste the wormwood on the nipple
> Of my dug and felt it bitter, pretty fool,
> To see it tetchy and fall out with the dug.

> (1.3.30–2)

Patch comments, 'As we thirst for her gifts, so Fortune gives us sweet and bitter to drink, by turns honey and gall'.[12] Romeo, as yet in thrall to Rosaline, invokes this commonplace: 'A madness most discreet,/A choking gall, and a preserving sweet' (1.1.190–1). It is repeated by Tybalt when restrained by Capulet at the feast: 'but this intrusion shall/Now seeming sweet, convert to bitt'rest gall' (1.5.90–1). Finally, the Nurse is linked to nature herself on whom 'divers kind/We sucking on her natural bosom find' (2.3.7–8). Like the Nurse and Fortune, nature provides honey or gall, or, in Friar Laurence's words, 'poison' or 'medicine'. The Friar's speech here (2.3.1–26) espouses a concept central to both Bakhtin's thought and Shakespeare's representation of death and carnival, and will be returned to. The Nurse's love and comedy provide a carnivalesque

contrast with romance and tragedy, but mock-Fortune is no match
for blind Cupid, blindfold Fortune and masked Death.

Bakhtin sees carnival as a cultural form of opposition, subversion
and liberation from what he terms the 'official' ideology pro-
pounded by the ecclesiastical orthodoxy of the Middle Ages,
whereas Shakespeare's use of the carnivalesque in *Romeo and Juliet*
provides a contrastive frame for the inherent values of romantic love
as it had developed in literature by the late sixteenth century into an
amalgam of courtly love, Petrarchism and neo-Platonism. Many
critics have looked at those elements variously considering them as
comic, satirical or burlesque. They have primarily looked at the first
half of the play, often without giving due weight to the later comic
scenes of the Nurse's response to Juliet's seeming 'death' and the
festive-funeral musicians (4.5). More broadly considered, comedy
can be seen to draw on the carnivalesque and to become something
of a touchstone in a cultural critique of romantic tragedy.

First, it might be said that it is difficult to understand how, if
Shakespeare had intended to present only a poignant tragedy of
ideal love, he chose to emphasize Romeo's first love, Rosaline, who
is swiftly passed over in the source. Garrick dropped all references
to her entirely. In the early exchanges between Benvolio and
Montague, Romeo is pictured as having ostracized himself for love,
and his behaviour is explained in heavily parodic Petrarchan language (1.1.116ff). Having discovered the identity of Romeo's lover
who is included in the list of Capulet's guests, Benvolio challenges
Romeo with:

> Go thither and with unattainted eye
> Compare her face with some that I shall show
> And I will make thee think thy swan a crow.

> (1.2.87–9)

Immediately on entering the Capulet festivity, with a single glance
at Juliet and without any prompting whatsoever from his friend,
Romeo confirms Benvolio's scepticism:

> So shows a snowy dove trooping with crows
> As yonder lady o'er her fellows shows ...
> Did my heart love till now? Forswear it, sight.
> For I ne'er saw true beauty till this night.

> (1.5.47–8, 51–2)

This change happens without any such externalized agency as the magic potion of love-in-idleness administered to the lovers by Puck in *A Midsummer Night's Dream.* The paradox of love as both arbitrary and absolute creates a richly comic moment which is developed in the scene and in what follows not least when Mercutio unwittingly echoes Romeo's words, 'Romeo! Humours! Madman! Passion! Lover!/... Cry but "Ay me!" Pronounce but "love" and "dove"' (2.1.7,10), and then goes on, unaware of Romeo's new love, to evoke the chaste Rosaline in comically inappropriate erotic terms. Again, Friar Laurence assumes that Romeo has been with Rosaline. This Romeo hastily denies with 'I have forgot that name, and that name's woe' (2.3.42), but his language inadvertently recalls Juliet's 'What's in a name?' (2.2.43) and their amorous wordplay on 'forgetting' (2.2.170–5). Little wonder that the Friar continues to chide:

> Is Rosaline, that thou didst love so dear,
> So soon forgotten? Young men's love then lies
> Not truly in their hearts but in their eyes.

> (2.3.62–4)

The dramatic interplay of such references serves to compromise, if not undermine, the evident partiality of a purely romantic response created by traditions of performance from Garrick to Franco Zeffirelli, in which most of the comedy was cut to emphasize romance and pathos.[13] Moreover, if we return to the Capulet festival aspects of the staging suggest a further comedic dimension.

As the young men make their way to the Capulet house visors are distributed. Most likely these would have been full-face visors, like those in *Much Ado About Nothing* (2.1), of a grotesque nature and attention is specifically drawn to this detail in Mercutio's dialogue:

> Give me a case to put my visage in:
> A visor for a visor. What care I
> What curious eye doth quote deformities?
> Here are the beetle brows shall blush for me.

> (1.4.29–32)

For Bakhtin the mask reveals 'the essence of the grotesque' (p. 40) in the carnivalesque conversion of the fearful into the funny, an analogue to carnival death in which the hideous becomes humorous. Tybalt identifies Romeo by his voice since his visage is 'cover'd with an antic face' (1.5.55); Capulet restrains Tybalt from violence; and Romeo pays court to Juliet with a quatrain which develops into a sonnet in an exchange on the Petrarchan commonplace of the lover as pilgrim worshipping at the shrine of his 'saint'. In the source 'All dyd unmaske',[14] but Shakespeare does not indicate any unmasking in an explicit stage direction. In fact the stage directions *He kisses her* at ll.105, 109 were provided by Rowe and Capell in response to the cue lines 'Thus from my lips' (l.106) and 'You kiss by th' book' (l.109). Romeo has seen Juliet's beauty, so she is not wearing a lady's half-mask. Harley Granville Barker simply assumed that 'Romeo, his mask doffed, moves towards her'.[15] This is far from certain. Although recognized by Tybalt and identified to Capulet, for Romeo to have unmasked would surely have given such provocation as to have cancelled the hospitality which initially admitted the masked revellers. But if Romeo remains masked until the kiss, it means that Juliet has instantly fallen in love with a visor and a quatrain. If Romeo unmasked at the beginning of the 'sonnet', then Juliet falls for someone she doesn't know, albeit handsome, who recites modish love verses. However it is seen, idealized romance is rather undermined in contrast with the source, which stresses that Romeo's love-lorn complexion convinces Juliet of his devotion.[16] The prologue to Act 2 may imply something less than ideal in the comment that both were 'Alike bewitched by the charm of looks' (l.6).

The Arden editor, Brian Gibbons, points out that the Act 2 scene division inaugurating the famous balcony exchange between Romeo and Juliet is traditional and convenient for reference, though in fact Romeo's first line – 'He jests at scars that never felt a wound' – rhymes with the preceding line of Benvolio, 'Go then, for 'tis in vain/To seek him here that means not to be found.' More significant, given this fluidity of the Elizabethan stage, is the fact that one of the most celebrated scenes in romantic literature begins with the grossest example of explicit bawdy in the play echoing in the audience's ears, Mercutio's

> O Romeo, that she were, O that she were
> An open-arse and thou a poperin pear!

> (2.1.37–8)

Surprisingly, Bakhtin only touches on bawdy in passing, though he recognizes that it is fundamental to the carnivalesque acceptance of life in its derisive 'degradation' of high to low: 'mockery and abuse is almost entirely bodily and grotesque. The body that figures in all the expressions of the unofficial speech of the people is the body that fecundates and is fecundated, that gives birth and is born, devours and is devoured, drinks, defecates, is sick and dying' (p. 319). Bawdy can give expression to revulsion and lead to porno- graphic hatred as in *Othello, Hamlet* and *Troilus and Cressida*. On the other hand, almost throughout *Romeo and Juliet* bawdy is used not only for structural and thematic contrast, but for something larger and more positive – the carnivalesque embrace of existence.

Bawdy reduces passion to the lower bodily stratum. It demystifies the romantic with the physical. Romantic love priva- tizes passion by subjectifying experience, and excludes life by claiming all existence. Perhaps John Donne summarizes the situ- ation most succinctly and ironically, 'She is all states, all Princes, I,/Nothing else is.'[17] The literary imagery of Petrarchan love alien- ates further with its elitist cult of suffering and isolation, and in the excesses of poets like Marino and Serafino subjectivity becomes merely a reified rococo artefact. Shakespeare sees both the comic and tragic implications of dramatizing Petrarchan conceits in con- trast with bawdy.[18] Bawdy reflects the collective levelling culture of carnival. Sex is part of life and bawdy imagery reflects not sonnet sequences but the marketplace, the tavern, the kitchen, the farm- yard, and so on – nature and society as one. However vulgar, bawdy is social in its humorous relation, person to person, in anec- dote, proverb or joke, and this is duplicated in the theatre with the collectivity of laughter.

Mercutio's vulgarism, though characteristic of his bawdy wit, here draws on folk culture in the dialect names for fruits popularly considered to resemble in shape the male and female sexual organs. Sex and fruit compound the carnival images of earth and body mutually sustaining and reproducing. From such a point of view this is not obscene but a comic affirmation shared by 'maids … when they laugh alone' (2.2.36), that is, amongst themselves. In contrast to such earthiness Romeo's romantic expostulation invokes the celestial: 'It is the east and Juliet is the sun!' (2.2.3). The incipient comedy of such contrast is increased by Juliet's seeming deafness at this point and Romeo's consequent descent into near- bathos: 'She speaks, yet she says nothing. What of that?' (1.12). Juliet's eventual interjection in what has been appropriated as one of the most celebrated of love overtures, again adding a touch of burlesque, is merely 'Ay me' (l.25), precisely fulfilling Mercutio's parodic prediction of 56 lines earlier. The staging here indicates that Juliet cannot see Romeo, who is listening – 'Shall I hear more' (l.37) – 'bescreen'd in night' (l.52), but she eventually recognizes his voice: 'Yet I know the sound' (l.59). Instead of romantic union in love, at this point the lovers are spatially, psychologically and socially separated from each other and others. Thus it is rather difficult to accept the idea of maturity accorded the thirteen-year-old Juliet in this scene. Later, awaiting fulfilment of 'amorous rites', Juliet's language of love (3.2.1–30) converts the physicality of orgasm – '... come Romeo ... when I shall die' – into the poetic transcendence of passion. Yet as we shall see, the literalness of death once more is anticipated. Here, in the balcony scene the Nurse's calling voice (ll.149, 151) is like the voice of reality, structurally placed in answer to Romeo's

> I am afeard
> Being in night, all this is but a dream,
> Too flattering sweet to be substantial.

(ll.139–41)

The social mode of bawdy is perhaps nowhere better seen in the play than in Mercutio's ribald chiding later in the act in which he effects a carnivalesque rescue of Romeo, a rescue albeit like carnival itself, only temporary. As we have seen in the alternating structure so far, after the balcony exchange Romeo has to endure Friar Laurence's sober criticism, and on entering in the following scene he faces Mercutio's welcoming witty play on his name.

> Without his roe, like a dried herring. O flesh, flesh, how art thou fishified. Now is he for the numbers that Petrarch flowed in. Laura, to his lady, was a kitchen wench – marry, she had a better love to berhyme her – Dido a dowdy, Cleopatra a gypsy, Helen and Hero hildings and harlots, Thisbe a grey eye or so ...
> (2.4.38–44)

Early in his introduction Bakhtin hints at the 'comic crownings and uncrownings' (p. 11) of carnivalesque inversion in Shakespeare and others. This is the case with Petrarch throughout the first half of *Romeo and Juliet* and here, in particular, the laureate poet is 'uncrowned'. Seizing on the anomaly of Petrarch's chaste love,

Mercutio laughs at the metamorphosis of carnival sex, 'flesh', into Lenten 'dried herring', as if this love was actually life-denying.[19] Brian Gibbons points out that the *OED* cites this passage as an illustration of 'roe' as the sperm of male fish.[20] Conversely the romantic heroines of legend and history are travestied in a mode anticipating a figure frequently referred to by Bakhtin – Scarron. Romeo responds with extensively witty word-play culminating in Mercutio's bawdy capitulation – 'I was come to the whole depth of my tale and meant to occupy the argument no longer' (ll.98–9) – which, in fact, is a victory, 'Now art thou sociable, now art thou Romeo' (l.89).

Mercutio's laughter at Petrarch's Laura as a kitchen maid has been anticipated earlier in a carefully structured scenic interpolation which is a perfect cameo of Shakespeare's carnivalesque method in *Romeo and Juliet*, and has a specifically Rabelaisian echo. This is Act 1, scene 5 where the stage directions. *'They march about the stage, and* Servingmen *come forth with napkins'* indicate the entry of Romeo's group into the Capulet household. Immediately preceding this is Romeo's speech of foreboding which recalls the tragic motif of the prologue:

> … my mind misgives
> Some consequence yet hanging in the stars
> Shall bitterly begin his fearful date
> With this night's revels, and expire the term
> Of a despised life clos'd in my breast
> By some vile forfeit of untimely death.

> (1.4.106–11)

As the servants enter a question immediately introduces a Rabelaisian note: 'Where's Potpan?' (1.5.1). Amongst the 64 cooks of book IV of *Gargantua and Pantagruel* is 'Pudding-pan' in Urquhart's translation, 'Piepan' in the modern Penguin edition.[21] Whereas Romeo has a fated assignation at the revels, the servants are arranging their high jinks below stairs.

> Away with the joint-stools, remove the court-cupboard, look to the plate. Good thou, save me a piece of marchpane, and as thou loves me, let the porter let in Susan Grindstone and Nell – Antony and Potpan!

> (1.5.6–10)

It seems unlikely that these lovers will exchange Petrarchan conceits – Susan Grindstone's carnivalesque surname says it all, alluding to motion in coition and an avid sexuality wearing out the male. Yet, as we have seen above, sex and the body are also combined with nature and sustenance in a regenerative cycle. All harvest corn will be threshed and the seed ground for flour to make bread to feed people. The servants and their girlfriends will enjoy food and sex with their own banqueting and revels while 'the longer liver take all' (1.5.15), a proverbial relegation of death, in direct contrast to Romeo's apprehension of 'some vile forfeit of untimely death' (1.4.111). Carnival death is subsumed into the social and natural cycle in which human and harvest seed ensure life, whereas Romeo and Juliet are singled out by another kind of death for extinction.

It has been argued, with some justification, that *Romeo and Juliet* in large part dramatizes the proverb *festina lente*, hasten slowly.[22] But much more central than this cautionary morality is the philosophy of nature as espoused by Friar Laurence drawing on proverbial knowledge encapsulating the carnivalesque. From this point of view the play dramatizes a dialogism between high and low cultures – between the Renaissance philosophy of love and proverbial folk wisdom, between emergent subjective individualism and communal consciousness. At the centre of the play we hear from the Friar:

> The earth that's nature's mother is her tomb:
> What is her burying grave, that is her womb;
> And from her womb children of divers kind
> We sucking on her natural bosom find.

> (2.3.5–8)

This proverbial knowledge gains particular force in English with the rhyming agnomination of 'womb' and 'tomb', a rhetorical figure at the heart of the play and a figure which both unites and divides the later middle ages and the Renaissance. In his lengthy chapter on 'The Grotesque Image of the Body' we find in Bakhtin:

> Death, the dead body, blood as a seed buried in the earth, rising for another life – this is one of the oldest and most widespread themes. A variant is death inseminating mother earth and making her bear fruit once more ... Rabelais speaks elsewhere of the 'sweet, much desired embrace of ... Mother Earth, which we call burial' ... This image of burial is probably inspired by Pliny,

who gives a detailed picture of the earth's motherhood and of burial as a return to her womb.

(p. 327)

In a speech combining the rhythm of the seasons, human growth and social festivity, Capulet explains of Juliet to Paris that 'Earth has swallow'd all my hopes but she;/She is the hopeful lady of my earth' (1.2.14–15). Carnival and capitalist notions seem to be played against each other here if the second 'earth' is taken as referring ambiguously to either Capulet's body, alive and dead, or to his lands. Given the prevalent references to age and youth, summer and winter, the cyclic carnival element is to the fore, earth as womb and tomb.

The design of *Romeo and Juliet* does not fall into a simple division of a tragic following upon a comic movement, and neither is there an unbridgeable dichotomy between the language of romantic love and sexuality, as we have seen above. Until Act 5 comedy and tragedy alternate. 'My grave is like to be my wedding bed' (1.5.134), Juliet remarks, while Romeo later declares, 'Then love-devouring death do what he dare' (2.6.7). Many proleptic notes like this are sounded throughout the play. In contrast, the carnival world persists in the midst of death; Menippus laughing in the underworld is a favourite image for Bakhtin (see p. 69), whereas in *Romeo and Juliet* Mercutio jests at death, 'you shall find me a grave man' (2.1.99). But carnival surrenders to tragedy at the close. More precisely, the reversals in Capulet's 'festival'/'funeral' speech (4.5.84–90), agnomination again, pattern Act 4 as a whole. In scene 1 Juliet evokes the horrors of the charnel house and death-shrouds, whereas scene 2 opens with proverbial jokes about cooks licking their fingers. In scene 3, just before taking the potion, the horrors of being entombed are vividly before Juliet. And then the carniva-lesque world of food and the body is heard once more – 'more spices', 'They call for dates and quinces', 'Look to the bak'd meats' (ll.1, 2, 5). The Nurse as weeping Fortune discovers Juliet's body in scene 4, and the festive musicians decide to stay on for a funereal free meal. The homiletic association of death and musicians is of great importance and will be touched on shortly. Suffice it here to note how the social festive world vies with the medieval horrors of death, and eventually with the development of death as lover.

In Act 5, in the Capulets' tomb, the festive is finally superseded by the counter-carnival triumph of death, and carnival day and festive light are extinguished by tragic darkness. Capulet's feast was to 'make dark heaven light' (1.2.25), but Montague had acknowledged that his son 'locks fair daylight out/And makes himself an artificial night', a 'black ... humour' that indeed proves 'portentous' (1.1.137–9). Yet 'night' also gives expression to the most potent love language in the play, touched on above.

> Come gentle night, come loving black-brow'd night,
> Give me my Romeo; and when I shall die
> Take him and cut him out in little stars ...

>   (3.2.20–2)

The orgasmic reading of 'die' is now commonplace and the proleptic punning equally so, but 'black-brow'd night' bears re-examination in a context in which Juliet recalls her first meeting with the masked Romeo on a festive occasion, 'So tedious is this day/As is the night before some festival' (3.2.28–9). The speech is remarkable for its affirmation and conversion of sexuality to poetry, and in effect offers an inherent rebuff to bawdy, but this in turn is severely qualified, yet again, by 'death-mark'd love'. 'Black-brow'd night' recalls the 'beetle [i.e. overhanging] brows' of Mercutio's grotesque visor and anticipates the 'overwhelming brows' (5.1.39) of the death-like apothecary who delivers the deadly potion. 'Black-brow'd night' seems part of a half-realized metaphor of night as a masquer at the revels. Romeo the antic masquer brings both love and death. In this the iconographic complex of death, festivity and romance in fifteenth- and sixteenth-century graphic art is recalled, particularly that of the 'Dance of Death'.

Shakespeare would have first encountered the iconography of the 'Dance of Death' as a child. John Stow noted in his copy of Leland's *Itinerary* that this imagery, common to all Europe by the beginning of the sixteenth century, was found on the wall of the parish church of Stratford-upon-Avon.[23] The 'Dance of Death' was otherwise known as the 'Dance Macabre' from its original attribution as 'The Dance of Machabree', as it appears in John Lydgate's translation.[24] The original fifteenth-century French poem with accompanying illustrations adorned the walls of the Church of the Holy Innocents in Paris. Lydgate's version was similarly used with illustrations in old St Paul's cathedral, where it became an object of devotion for Sir Thomas More contemplating death without us, and within us.[25] Holbein's 41 woodcuts for his work, commonly referred to as *The Dance of Death*, are well known and they became the basis for the psaltery of Queen Elizabeth's *Book of Common Prayer* (1569) with the number of border illustrations of *The Dance of Death* expanded to 71.[26]

The Dance of Death might well have arisen in response to the horrors of the Black Death, but from a larger perspective it was a development of the death obsession of the Middle Ages as exemplified in Pope Innocent III's *De Miseria Condicionis Humane* (1195) which was circulated throughout Europe in manuscripts and books, and translated by George Gascoigne in his *The Droomme of Doomes Day* (1576).[27] This literature focused on bodily corruption, death, burial and decomposition, with Death the leveller used to reinforce the hierarchy of the Church. In *The Dance of Death* the estates of man, and eventually woman, are led off to their inevitable end. Tomb sculpture often reflected this worm-ridden fate.[28]

The Dance of Death strikes at the heart of carnival since it concentrates on final bodily putrefaction, whatever might await the soul, whereas carnival celebrates bodily regeneration on earth. As the word 'dance' implies, music and dancing reflect the festive world of carnival, banqueting and romance. Throughout *Romeo and Juliet* Capulet's household reflects both this revelry and impending death. As we have seen with the old Capulets looking on at the revels (1.5) the carnivalesque is affirmed in spite of Romeo's forebodings. Acts 4 and 5 with the preparations for the wedding feast, festive musicians, and so on, reverse this, finally succumbing to death, tragedy and the tomb. *Romeo and Juliet* was performed within a culture in which the iconography of death had persisted, yet with some degree of development in which moral censure of the carnivalesque and festive partly displaced the homiletic corpse or skeleton. All this is reflected in the design of play.

Arthur Brooke's source had provided the commonplace from which Shakespeare developed. In Brooke Romeo pursues his love 'till Fortune list to sawse his sweete with sowre', until 'all his hap turnes to mishap, and all his myrth to mone'.[29] *Romeo and Juliet*'s 'womb'/'tomb', 'festival'/'funeral' have been touched on. Brooke's figure of agnomination, 'myrth'/'mone', echoes what seems to have been a source for English Renaissance rhetoric, St Gregory the Divine (Gregorius Nazianzen). In his translation of Innocent III, Gascoigne cites St Gregory on the contrasts to joy in a heavenly

Creator; 'all other myrth is mournyng, all other pleasure is payne, all sweete soure, all leefe lothsome, and all delyghtes are dollorous'. John Lyly's Euphuism would appear to owe something to Church Fathers like St Augustine and St Gregory as John Hoskins notes, while providing his own carnivalesque–lenten example in 'feasting'/'fasting'.[30] The conflation of antitheses in the iconography of death partly developed from this homiletic rhetoric, and particularly seized on images of the carnival and festive, above all music, masks and dancing. In Thomas Nashe's diatribe *Christ's Teares Over Jerusalem* (1593), just a few years before *Romeo and Juliet*, we find: 'Your morne-like christall countenances shall be netted over and (Masker-like) cawle-visarded with crawling venomous wormes'.[31] The most well-known dramatic example is, of course, Vindice in Middleton's *The Revenger's Tragedy* (1607) holding a skull and declaring; 'It were fine, methinks/To have thee seen at revels, forgetful feasts', to 'put a reveller/Out of his antic amble' (3.5.89–93). This is precisely what the illustrations of death did.

In Bruegel's still harrowing painting 'The Triumph of Death', which included several motifs from the 'Dance of Death' sequences, we see in the lower right-hand corner a cloaked and masked death overturning flagons of wine, disrupting feasting and gaming as a jester tries to hide, while two lovers, blithely unaware, sing and play music accompanied by another unseen death (figure 1).[32] Similarly, in a Dürer woodcut a shrouded figure introduces a corpse into a banquet. Most of the guests, including two lovers, are too engrossed to notice.[33] In Ripa's *Iconologia* (1603) Death is masked and in a burden carries 'musical instruments … of worldly joys' along with symbols of power and pleasure.[34]

Shakespeare's musicians in Act 4 do not convert festival to funeral, mirth to moan, but persist in a carnival humour with Peter, the Capulet servant. The carnivalesque element is uppermost as, before their actual entry, the musicians' festive music is heard even as Juliet's 'dead' body is discovered. The original stage direction at 4.4.20 is '*Play music*', as Capulet says, 'The County will be here with music straight,/For so he said he would. I hear him near' (4.4.21–2). As the Nurse, Capulet and Lady Capulet heavily bemoan death, comedy supervenes since the audience knows that Juliet is drugged, not dead – in the midst of death we are in life, the reverse of the iconographic tradition.

In at least nine of Holbein's woodcuts for *The Dance of Death* death and music are associated, nearly always, with death as a

Figure 1   'The Triumph of Death' by Bruegel (detail).

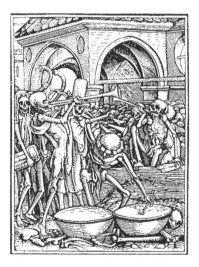

Figure 2 From 'The Dance of Death' by Holbein.

Figure 3 From 'The Dance of Death' by Holbein.

Figure 4   'Dance aux aveugles'.

musician. Number 35 shows newlyweds seemingly engrossed in
each other while Death dances before them striking a festive tabor
(figure 2), an image reflected in the Bruegel painting. The fifth illustration shows the entrance to a tomb with half a dozen partly
clothed skeletons playing instruments which compound festival
with funeral – crumhorns, kettle drums, a hurdy-gurdy, a shawm,
and so on (figure 3). There is an apocalyptic element here whereas
some earlier sequences, such as the 1491 *La grande Danse macabre*
had included 'The Orchestra of Death'.[35] A variant of this tradition
is found in Pierre Michault's fifteenth-century poem *La Dance aux
aveugles* (figure 4) which in an illustrated Geneva manuscript shows
the three 'blind' – or blindfolded – ones, Cupid, Fortune and Death,
disposed in a triptych. At the foot of each panel seated musicians
look on awaiting those led to this dance of death.[36] *Romeo and Juliet*
reflects Michault's structure as the lovers move from Cupid's blind,
or masked, passion through fatal misfortune to death with, at one
point, musicians in attendance. Queen Elizabeth's prayer book sep-
arates the musicians from death. As they play a skeleton looms
behind (figure 5). And in contrast to the carnivalesque death–birth,
tomb–womb cycle we have seen in the Nurse's speech particularly,

Figure 5   From Queen Elizabeth's *Book of Common Prayer* and *Psaltery.*

one of the woodcuts shows Death behind a nurse cradling her charge, with the words 'give suck no more; for I am at the door' (figure 5).

Emblems and paintings not directly concerned with eschatological death nevertheless endorsed an anti-carnivalesque view of music, dancing and love. Joos van Winghe's *Nocturnal Party* (1588) depicts masked musicians joining in with dancers before a statue of Venus.[37] Drunken abandon make the moral implications quite clear. More directly pertinent to *Romeo and Juliet* is Otto van Veen's emblem entitled 'Voluptatum Usurae, Morbi et Miseriae' ('Pleasure's Usury, Sickness and Misery') in his *Horatii Emblemata,* 1612 (figure 6).[38] Masked dancers accompanied by a masked musician with a drinker and a venal couple looking on dominate the

Figure 6   From Otto van Veen *Horatii Emblemata.*

foreground. In the background gamblers play, an old man grasping
a cupid-putto is admitted, while at the rear on a darkened sickbed
reclines a figure whose urine is being examined in a glass bottle by
a physician. Arthur Brooke's source for *Romeo and Juliet* indirectly
provides a comment since precisely at that point quoted above
where he considers 'myrth' and 'mone', he draws on the same

moral commonplace which gave van Veen his title, the metaphor of usury for pleasure; Fortune 'payd theyr former greefe with pleasures doubled gayne,/But now for pleasures usery ten folde redoubleth payne.'[39] In the polyglot verses beneath several lines from Latin sources once again we find predictable antitheses of pleasure and pain, joy and tears, glossing van Veen's picture. Van Veen and Brooke both share a common moralizing outlook. Sickness and death follow upon indulgence of vice. Shakespeare's comparable scene, the revels with the aged Capulets looking on, affirms the carnivalesque by including age with youth suggesting a triumph of life.

But this is not to be. As James Black has noted of the repeated stage picture of the prince of Verona and his feuding subjects, with youth killed off and the aged solemnly gathered; it 'is made progressively tragic as it becomes more and more a pageant of death'.[40]

On entering the tomb Romeo's language recalls the carnivalesque death-earth-womb but transforms it into death as a ravenous monster, a traditional hell-mouth.

> Thou detestable maw, thou womb of death
> Gorg'd with the dearest morsel of the earth,
> Thus I enforce thy rotten jaws to open,
> And in despite I'll cram thee with more food.

> (5.3.45–8)

Inside, the sight of Juliet's beauty transforms her surroundings. Complementing her earlier speech when she had related night, death, and festival, Romeo says, 'her beauty makes/This vault a feasting presence, full of light' (5.3.85–6). As his first glimpse of Juliet was in the midst of revels and banqueting, an image as we have seen associated with the entrance of death, so the tomb scene inverts this and festival enters into the midst of death. Analogously, as he was lover at the festival, so death is lover here:

> Shall I believe
> That unsubstantial Death is amorous,
> And that the lean abhorred monster keeps
> Thee here in dark to be his paramour?

> (5.3.102–5)

And so Romeo rivals death who can only be the final triumpher as Bruegel rehearsed in a title which Petrarch bequeathed to the Renaissance in *The Triumph of Death* from his *Trionfi*.[41] In carnival there can be no triumph of death, only a triumph of life in human generation. Echoing the sonneteers, Romeo had said that Rosaline's chastity 'Cuts beauty off from all posterity' (1.1.218). Romeo and Juliet were briefly lovers but now it is her beauty which is cut off from all posterity. This is the larger, more inclusive sense of tragedy, from a carnivalesque perspective: not simply the poignancy of their deaths, but that only death came from their love, not the renewal and thus reaffirmation of life. When Capulet follows Juliet to the tomb that will be the end of his line. And the same for the Montagues since Brooke included the detail that Romeo's 'parentes have none other heyre, thou art theyr onely sonne'.[42] The funereal gold statues are no substitute for the warmth of new life. But carnival can never really be defeated. It finds new life in new forms as long as there is comedy. It is said that *The Dance of Death* itself arose partly as a homiletic reaction to a peasant custom – of dancing in graveyards.[43]

NOTES

1. This essay, a slightly edited version of that published by *Shakespeare Survey* (49, 1996: pp. 69–85), has benefited from comments on readings of preliminary drafts at the Reading Renaissance Research Seminar, and the 'Shakespeare, Carnival and Society' wing of Reading's Literature and History Conference, 1995. At the former my attention was drawn to Kent Cartwright's extensive and subtle chapter 'Theater and Narrative in *Romeo and Juliet*', in his *Shakespearean Tragedy and Its Double: The Rhythms of Audience Response* (Pennsylvania: Pennylvanian State University Press, 1991). In his concentration on the central topic of 'spectatorial distance' he alludes several times to the Bakhtinian carnivalesque functioning within the play in ways close to my own, but we differ fundamentally concerning Romeo and Juliet's love. He sees it as *part* of, I see it as *opposed* to, the carnivalesque.
2. All references are to Brian Gibbons (ed.), *Romeo and Juliet*, The Arden Shakespeare (London and New York: Methuen, 1980).
3. Terence Hawkes (ed.), *Coleridge on Shakespeare* (Harmondsworth: Penguin, 1969), pp. 87–8.
4. Geoffrey Bullough, *Narrative and Dramatic Sources of Shakespeare*, Vol. I (London, Routledge and Kegan Paul; New York, Columbia University Press, 1964), pp. 295, 1.344.

5. 'Shakespeare ad Infinitum', in Oswald Le Winter, *Shakespeare in Europe* (Harmondsworth: Penguin, 1963), p. 66.
6. Howard R. Patch, *The Goddess Fortuna in Medieval Literature* (Cambridge, Mass.: Harvard University Press, 1927).
7. Ibid., p. 56. F.N. Robinson (ed.), *The Complete Works of Geoffrey Chaucer* (Oxford: Oxford University Press, 1957), p. 330.
8. Ibid. Achille Bocchi, *Symbolicarum Quaestionum de Universo Genere* [Bologna, 1574], ed. Stephen Orgel (New York and London: Garland, 1979), G1ʳ.
9. Patch, p. 44.
10. Ibid., p. 37, Robinson, p. 273, l.622.
11. Bullough, p. 303, l.673.
12. Patch, p. 52.
13. See Jill L. Levenson, *Shakespeare in Performance: Romeo and Juliet* (Manchester: Manchester University Press, 1987).
14. Bullough, p. 290, l.169.
15. *Prefaces to Shakespeare*, second series (London: Sidgwick and Jackson, 1930), p. 8.
16. Bullough, p. 297, ll.413ff.
17. A.J. Smith (ed.), *John Donne. The Complete English Poems* (Harmondsworth: Penguin, 1971). See 'The Sun Rising' p. 80, ll.21–2. Romeo exclaims: 'Turn back, dull earth, and find thy centre out' (2.1.2); cf. 'The Sun Rising' 1.30 – 'This bed thy centre is, these walls thy sphere'.
18. For an argument opposite to that made here, see Ann Pasternak Slater, 'Petrarchism Come True in *Romeo and Juliet*', in *Images of Shakespeare*, ed. Werner Habicht, D.J. Palmer and Roger Pringle (Newark: University of Delaware Press, 1988), pp. 129–50.
19. For a parallel interpretation see François Laroque, *Shakespeare's Festive World* (Cambridge: Cambridge University Press, 1991), p. 210.
20. Gibbons, p. 144.
21. *The Works of Francis Rabelais* by Sir Thomas Urquhart and Peter Motteux (London: H.G. Bohn, 1849), Vol. 2, p. 311. *The Histories of Gargantua and Pantagruel*, trans. J.M. Cohen (Harmondsworth: Penguin Books, 1965), p. 535.
22. Marjorie Donker, *Shakespeare's Proverbial Themes* (Westport and London: Greenwood Press, 1992), ch. 2.
23. J.M. Clark, *The Dance of Death* (Glasgow: Jackson Son and Co., 1950), p. 15.
24. Two manuscript versions of Lydgate's poem, with further collation, ed. Florence Warren and Beatrice White, are published as *The Dance of Death* (The Early English Text Society, no. 181, London: Oxford University Press, 1931).
25. 'The Four Last Things', *The English Works of Sir Thomas More* (London, Eyre and Spottiswoode; New York, Lincoln MacVeagh, 1931), Vol. I, p. 468.
26. See Francis Douce, *Holbein's Dance of Death* (London: Henry G. Bohn, 1898). The Queen Elizabeth prayer book reproduced here is the version by William Pickering, London, 1853. See Ruari McLean, *Victorian Book Design* (London: Faber: 1963), pp. 10–12. The woodcuts

Ronald Knowles

were by Mary Byfield. I am indebted to Christopher and Phillipa Hardman for help with this reference.

27. Robert E. Lewis (ed.), *De Miseria Condicionis Humane* (Athens: The University of Georgia Press, 1978), pp. 3–5 survey the transmission of manuscripts. John W. Cunliffe (ed.), *The Complete Works of George Gascoigne* (Cambridge: Cambridge University Press, 1910), Vol. II, *The Glasse of Government and Other Poems and Prose Works*, pp. 209–450.

28. See 'The Vision of Death', ch. XI of J. Huizinga, *The Waning of the Middle Ages* (New York: Doubleday, 1954).

29. Bullough, p. 310, ll.932–46.

30. *Directions for Speech and Style* (1599), ed. Hoyht H. Hudson (Princeton, NJ: Princeton University Press, 1935), pp. 16, 37. Gascoigne, p. 398.

31. Ronald B. McKerrow, *The Works of Thomas Nashe* (London: A.H. Bullen, 1904), Vol. II, pp. 138–9.

32. See Walter S. Gibson, *Bruegel* (London: Thames and Hudson, 1977), p. 116.

33. Willi Kurth, *The Complete Woodcuts of Albrecht Dürer* (New York: Arden Book Co.), illustration 15. I am indebted to Pat Righelato for this reference.

34. Georg Olms Verlag, Hildesheim and New York, 1970, 'istromenti de l'allegrezze mondane', p. 340.

35. *Le Sentiment de la Mort au Moyen Age* (Montreal: L'Aurore, Les Editions Univers Inc., 1979), p. 199.

36. Bruno Roy, 'Amour, Fortune et Mort: La danse des trois aveugles', in *Le Sentiment de la Mort au Moyen Age*, pp. 121–37. The illustration is reproduced in Erwin Panofsky's seminal chapter 'Blind Cupid', in *Studies in Iconology* (New York: Harper and Row, 1962), plate XLVI.

37. *Masters of Seventeenth-Century Dutch Genre Painting* (Philadelphia Museum of Art, 1984), p. 177.

38. Otto van Veen, *Horatii Emblemata*, New York and London: Garland Publishing Inc., 1979, pp. 38–9.

39. Bullough, p. 310, ll.953–4.

40. James Black, 'The Visual Artistry of *Romeo and Juliet*', *Studies in English Literature* 15 (1975), p. 250.

41. D.D. Carnicelli in his edition of *Lord Morley's Tryumphes of Frances Petrarcke* (Cambridge, Mass.: Harvard University Press, 1971) provides much useful introductory material, pp. 1–74.

42. Bullough, p. 289, l.120.

43. See Lydgate, *The Dance of Death*, p. xiii.

4

The Carnivalesque in *A Midsummer Night's Dream*

David Wiles

Carnival theory did not begin with Bakhtin, and we shall understand Bakhtin's position more clearly if we set it against classical theories of carnival.[1] From the Greek world the most important theoretical statement is to be found in Plato:

> The gods took pity on the human race, born to suffer as it was, and gave it relief in the form of religious festivals to serve as periods of rest from its labours. They gave us as fellow revellers the Muses, with Apollo their leader, and Dionysus, so that men might restore their way of life by sharing feasts with gods.[2]

This is first a *utopian* theory, maintaining that carnival restores human beings to an earlier state of being when humans were closer to the divine. And second, it associates carnival with communal *order*. Plato argues that festive dancing creates bodily order, and thus bodily and spiritual well-being. He clarifies his orderly view of carnival by dissenting from an alternative view, relating specifically to the worship of Dionysus, which maintains that Hera caused Dionysus to lose his reason, and Dionysus inflicts his revenge upon mortals, making them drunk and wild in their dancing.[3] Plato thus dissents from an *anarchic* view comparable to the later Christian idea that carnival is an expression of the Devil.

Aristotle's most relevant discussion concerns the music of the pipes, which troubles him because of its effect upon the emotions of player and listener. He cites the myth that Athena invented the pipes, but being rational threw them away. Orgiastic music, and implicitly the festivals associated with such music, placed Aristotle in a dilemma. He refused to let upper-class youth meddle with the

61

pipes, but allowed the lower classes with their disordered minds and bodies to indulge; nevertheless he accepted some usage by the elite on the grounds of 'catharsis', observing that 'enthusiasm' (i.e. possession by the god)

> affects some people very strongly ... They are, as it were, set on their feet, as if they had undergone a curative and purifying treatment ... Cathartic music brings men an elation which is not at all harmful.[4]

Aristotle introduces two important notions to the debate about festive practice. One is *popular culture*, a debilitating or demoralizing form of recreation which the upper class must avoid. The other is catharsis, normally termed in discussions of carnival as '*safety-valve* theory'.[5] It is an important aspect of Aristotelian 'safety-valve' theory that it analyses the individual rather than the social process. Where Plato was concerned with the way choral dance binds the community together, Aristotle's analytic approach is concerned with the breeding of individual leaders.

In the Roman republic the Dionysia was suppressed and in the course of the imperial period the Saturnalia emerged as the major festival. The festive focus shifted from the spring equinox to the winter solstice. Macrobius cites two major theories of the Saturnalia.[6] The dominant theory is *utopian*, locating Saturn as the god who brought fertility to Italy in the golden age, teaching Janus the art of agriculture. There was no war in the age of Saturn, and most importantly no class distinction. The inversion of master and slave at the Saturnalia is seen as a means of honouring the god who symbolizes this uncorrupted, egalitarian past. The theme of class inversion becomes dominant in Roman rather than Greek carnival because Roman society at all levels was rigidly stratified. We should also take note in Macrobius of the explicit calendrical symbolism, for Saturn suddenly vanishes leaving two-faced Janus (January) to face forwards towards the new year. Saturn is associated with the Greek C[h]ronos, who symbolizes time and the *orderly* progress of the seasons. The main competing theory, which Macrobius attributed to Varro at the end of the Republican period, is *propitiatory*, and relates to the Greek settlement of Sicily. Masks and lights are a symbolic substitute for human sacrifice, and Saturn is linked to the god of Death. Varro's theory is rationalistic and historicizing, and presumes that the human condition is advancing rather than declining. But it points up a negative aspect of Saturn, whose sickle is used to castrate the father as well as to reap the harvest.

In the medieval period the Saturnalia, in its new guise as the 12 days of Christmas, remained important, but the focus of communal celebration in continental Europe shifted to *Mardi gras*, 'carnival' in the strict sense of 'farewell to flesh', flesh in the dual form of sexual intercourse and eating meat. Medieval education was steeped in Aristotle, and Aristotelian 'safety-valve' theory provided an obvious means of theorizing carnival. Udall in the preface to *Ralph Roister Doister* speaks of how 'mirth prolongeth life, and causeth health; mirth recreates our spirits and voideth pensiveness.'[7] The explanation turns on the Aristotelian and Hippocratic theory of the four humours. Celebration evacuates melancholy and thus restores the body to equilibrium. Similar thinking underlies the famous Parisian apologia of 1444:

> We do these things in jest and not in earnest, as the ancient custom is, so that once a year the foolishness innate in us can come out and evaporate. Don't wine skins and barrels burst very often if the air-hole is not opened from time to time?[8]

The humoral conception is here linked to a Christian conception, for the jest/earnest dichotomy relates to the Manichaean division of Devil and God within the human individual. If the Devil is innate, then by definition it cannot be overcome and must be rendered harmless in other ways.

For scholars of the Enlightenment and Romantic periods, carnivalesque phenomena were either distasteful, or symbols of an idealized past. Whereupon, enter Bakhtin, with the impetus of Marxism behind him. In his study of Rabelais, Bakhtin identified 'carnival' as the basis of an autonomous and historically progressive popular culture. The 'carnivalesque' is for Bakhtin a genre synonymous with 'grotesque realism', but becomes also a sociological category. In the ancient world Bakhtin seems to have envisaged a homogeneous community with no distinctive 'popular' culture. The satyr play is cited as an example of how each genre has 'its own parodying and travestying double, its own comic-ironic *contre-partie*'.[9] In the ancient world, Bakhtin declares, 'there could be no sharp distinction between official and folk culture, as later appeared in the Middle Ages.'[10] In the seventh, eighth and ninth centuries

feudalism had yet to take root, and the homogeneous classical tradition was still strong,[11] and Bakhtin's folk culture seems to have
appeared somewhere in the early Middle Ages. Rabelais is interpreted as a historically progressive figure, whose use of a residual
popular culture supported monarchy against feudalism.[12] Bakhtin
sees this historically-specific popular culture as the means whereby
people overcame their fears and freely expressed their views about
authority. Bakhtin's theory of carnival is not a 'safety-valve' theory,
and he extrapolates from the 1444 text cited above the alternative
principle that human beings have two separate natures.[13] Bakhtin's
theory is, in the tradition of Plato and Macrobius, a *utopian* theory,
positing a primal wholeness to which fallen humanity, ruined in
this case by the devil of class, is temporarily restored.

Bakhtin's most influential contribution to subsequent discussion
of carnival is his semiotics of the body. The carnivalesque body
with its orifices, protuberances and excretions is related to the flux
of the self-renewing cosmos, whilst the hermetic classical body is
individualized and sterile.[14] One of the difficulties in using this
theory is Bakhtin's tendency to lump all festivals together, slipping
from carnival in the narrow sense of *carnevale* or *mardi gras* to the
wide sense of popular celebration. 'Carnival' in the narrow sense is
specifically concerned with the body, which has to be mortified
during Lent, and its most potent symbol is the fat man who bloats
his body to the point of expiry. The symbol of the classical Dionysia
was the erect phallus, appropriate to the spring season and the
renewal of life. The ithyphallic satyr of the Dionysia was sexually
rampant, but not bloated, and his grotesqueness was specifically
goat-like. The Saturnalia focused on structures of authority, and the
ugliness of an inversionary Christmas king was in the first instance
a symbol of class, not eating. Midsummer giants were grotesque in
a very specific way, being occasions for setting a fire high above the
ground on the night of the solstice.[15] Bakhtin's generalizing tendency encourages us to see popular culture and the carnival
grotesque as a more uniform entity than it is.

The assumption that we can usefully separate out popular
culture from official culture in the Middle Ages cannot pass unchal-
lenged. Peter Burke, drawing his terminology from Redfield, allows
a binary model of society, but argues that:

> There were two cultural traditions in early modern Europe, but
> they did not correspond symmetrically to the two main social

groups, the elite and the common people. The elite participated in the little tradition, but the common people did not participate in the great tradition.[16]

The educated elite had access to a language and tradition from which the many were excluded, but the many had no autonomous cultural tradition of their own. Ladurie's analysis of carnival practices in Romans in the Shakespearean period demonstrates that all the different social fractions in the town had their independent carnival traditions which served to emblematize local solidarities. It was members of the elite who constituted the jocular 'Abbey of Misrule', erected the annual maypole, and policed marriage within the community.[17] Bercé's wide-ranging analysis of French festival and rebellion in the period concludes that festival only thrives in a town where there is social solidarity. When solidarity breaks down, festive symbolism can be used temporarily to express dissidence, but the framework for such symbolism rapidly evaporates.[18] Bercé emphasizes the discontinuities in festive traditions, which are for ever being renewed and reinvented, and he sees timeless ritual practice as a utopian myth.[19] The work of Burke, Ladurie and Bercé obliges us to view with scepticism Bakhtin's overarching notion of an on-going autonomous popular culture.

The situation in England in the Shakespearean period is in many specific respects hard to accommodate with the Bakhtinian paradigm. In Marxist terms one cannot see festivals as historically 'progressive', for the land-owning aristocracy began to use rites associated with the land to lay claim to authentic Englishness in opposition to the urban and bourgeois Puritan movement.[20] King James' *Book of Sports* (1618) is the most blatant example of such ideological manipulation of carnival, but Elizabeth engaged in the same strategy. At court Shakespeare's plays were performed according to the rhythm of the festive calendar, whilst in the city his plays were performed according to the sabbatarian rhythm of the Reformation. When we look at the plays in their performance context, the festive or carnivalesque dimension relates to the experience of the aristocratic audience much more closely than it does to the experience of the 'popular' audience.

'Carnival' is a troublesome term because in its narrow sense the English festival bears the penitential term 'Shrovetide'. The festival was not the occasion for public processions as on the continent,[21] and the 'King of Christmas' is the dominant celebratory figure, not the continental 'Carnival' who engages in mortal combat with Lent. Bakhtin's generalized view of carnival renders him blind to the highly specific way in which festivals organize and give meaning to the passage of time. He does not explore, for example, how the pattern of early modern festivals relates both to the narrative of Christ's life-cycle and to the major points of transition in the life-cycle of Everyman and Everywoman. Bakhtin's concern is with epochs, not with chronological minutiae, and he is content to identify a general festive merging of death with birth apparent in images of the harvest or the marriage bed. His concern as a critic is with genre rather than performance, and so for example the life/death nexus that he discerns in Aristophanes finds a 'significant kinship' in the Shakespearean clown.[22] He is also pre-occupied with the novel rather than drama, which, perhaps because of the dominance of naturalism at the time when he wrote, seemed to him a relatively monologic medium.[23] The carnivalesque is experienced as a textual artefact belonging to a given historical moment rather than as a performance belonging to a specific calendrical moment.

Michael Bristol, a critic sympathetic to Bakhtin, offers a reading of *A Midsummer Night's Dream* along broadly Bakhtinian lines. He criticizes C.L. Barber's 'saturnalian' approach to Shakespearean comedy as a version of 'safety-valve' theory. For Barber, 'release' is followed by a 'clarification' that Bristol rightly interprets as a reaffirmation of the status quo.[24] For Barber, the maying in which Theseus engages is the dominant festive motif, the single critical key that unlocks the whole. Bristol attempts to effect a dialogic reading, contrasting the official discourse of the aristocracy with the heteroglossia of the mechanicals, so that the latter provides a critique of the former and the text becomes an open one. In the mechanicals he sees an emphasis on the body, and a denial of individual subjectivity.[25] Bristol's reading offers us a more radical and progressive Shakespeare than before, but seems in some ways to force the play to fit the theory. Bristol emphasizes the aristocratic/popular binary in a play that is more obviously trinary, with its three layers of commoners, aristocracy and fairies. The activities of the fairies provide a more obvious critique of marriage than the activities of the mechanicals. It seems to be the unspoken assumption of a materialist modern age that the fairy couple are the super-egos of Theseus and Hippolyta, and thus no more than psychoanalytic projections. The binaries of youth/age and male/female remain subordinate in Bristol's reading to the overarching Bakhtinian paradigm of them-and-us, officialdom and the folk. Another critic who has attempted a Bakhtinian reading of Shakespeare is Manfred Pfister, who adopts a position much closer to Barber, finding that the multiple inversions of the early comedies are safely contained 'within an over-ruling framework of a benign and flexible order'. Pfister dismisses these inversionary plot structures as 'instances of saturnalian revelling rather than subversive carnivalesque revelling'.[26] A Bakhtinian reading leads Bristol and Pfister to focus on an apparently straightforward question: Are the texts univocal or dialogic? Are they ordered classical structures or open-ended carnivalesque structures?

Posed in these terms, the question, I would suggest, is an unsatisfactory one because it implies that the text has immanent properties. The text under investigation has been extracted from its historical context of performance, and defined as a self-contained and complete entity. To bind the text between the covers of a book is already to impose an over-ruling framework, and to define its level of discourse. The alternative, however, is not easy, for in addition to the literal heteroglossia provided by the multiple voices of the actors, and the more subtle heteroglossia provided by the different linguistic registers in the dialogue, we also have the language of gesture which may speak against the words. The twentieth-century director will often seek to create dialogism by playing against the text, and we may wonder whether Elizabethan performers did not also have critical attitudes to the texts they were given. More important still we have the voice of the audience. Through laughing, clapping, hissing and by their visible socially structured presence, the Elizabethan audience were necessarily an integral part of the performance event, interacting with the players far more than a modern audience would do.

The starting point for my own analysis will be the proposition that although we encounter *A Midsummer Night's Dream* as a text, it was historically part of an aristocratic carnival. It was written for a wedding, and part of the festive structure of the wedding night. The audience who saw the play in the public theatre in the months that followed became vicarious participants in an aristocratic festival from which they were physically excluded. My purpose will be to demonstrate how closely the play is integrated with a historically specific upper-class celebration.

I have argued at length elsewhere[27] that the play was written for the marriage of Elizabeth Carey, daughter of George Carey, who became patron of Shakespeare's company of actors and later commissioned *The Merry Wives of Windsor*. The argument, in brief, is that aristocratic weddings customarily took place on significant calendrical dates. The Careys eschewed Saint Valentine's Day in favour of 19 February 1596, because that day saw the planetary conjunction of the new moon and Venus, the most favourable conditions an astrologer could imagine, and both parties to the wedding took astrology very seriously. The parents of the bride and groom must have consulted an almanac, just as Bottom tells Quince to do. The moon changed (whilst remaining occluded) on 18 February and thus the fictitious setting of the action announced in the first lines of the play when 'four happy days bring in another moon' became Saint Valentine's Day, 1596. Lest the audience miss the point, Hippolyta repeats that

> Four days will quickly steep themselves in night:
> Four nights will quickly dream away the time:
> And then [*on the fifth night*] the Moon, like to a silver bow,
> Now bent in heaven, shall behold the night
> Of our solemnities.

$$(1.1.7-11)^{28}$$

The central action of the play inhabits a liminal, dream-like space characterized by the inversion of real conditions, being set out-of-doors, in the country, in summer and under a full moon.

Saint Valentine's Day is only mentioned once, at the moment when the lovers return from the liminal world of their dream to the courtly world of Theseus. Within the closed system of the text, Theseus' jest on May Day seems inconsequential: 'Saint Valentine is past: Begin these wood-birds but to couple now?' (4.1.138–9). The importance of Saint Valentine's Day rites in structuring the narrative of the play has long been overlooked, because critics viewing the play as a purely textual entity have been fixated by the overt verbal references to May. Let us spend a while investigating those forgotten rites.

If we step back to the world of John Paston, we can see how the Saint Valentine tradition shaped medieval courtship. Financial negotiations were under way, the girl was getting impatient, and the romantic interview had yet to take place when John Paston's prospective mother-in-law wrote inviting him to visit on Saint Valentine's eve:

> Cousin, upon Friday is Saint Valentine's Day, and every bird chooseth him a mate. And if it like you to come on Thursday at night, and so purvey you that ye may abide there till Monday, ye shall so speak to my husband.

Soon afterwards, the prospective bride wrote a love-letter to Paston, her 'right well-beloved Valentine', lamenting that her father would not increase her portion. Her next letter, written in mounting distress, urged her 'good, true and loving Valentine' not to pursue the matter of marriage if he could not accept her father's terms. She signed herself 'your Valentine'.[29] We discern from these letters the important part which Saint Valentine rituals played in shaping the emotional aspect of relationships within a system of arranged marriages.

Like Paston's mother-in-law, Theseus alludes to the proverbial notion that birds choose their mates on this day when he asks: 'Begin these wood-birds but to couple now?' The major medieval poets – Chaucer, Gower, Lydgate – all made play with this tradition, and it continued to flourish in Surrey and Herrick.[30] The tradition is strictly literary, for birds do not pair off at this time of year in the English climate.[31] The poet normally seeks to develop a contrast between the natural behaviour of birds and unnatural behaviour amongst human beings. George Wither, in his epithalamium written for the marriage of James I's daughter on Saint Valentine's Day, reverses the motif, and suggests that the blackbird and thrush have learned from the human couple.[32] Lydgate lists numerous wood-birds, while Chaucer and Gower both use the image of a 'parliament' of birds. John Donne, in his epithalamium for James' daughter, produces a similar listing of birds, both common birds like the robin and blackbird, and aristocrats like the goldfinch and kingfisher; at the head of this unparliamentary hierarchy, the marrying couple are likened to phoenixes.[33]

The tradition of a parliament of courting birds establishes a generic context for Bottom's musical catalogue of wood-birds: the ousel cock, the thrush, the wren, the finch, the sparrow, the lark and the cuckoo (3.1.120ff.). Bottom's song evokes the different musical qualities of the different birds. The birds in the first stanza are explicitly masculine, and implicitly phallic:

> The ousel cock, so black of hue,
> With orange-tawny bill,
> The throstle, with his note so true,
> The wren with little quill –

While Donne's poem ends gloriously with the phoenix, Bottom ends with bathos. No man can deny that he is a cuckoo/cuckold:

> The finch, the sparrow, and the lark,
> The plain-song cuckoo grey,
> Whose note full many a man doth mark,
> And dares not answer nay.

Bottom's mating-song, which identifies the singer as the sexually inadequate cuckoo, culminates in the emergence of Titania the dominant female from her flowery bed, enraptured by what she hears. Perhaps the bed ressembled a nest as in Brook's production, we do not know. Certainly, Bottom's bird-song contrasts grotesquely with the lullaby which laid Titania to rest in her bed, where the sounds are supposedly uttered by Philomel the nightingale (2.2.13). The bird motif ties the love of Bottom and Titania to the important Saint Valentine tradition, which likes to contrast the natural coupling found in the greenwood with the constraints which society imposes on human beings.

Two other aspects of Saint Valentine's day relate closely to the plot structure of *A Midsummer Night's Dream*. First is the tradition of drawing lots on the night before Saint Valentine's day. This custom derives from the Roman Lupercalia on February 15th, when men drew lots with the names of women. One medieval poet describes how

> Of custom year by year
> Men have an usaunce in this region
> To look and search Cupid's calendar
> And choose their choice by great affection –
> Such as been moved with Cupid's motion
> Taking their choice as their sort doth fall ...[34]

'Sort' is of course the French word for 'lot'. The drawing of lots on Saint Valentine's eve is documented at Jesus College, Cambridge in 1608: a man was expected to give a pair of gloves to the girl whose name he drew.[35] The custom is described in some detail by the Frenchman, Henri Misson, at the end of the seventeenth century:

> An equal number of maids and bachelors get together, each writes their true or some feigned name upon separate billets, which they roll up, and draw by way of lots, the maids taking the men's billets, and the men the maids'; so that each of the young men lights upon a girl that he calls his Valentine, and each of the girls upon a young man which she calls hers. By this means each has two Valentines; but the man sticks faster to the Valentine that is fallen to him, than to the Valentine to whom he is fallen. Fortune having thus divided the company into so many couples, the Valentines give balls and treats to their mistresses, wear their billets several days upon their bosoms or sleeves, and this little sport often ends in love.[36]

From an anthropological perspective, the drawing of lots is functional in relation to village life. Couples are not formed on the basis of individual inclinations (though force of personality must play a part in determining whether the boy finishes up with the girl who chases him or the girl whom he chases), nor are pairings going to reflect economic and political power blocs, as they must do in any system where marriages are arranged according to parental choice. The Saint Valentine's lottery was profoundly egalitarian.

Ben Jonson's nostalgic Caroline reconstruction of Elizabethan life, *A Tale of a Tub*, was written soon after the reissue of James I's *Book of Sports*,[37] and the play has a Saint Valentine's Day setting. The main plot centres on the attempt by the constable to marry his daughter, Audrey Turf, to a bridegroom called Clay. Squire Tub (i.e. a tub of fertilizer) is a rival, as is young Justice Bramble. The constable has chosen Clay because

> Mistress Audrey Turf
> Last night did draw him for her Valentine:
> Which chance it hath so taken her father and mother,
> Because themselves drew so on Valentine's Eve
> Was thirty year, as they will have her married
> Today by any means.

(1.1.45–50)

Another character reminisces in similar vein that 'Sin' Valentine

> had a place, in last King Harry's time,
> Of sorting all the young couples, joining 'em,
> And putting 'em together; which is yet
> P'rformed as on his day ...

(1.2.22–5)

Jonson goes on to give his plot the structure of a Saint Valentine's lottery. The audience have no idea whom the heroine will marry, and it is pure chance that leads her at the last into the arms of a stranger, 'Pol Marten'. Apparently a bird (and thus an appropriate hero for Saint Valentine's Day), it transpires that the groom is really 'Martin Polecat', and knows how to burrow into the 'turf'.

The game played on Saint Valentine's day whereby boy A chases girl B who chases boy C who chases girl D is startlingly analogous to the plot structure of *A Midsummer Night's Dream*. A random principle seems to govern the pairing of the young couples, and Shakespeare provides no clues to character which might suggest that the choices made by Hermia and Helena are anything other than arbitrary. Despite all odds, the two women pursue the men whom fate seems to have allotted them. Puck views the proceedings as a 'fond pageant' and a 'sport', and functions as a master of ceremonies by manipulating his magic potion (3.2.114, 119). Initially, Helena → Demetrius → Hermia → Lysander. The circle is complete when, thanks to the potion, Lysander → Helena. Oberon begins to move the game to a conclusion when Demetrius → Helena, and the final resolution is achieved when Lysander's eyes are re-anointed.

The second custom which characterizes Saint Valentine's Day is the custom whereby one's 'Valentine' is the first person whom one sees when one wakes in the morning. For a full picture of this ritual, we can turn to Pepys' entries for 14 February. In 1666, the early morning ritual is associated with the lot-drawing of the night before. Pepys records that he was

> called up by Mr Hill, who my wife thought had come to be her Valentine, she it seems having drawn him last night, but it proved not; however, calling him up to our bedside, my wife challenged him.

Mrs Pepys subsequently went off with her Valentine to an all-night party. The next day a lady who had drawn Pepys' name in a lottery appeared 'with my name in her bosom, which will cost me money'. Young people frequently present themselves at the Pepys' bedside, motivated by the fact that the wealthy older person will have to provide a present of money or gloves. There is a colourful entry for 1665, when Pepys was visited by the young wife of a ship's carpenter. Three weeks previously, his wife being incapacitated with period pains, Pepys had dined and had his pleasure with this lady, who wanted him to find work for her husband, and he subsequently swore an oath to let women go, in order to concentrate on business. He now complains on 14 February that this woman

> had the confidence to say she came in time enough to be my Valentine, and so indeed she did – but my oath preserved me from losing any time with her.

There was always the risk that one might clap eyes upon a wholly inappropriate Valentine. When he went visiting in 1661, Pepys had to ask whether the servant about to open the door was male or female, and the servant, a negro male, teased him by answering 'a woman'. The next year, his wife had to cover her eyes with her hands all morning in order not to see the painters who were gilding the plasterwork.[38]

These early morning visitations, resurrected at the Restoration, were common practice in the Elizabethan period. In Hamlet, Ophelia's ballad describes the tragic plight of a girl who goes out early in the morning to seek her Valentine:

> Tomorrow is Saint Valentine's day,
> All in the morning betime,
> And I a maid at your window,
> To be your Valentine.
> Then up he rose, and donned his clothes,
> And dupped the chamber door –
> Let in the maid, that out a maid
> Never departed more.

> (4.5.48–55)

Nashe, in a rather different vein, also drains Saint Valentine's day of all idealism. His poem 'The Choice of Valentines' describes how young men rise before day-break in order to seek Valentines whom they will accompany dancing, eating cream and cakes, or watching a play. The girl whom the poet is seeking turns out to be a prostitute, who has been driven from her home and now works in a brothel.[39]

The sub-plot of *Tale of a Tub* centres on the middle-aged mother of Squire Tub, who decides to set off across the frosty fields to find a Valentine for herself. She wants her son for company, but he is said to be asleep, so she takes her serving-woman, Wispe. Since both are women, this causes complications. When they knock at the constable's house, the servant Hannibal Puppy comes to the door, and both women claim him:

Lady: Come hither, I must kiss thee, Valentine Puppy.
     Wispe, ha' you got you a Valentine?
Wispe: None, Madam.
     He's the first stranger that I saw.
Lady: To me
     He is so, and such. Let's share him equally.

                    (3.4.23–6)

Puppy calls for help as the two women set upon him in order to claim him with a kiss. The women resolve that they will divide him in half: the right-hand side will belong to one, the left-hand side to the other. Lady Tub passes money to her servant in order that both can complete the ritual by giving a gift to the Valentine whom both have claimed. At the end of the play, courtship leads to marriage, and Wispe and Puppy marry.

Lots were drawn on the eve of Saint Valentine's Day, and the game was thus a nocturnal one. We saw in Pepys that if one drew a name in the lottery, one might well choose to accost that person the next morning – or attempt to do so. Oberon's love juice, derived from Cupid's arrow, 'Will make or man or woman madly dote/Upon the next live creature that it sees' (2.1.171–2), in a way that is precisely analogous to the rules which ritual prescribed for the morning of Saint Valentine's Day. When Theseus greets the lovers with the words: 'Good-morrow friends. Saint Valentine is past: Begin these wood-birds but to couple now?' the stage direction which immediately precedes his words in the Quarto text

reads: 'Shout within: they all start up. Wind horns.'⁴⁰ To the sound
of horns, the ritual of 14 February is accomplished. The lovers
transmit the kisses which secure their Valentines and bring the
game to an end. Hermia confirms her choice via a socially prescribed ritual designed precisely to override parental efforts at
match-making.

The custom that one could claim as one's Valentine the first
stranger of the opposite sex whom one saw could result in embar-
rassment for the gentry. We have seen Mrs Pepys' fear of being
accosted by a workman, and Samuel Pepys' anxiety on account of a
negro, and in a fictional context we have seen how a young male
servant benefited from the largesse of Lady Tub. Titania's awaken-
ing to the sight of an ass represents an extreme version of a
common occurrence, a temporary liaison between people of diver-
gent status. When Titania plies Bottom with gifts and goes about
the wood 'Seeking sweet favours for this hateful fool' (4.1.48) she
behaves precisely as a Valentine ought towards a social inferior. As
permitted by the ritual, the liaison ends as abruptly as it begins.

The rituals of Saint Valentine's Day imply a considerable degree of
sexual equality. While in ordinary life the male always initiated
courtship, on Saint Valentine's Day women seem to have been free to
approach men. A writer at the start of the eighteenth century commented that according to the rules of the lottery system 'the obliga-
tions are equal, and therefore it was formerly the custom mutually to
present [gifts], but now it is customary only for gentlemen.'⁴¹ Helena
and Hermia are forced in the play to pursue their respective men,
and Helena complains that Daphne now has to chase Apollo:

> Your wrongs do set a scandal on my sex.
> We cannot fight for love, as men may do;
> We should be woo'd, and were not made to woo.

> (2.1.240–2)

The difference between the women's role in the greenwood, governed by festive laws, and the women's role at court, governed by
social norms, becomes striking when the young women sit in
respectful silence through 'Pyramus and Thisbe'.

The rites of May, though more overt in the play, are no less pertinent to the narrative structure of *A Midsummer Night's Dream* than
the rites of February. Although the journey into the greenwood

before dawn is normally associated with May Day, we should
remember that on Saint Valentine's Day likewise the young rose
very early – though the weather did not encourage expeditions into
the greenwood. It was not difficult for Shakespeare to draw the two
festive contexts together. The literary tradition, whereby the poet
on Saint Valentine's Day goes out into the greenwood into a surprisingly summery landscape to look at the pairing of the birds,
helped to make the link an easy one. We find this linkage in one of
Shakespeare's source texts, Chaucer's *Legend of Good Women*, where
the poet goes out into the meadows on the morning of May Day
and hears the birds singing of Saint Valentine's Day.

I shall not dwell on the rites of May because Barber, Young and
others have sufficiently signalled their importance.[42] The expedi-
tion into the greenwood, the gathering of dew and the importance
of the hawthorn bush all complement the scene in which Theseus
and Hippolyta enter wearing (as we must assume) the garlands of
hawthorn which were the main visual emblem of the ceremony.
Perhaps less obvious is the relationship between the play and a
'midsummer night', for there is no trace of the corporate processions and bonfires that marked the solstitial ceremony.

Shakespeare's title is in the first instance a homage to Spenser,
whose 'Epithalamion' was published in 1595, and has been
identified as a Shakespearean source.[43] The poem celebrates
Spenser's own wedding on the day of the summer solstice in 1594,
and develops tight parallels between the internal structure of the
poem, the hours of the day, the days of the year, and the bride's rite
of passage.[44] The transition of the year from its waxing to its
waning correlates with the bride's transition from virgin to woman.
It is relevant that maidens on midsummer night were supposed to
dream of the man they were to love.[45] Young women who had
missed out on the annual cycle of renewal in one year positioned
themselves for the next. Shakespeare creates an important image of
midsummer night through the medium of stage iconography.
While Hermia is short and dark – a 'minimus', an 'Ethiope' –
Helena is tall and fair like a 'painted maypole'. As a pair, Hermia
and Helena constitute an emblem of midsummer when the bright
day is very long and the dark night is very short. The conflict
between them reflects the battle of day and night, a battle which
reaches its turning point at midsummer.

The three festivals of Saint Valentine's day, May Day and
Midsummer are interwoven in the central, liminal portion of

A Midsummer Night's Dream, framed by the scenes at court. They are not selected at random for they reflect symbolically three phases in the life cycle of a young person: mate selection, courtship and marriage. And this is the process through which the young aristocrats pass in the liminal, greenwood section of the play. Calendar festivals provided Shakespeare and his audience(s) with a symbolic vocabulary which allowed them to relate the phases of an individual life to laws of nature inscribed in the cosmos. The three festivals thrived in the relatively stable social structure of rural early modern England, and were cherished by an Elizabethan aristocracy that wanted to preserve social stability.

And so we return to the question of theorizing the carnivalesque. One of my favourite images of *A Midsummer Night's Dream* is a fresco at Buscot House in Oxfordshire, evidently of the 1930s. The image is part of a diptych, located under an arch that leads aristo-cratic bathers from their swimming pool to a view of the estate. One half of the diptych shows the local Faringdon Communist Party marching in the background, whilst in the foreground Lord Faringdon, the lord of the house, stands on a hay cart as if at the hustings, and is evidently warning his employees (who were doubtless fortunate to be employed during the depression) not to follow the red flag. On the other side Titania in her bower embraces the ass. The bower is constituted by a white valance at head height supported by four spears and embroidered with Tudor roses. The fairies who look on are evidently young women of the family. Oberon's green costume and position link him as a nature spirit to the estate that lies behind. The vista in the painting leads down a long avenue to an artificial lake, and precisely replicates the real landscape that belongs to Lord Faringdon and confronts him as he passes through the arch. The play is thus conceived as an idyll justifying in symbolic terms the appropriation of nature as property. Its political message is overt.

On what grounds can we claim that the artist of the 1930s sub-verted Shakespeare's play? Or was he rather in a position that allowed him to share the viewpoint of the aristocrats who commis-sioned? It may be that the fairies were played by choristers in a wedding performance, and that those roles were taken over by adults in the public playhouse,[46] introducing a new element of the grotesque to the public performance. It is, however, not upon the fairies but upon the slim and melancholy ass that we must focus if we are to mount a serious challenge to Lord Faringdon's painting and salvage some elements of the Bakhtinian carnival grotesque for a wedding performance in 1596. The ass-head has always pushed productions of the play towards sentimentality, and Peter Brook substituted a simple black rubber nose in his production which sought to emphasize the rampant sexuality of Bottom, following Jan Kott's vision of the play. The time-honoured ass-mask has long helped to obscure in performance the symbolism of the bird song which is so important to the Saint Valentine motif. It seems to me far more likely that a fool's cap with ass ears was used to create Bottom's 'transformed scalp' (4.1.63). The ears could have been held up as a cuckold's horns when Bottom at the end of the song becomes the 'cuckoo'. The figure of Bottom/clown/Kemp seems to refer back to this fool's attire when he recalls

Man is but an ass if he go about to expound this dream. Methought I was – there is no man can tell what. Methought I was – and methought I had – but man is but a patched fool if he will offer to say what methought I had.

(4.1.205–8)

The wooing of the fool seems more appropriate to the recurrent festive motif than the wooing of the ass.[47] It is in the figure of Bottom the clown, the lower-class male locked in the arms of a queen, that we must seek the elusive Bakhtinian grotesque, the dimension of ugliness not proffered to the elegant bathers at Buscot.

Bottom is part of a company of players. These players are a metaphor for Shakespeare's own company who, by performing A Midsummer Night's Dream at a wedding, intruded upon an elite gathering to which they would not normally have been admitted. Their 'Pyramus and Thisbe' is, as has long been recognized, a parody of the company's recent Romeo and Juliet. To present the players of 'Pyramus and Thisbe' as grotesques may thus be construed, in the context of a wedding performance, as a sign of deference, a humorous apology for the fact that the entertainment on such an important night is provided not be illustrious aristocratic masquers but by common players.[48] The case becomes rather more complex in the public playhouse, where the audience are simultaneously positioned (a) as fellow spectators with Theseus, laughing at the folly of the players, and (b) as fellow commoners alongside the players, granted through their visit to the playhouse vicarious access to an elite private gathering.

In the context of a wedding performance we may see Bottom's copulation with Titania as a kind of preparation for the real bedding ceremony. The 'grotesque realism' of Bottom would be a means of preparing the bride and groom for the intimidating and embarrassing rite of passage that social custom required of them. There is a clear correlation between Bottom's low social station and a low carnal aspect of human identity. Within the frame of an aristocratic wedding night, however, there is no cause to see the scene as a critique of marriage, or as a celebration that belongs in any way to the folk. There is nothing inherently subversive in the proposition that aristocrats have bodies just as estates have workers, and that these indispensable bodies/workers need to be controlled. In the context of a public performance the scene works rather differently, of course. The clown, representative of the commons, gains temporary access to the forbidden body of the aristocratic lady.

To summarize: I have located Bakhtin's theory of carnival within a classical tradition which locates festival as the return to a lost Utopia. While 'safety-valve' theories stress how individuals adapt to the status quo, 'utopian' theories show how carnival envisages a better way for society to be organized – and they thus offer a more dynamic and positive view of popular culture. Bakhtin's theory is a blunt critical instrument, however, because the concept of 'carnival' is effectively monologic, postulating a single model and obscuring the differences which allowed festivals to function as a complex semiotic system – as we see in the interplay of festivals in *A Midsummer Night's Dream*. Dionysia, Saturnalia, Mardi Gras and English summer festivals are molten by Bakhtin into a single entity. The assumption that this entity dubbed 'carnival' is the property of the folk as distinct from the elite seriously obscures the mechanisms by which power was validated and maintained in the early modern period. Bakhtin's logocentric methodology is not easily adapted to the phenomenon of performance. In the analysis of theatre, the time and place of the performance, the placing and status of the audience all have to be considered before we can effect a satisfactory analysis of festive or carnivalesque elements.

80   *David Wiles*

NOTES

1. By permission of the publisher, this essay reproduces some passages from chapter 6 of my *Shakespeare's Almanac: A Midsummer Night's Dream, Marriage and the Elizabethan Calendar* (Woodbridge: D.S. Brewer, 1993).
2. Plato, *Laws*, 654: translation adapted from that of T.J. Saunders in *The Laws* (Harmondsworth: Penguin, 1970), p. 86. The untranslatable phrase *epanorthontai tas ge trophas* could be literally rendered 'set straight again their upbringings'.
3. *Laws*, 672, Penguin edn., pp. 113–14.
4. *Politics*, viii.5–7, *The Politics* trans. T.A. Sinclair (Harmondsworth: Penguin, 1962), pp. 307–14.
5. Important discussions include Peter Burke, *Popular Culture in Early Modern Europe* (London: Temple Smith, 1978), pp. 202–5; and Michael D. Bristol, *Carnival and Theater: Plebeian Culture and the Structure of Authority in Renaissance England* (New York & London: Routledge, 1989), pp. 27–32.
6. A.T. Macrobius, *The Saturnalia*, i.7–8, trans. P.V. Davies (New York & London: Columbia University Press, 1969), pp. 55–65.
7. *Dramatic Writings of Nicholas Udall*, ed. J.S. Farmer (London: Early English Text Society, 1906), prologue.
8. Cited in Burke, p. 202.
9. 'From the prehistory of novelistic discourse' in *The Dialogic Imagination*, pp. 53–4. Contrast Tony Harrison's vision of the satyr play as popular culture in his play *Trackers*.
10. *Rabelais and His World*, trans. by Hélène Iswolsky (Bloomington: Indiana University Press, 1984), p. 121.
11. *Ibid.*, p. 76.
12. *Ibid.*, pp. 97, 452.
13. *Ibid.*, p. 75.
14. *Ibid.*, p. 312ff.
15. For examples, see François Laroque, *Shakespeare's Festive World*, trans. J. Lloyd (Cambridge: Cambridge University Press, 1991), p. 141, with note p. 242.
16. Burke, p. 28.
17. Emmanuel Le Roy Ladurie, *Carnival in Romans: A People's Uprising at Romans 1579–1580*, trans. M. Feeney (Harmondsworth: Penguin, 1981), pp. 274–6.
18. Yves-Marie Bercé, *Fête et révolte* (Paris: Hachette, 1976), p. 88.
19. *Ibid.*, pp. 9ff., p. 189.
20. See especially Leah S. Marcus, *The Politics of Mirth. Jonson, Herrick, Milton, Marvell and the Defense of Old Holiday Customs* (Chicago: University of Chicago Press, 1986); Peter Stallybrass, '"We feaste in our Defense": Patrician carnival in early modern England and Robert Herrick's "Hesperides"', *English Literary Renaissance* 16 (1986), pp. 234–252; also Laroque, *Shakespeare's Festive World*, p. 70.
21. Laroque, pp. 96–7. Bristol makes the most he can of the festival in *Carnival and Theater*, pp. 72–87. I have examined the festival in

London in '"That day are you free": *The Shoemaker's Holiday'*, *Cahiers Élisabéthains* 38 (1990), pp. 49–60.
22. 'Forms of Time and Chronotope in the Novel', in *The Dialogic Imagination*, pp. 216–19.
23. See Marvin Carlson, 'Theater and Dialogism', in *Critical Theory and Performance*, ed. J.G. Reinelt and J.R. Roach (Ann Arbor: University of Michigan Press, 1992), pp. 313–23.
24. Bristol, pp. 30–2; C.L. Barber, *Shakespeare's Festive Comedy* (Princeton, NJ: Princeton University Press, 1959), p. 9.
25. *Ibid.*, pp. 172–8, following the discussion of Bakhtin on pp. 19–25.
26. Manfred Pfister, 'Comic Subversion: a Bakhtinian view of the comic in Shakespeare', *Deutsche Shakespeare Gesellschaft West Jahrbuch* (1987), pp. 27–43: p. 39.
27. Wiles, *Shakespeare's Almanac*, chapter 10.
28. Whilst 'Now bent' is the Quarto and Folio reading, modern editors prefer 'New bent'. All quotations are from Harold F. Brooks' Arden edition.
29. *The Paston Letters*, ed. J. Gairdner (London: Chatto & Windus, 1904), v.266–9.
30. See Chaucer, *Parliament of Fowls*, *The Complaint of Mars*, *Complaint d'amours;* Gower, *Balades*, xxxiiii, xxxv; Lydgate, 'The Flower of Courtesy' in *Minor Poems* Vol. II (London: Early English Text Society, 1934); Clanvowe, *The Cuckoo and the Nightingale;* Herrick, 'To his Valentine, on S. Valentine's day', in *Poetical Works* , ed. L.C. Martin (Oxford: Oxford University Press, 1956), p. 149; Surrey, *Poems*, ed. E. Jones (Oxford: Oxford University Press, 1964), no. 15.
31. Note that 14 February in the Julian calendar is equivalent to 4 February on the modern calendar.
32. *Juvenilia* (Manchester: Spenser Society, 1871), ii.474.
33. *Complete Poetry and Selected Prose*, ed. J. Hayward (London: Nonesuch Press, 1946), pp. 103–6.
34. First printed by Joseph Strutt in *Horda Angel-Cynna* (London, 1776), iii.179, and attributed to Lydgate. R.T. Hampson, in *Medii Aevi Kalendarium* (London, 1841), i.162, cites the manuscript reference as Harl. MSS Cod.v.2251 fo.268b. The origins of St Valentine's Day were explored by Francis Douce, in *Illustrations of Shakespeare* (London, 1807).
35. William Boswell, cited in John Brand and W.C. Hazlitt, *Popular Antiquities of Great Britain* (London: J.R. Smith, 1870), i.32.
36. *Misson's Memoirs and Observations in his travels over England*, trans. J. Ozell (London, 1719), pp. 330–1.
37. For the ideological context, see Marcus, *The Politics of Mirth*, pp. 133–5.
38. *Pepys' Diary*, ed. R.C. Latham and W. Matthews (London: G. Bell & Sons, 1970–83), vii.42–4, vi.35, 20, ii.36, iii.29, etc.
39. Nashe, *Works*, ed. R.B. McKerrow (Oxford: Oxford University Press, 1958), iii.403.
40. The stage direction in the Folio reads: 'Horns and they wake. Shout within, they all start up.' With the separation of music and ritual

action, the festive context seems to have become lost. Perhaps Jacobean performers no longer associated the play with Saint Valentine's Day.

41.   *British Apollo* (1709), cited in Brand and Hazlitt, *Popular Antiquities of Great Britain*, i.33.
42.   Barber, *Shakespeare's Festive Comedy*; David P. Young, *Something of Great Constancy* (New Haven, Conn.: Yale University Press, 1966).
43.   See the Arden edition, ed. Harold F. Brooks (London: Methuen, 1979), pp. xxxv–xxxvi.
44.   See A. Kent Hieatt, *Short Time's Endless Monument* (New York: Columbia University Press, 1960); also Wiles, *Shakespeare's Almanac*, pp. 67–9.
45.   Young explores some of these links in *Something of Great Constancy*.
46.   William A. Ringler 'The Number of Actors in Shakespeare's Early Plays', in G.E. Bentley (ed.), *The Seventeenth-Century Stage* (Chicago: Chicago University Press, 1968), pp. 110–34. For the suggestion that choir boys were used, see E.K. Chambers, *William Shakespeare* (Oxford: Oxford University Press, 1931), ii.86. T.J. King, in *Casting Shakespeare's Plays* (Cambridge: Cambridge University Press, 1992), opposes Ringler's view of the doubling.
47.   See Laroque's documentation of the morris dance, in *Shakespeare's Festive World* , pp. 121–36. On Kemp as Bottom, see David Wiles, *Shakespeare's Clown* (Cambridge: Cambridge University Press, 1987), pp. 74–5 and passim.
48.   It is sometimes falsely asserted that plays were not performed at Elizabethan weddings, only masques. Players did perform at the marriage of the Earl of Northumberland in 1594 for a fee of ten pounds: Wiles, *Shakespeare's Almanac*, p. 44.

5

Shakespeare's 'Battle of Carnival and Lent': The Falstaff Scenes Reconsidered (1&2 Henry IV)

François Laroque

In his pioneering book, Mikhail Bakhtin analyses the carnivalesque as the victory of the old world over the new, as the force which illustrates the way the principles of inversion and permutation work underneath the surface of carnival and festive misrule.[1] There 'Billingsgate', the language of the marketplace, takes precedence over the idiom of the learned, of Church and university culture. For Bakhtin, the carnivalesque is another version of the grotesque, it is the moment in the year when it is dynamically expressed in strings of abuse, in a number of comical and unexpected images; this shows how the aesthetics of the grotesque had become tied up with calendrical customs which served both to regulate and discharge the energies of popular festivity.

By creating a character like Falstaff, Shakespeare comes as close as he possibly could to Rabelais's particular style of comedy which, as we know, centres on the body and on the belly as well as on the world of the tavern and of the carnivalesque celebration of life. At the same time, the stress placed on this lower sphere is being used as a distorting mirror to reflect and undermine the upper level of court life and of the law as it is embodied by the Lord Chief Justice.

The Falstaff scenes in 1 & 2 Henry IV provide the spectator with a dramatic counterpart of Pieter Bruegel's famous painting 'The Battle of Carnival and Lent'. As I shall show, Shakespeare's ten-act play is shaped by an underlying opposition between those two principles. Although we can find no proof that Shakespeare knew of Bruegel's painting nor of the contrary (he might have seen it in the form of Flemish engravings or prints which were widely circulated at the time), it is quite clear that a Bruegel-like atmosphere pervades the two parts of the play.

The second scene of *1 Henry IV* presents an inverted version of the vision of time, which is expressed in King Henry's first words at court: 'So shaken as we are, so wan with care,/Find we a *time* for frighted peace to pant...' (my emphasis). The problem indeed is to find a truce, a respite to the intestine wars of the kingdom. This hope is immediately belied by Westmoreland's news of the battle on Holy-rood day (1.1.52). In the next scene, what we first discover is Falstaff surprised by Prince Hal turning day into night as he lies sleeping on a bench in the afternoon:

Fal. Now, Hal, what *time* of day is it, lad?
Prince Thou art so fat-witted with drinking of old sack, and unbuttoning after supper, and sleeping upon benches after noon, that thou hast forgotten to demand that truly which thou wouldst know. What a devil hast thou to do with the time of the day? Unless hours were cups of sack, and minutes capons, and clocks the tongues of bawds, and dials the signs of leaping-houses, and the blessed sun himself a fair hot wench in flame-coloured taffeta, I see no reason why thou shouldst be so superfluous to demand the time of the day.

                                        (1.2.1–12; my emphasis).

Falstaff's heavy, fuddled sleep provides a powerful contrast to the breathless tempo of war and peace ('for frighted peace to pant ...') which, like its sleepless king, fails to come to rest. Falstaff also stands as an ironical objective correlative to Hal, who must find something to do because of the non-vacancy of the throne. Killing time may thus be for him nothing but a means to kill his father by proxy. Prince Hal levels his sarcasm at the grotesque caricature of the king represented by Falstaff, while his father Henry laments the unworthy dissipation of the heir to the throne.

In the Prince's speech, time is seen from the point of view of various concrete manifestations (hours, minutes, clocks and dials) and it is emblematized in a burlesque procession with Sir John's pet sins marching by: 'cups of sack', 'capons', 'bawds', 'leaping-houses' and 'hot wench'. A similar device to materialize time under the form of carnival pageantry appears in the allegory of Rumour at the outset of *2 Henry IV*:

> *Enter Rumour painted full of tongues*
>
> Open your ears ...
> Upon my tongues continual slanders ride,
> The which in every language I pronounce,
> Stuffing the ears of men with false reports ...
> And who but Rumour, who but only I,
> Make fearful musters, and prepar'd defence,
> Whiles the big year, swoln with some other grief,
> Is thought with child by the stern tyrant War,
> And no such matter? Rumour is a pipe
> Blown by surmises, jealousies, conjectures,
> And of so easy and so plain a stop
> That the blunt monster with uncounted heads,
> The still-discordant wav'ring multitude,
> Can play upon it. But what need I thus
> My well-known body to anatomize
> Among my household?
>
> (*Induction*, 1–22)

With its tongue-studded cloak, Rumour is a visual metonymy of the many-headed monster and the several venomous mouths that swell the body politic with the ill wind of calumny or false news and, in its final metaphor, it reveals the aesthetic principle which lies at the background of carnivalesque discourse in the play. Such concrete figuration of the abstract (time, rumour), as picturesque as it is theatrical, comes from an anatomy or dissection of the body. It is a form of comic surgery, an art which was then regarded as a ceremonial practised in the 'anatomic theatres'.[2] Such variations remind us of the anti-masque, a device consisting in using a burlesque, popular or satirical sequence to be used as a contrast or as an introduction to the more lofty theme of the masque itself.

The rest of the exchanges between the Prince and Falstaff indeed take us towards a lyrical outburst, which is reminiscent of the verbal refinements of the masque:

Fal. Marry then sweet wag, when thou art king let not us that are squires of the night's body be called thieves of the day's beauty:

let us be Diana's foresters, gentlemen of the shade, minions of
the moon; and let men say we be men of good government,
being governed, as the sea is, by our noble and chaste mistress
the moon, under whose countenance we steal ...

                                                              (1.2.23–9)

Besides the string of puns on 'night'/'knight', 'body'/'bawdy',
'beauty'/'booty' and the alliterative sequence, one remarks a style
that parodies Lyly's Euphuism in *Endymion* (1591), a comedy where
the title-part is a young man in love with the goddess Cynthia, the
inconstant moon. The prologue of the play presents it as 'a tale of
the Man in the Moone' and one finds in the buffooneries of the sub-
plot a passage close to Prince Hal's first soliloquy.[3]

In this burlesque idealization of a rather sordid situation of cony-
catcher and parasite, Shakespeare lends a euphuistic accent to his
character to suggest an association between Falstaff and Robin
Hood and to make his tavern the urban counterpart of Sherwood
Forest. At the same time, the allusion to Diana and the moon con-
tributes to making Falstaff the champion of carnivalesque misrule
in the history plays linked to the 'monstrous regiment of women' –
by witches like Joan of Arc or amazons like Margaret (wasn't
misrule essentially regarded then as a 'rule of mis(s)?').[4] Indeed
Falstaff will later say that 'his skin hangs about him like an old
lady's loose gown' (3.3.2–3) and, in *The Merry Wives of Windsor,* he
will leave Mrs Ford's house disguised as Mother Prat, also known
as 'the fat' or 'the old woman' of Brainford (4.2.67, 69, 168). So, it
would seem that, under his cloak, Falstaff might embody the roles
of both Robin Hood and Maid Marian before the latter becomes
identified with Mrs Quickly later in the play (3.3.112). Transvestism
and gender change were indeed one of the common customs and
features of carnival games. Moreover, to the popular audiences of
the Globe, the folklore linked to Robin Hood combined the conservative flavour of 'Merry England' with the rebellion against the
king's authority. An Eastcheap tavern, like the forest of yore, seems
to enjoy the privilege of a 'liberty', i.e. of a form of extraterritorial
status, where the outlaws and the merry souls could find a refuge.
(Doesn't the name 'Boar's Head' symbolically refer to hunting, the
main sport and means of sustenance of the big-hearted rebels and
thieves?) So the territorial enclave gives a 'habitation and a name'
to the carnivalesque theme, itself enclosed within a parenthesis,
that of the calendar interval.

Falstaff's rebellion is first and foremost that of the belly and it is made to look like the general leading Carnival's army against the soldiers of famine[5] and the spare practitioners of Lent. The successive waves of assault of the fat against the lean make up a leitmotif running through both parts of *Henry IV* and they are a comic counterpoint to the real battles opposing the rebels to the king. This is a form of popular psychomachia where the strings of parodic litanies belong to the genre which Bakhtin calls 'praise-abuse'.[6] Many examples of it can be found in *1 Henry IV*, as, for instance, in this exchange between the Prince and Falstaff:

Prince Why, thou clay-brained guts, thou knotty-pated fool thou whoreson obscene greasy tallow catch ... This sanguine coward, this bed presser, this horse back breaker, this huge hill of flesh, –
Falstaff 'Sblood, you starveling, you eel-skin, you dried neat's tongue, you bull's pizzle, you stock-fish ... you tailor's yard, you sheath, you bow-case, you vile standing tuck

(2.4.221–44)

In the second half of this same scene, we attend a highly theatrical rendering of the game in a scene of a play within the play. Initially presented as a parody of the king's rebuking his son Hal, it soon veers off in the direction of the belly Falstaff, who is then put on trial like King Carnival on the eve of Ash Wednesday. What should have been for Hal a rehearsal and an exorcism of his father's angry sermonizing quickly turns into a carnivalesque show and the condemnation of Falstaff, the Prince's punching bag:

Prince Why dost thou converse with that trunk of humours, that bolting-hutch of beastliness, that swollen parcel of dropsies, that huge bombard of sack, that stuffed cloak-bag of guts, that roasted Manningtree ox with the pudding in his belly ...?

(2.4.442–47)

The string of adjectives is the form taken up by these oral and tribal jousts, where the totem of Falstaff is the fat ox of Manningtree fair, in Essex, or the little boar-pig of Bartholomew Fair in London ('little tidy Bartholomew boar-pig', *2 Henry IV*, 2.4.227), while Hal is identified with a form of dried ling (stockfish) and with an eel's skin (if that word is used rather than 'elf-skin', which would assimilate him to the 'changeling' mentioned by the king in the first scene of the play [*1 Henry IV*, 1.1.85–90]).

These facetious as well as injurious appellations are complemented by a number of pet-names which play upon patronyms as well as on the physical appearance of the two antagonists. Thus, Hal is associated with 'egg and butter' (1.2.21), i.e. to lean fare, in the beginning, and he becomes opposed to the one whom Poins calls 'Sir John Sack and Sugar' (1.2.110) in the same way as Sir John Paunch appears as the antithesis of John of Gaunt (2.2.63–4). This brilliant pun of Falstaff's turns the bodily variations on the carnivalesque body into the negative counterpart of the heroic dimension since this apostrophe takes up again John of Gaunt's variations on his name in *Richard II*, when he is about to die:

Richard How is't with aged Gaunt?
Gaunt O, how that name befits my composition!
 Old Gaunt indeed and gaunt in being old,
 Within me grief hath kept a tedious fast,
 And who abstains from meat that is not gaunt?
 For sleeping England long time have I watch'd,
 Watching brings leanness, leanness is all gaunt …
 Gaunt am I for the grave, gaunt as a grave,
 Whose hollow womb inherits nought but bones …

(2.1.72–83)

In *2 Henry IV*, when the body appears more and more afflicted by disease and symbolizes the progressive exhaustion of the king, food is lean and it goes against the grain of Falstaff's pun which transforms 'gravy' into 'gravity' before a rather pompous Lord Chief Justice. The time of penance has arrived, even if certain champions of leanness like Shallow have now become fatter:

Falstaff I do remember him at Clement's Inn, like a man made after supper of a cheese-paring. When a'was naked, he was for all the world like a forked radish, with a head fantastically carved upon it with a knife … I saw it and told John a Gaunt he beat his own name, for you might have thrust him and all his apparel into an eel-skin – the case of a treble hautboy was a mansion for him, a court; and now has he land and beefs.

(3.2.302–22)

Doll calls Falstaff a 'muddy conger', while both, according to the Hostess, are 'as rheumatic as two dry toasts' (*2 Henry IV*, 2.4. 53, 56). Speaking of Pistol, Doll says that 'he lives upon mouldy stewed prunes and dried cakes' (2.4.142–3). Falstaff compares Poins to Prince Hal, because 'he eats conger and fennel, and drinks off candles' ends for flap-dragons' (2.4.242–3). As to the army of down-at-heel rogues whom he recruits for the battle, it only includes a bunch of pathetic starvelings with predestined names: 'Mouldy', 'Shadow', 'Feeble', 'Wart' and 'Bullcalf' (only the latter might seem worthy to join the army of King Carnival!). Life's energy has dwindled away, the 'wassail candle' is almost burnt out and Falstaff's purple piece on the praise of sherris sack, which he delivers on the eve of the battle of Gaultree forest (4.3), is like his last will and testament. This meditation on the virtues of wine that warms the blood reminds us of Rabelais's praise of the 'Dive bouteille' while it lays down the main commandments of Falstaff's carnivalesque catechism:

Good faith, this same young sober-blooded boy doth not love me, nor a man cannot make him laugh; but that's no marvel, he drinks no wine. There's never none of these demure boys come to any proof; for thin drink doth so over-cool their blood, and making many fish meals, that they fall into a kind a male green-sickness; and when they marry they get wenches. They are generally fools and cowards – which some of us should be too, but for inflammation. A good sherris-sack hath a twofold operation in it. It ascends me into the brain, dries me there all the foolish and dull and crudy vapours which environ it, makes it apprehensive, quick, forgetive, full of nimble, fiery and delectable shapes, which, delivered o'er to the voice, the tongue, which is the birth, become excellent wit. The second property of your excellent sherris is the warming of the blood … It illumineth the face, which, as a beacon, gives warming to all the rest of this kingdom, man, to arm; and then the vital commoners, and inland petty spirits, muster me all to their captain, the heart; who, great and puffed with this retinue, doth any deed of courage; and this valour comes of sherris … If I had a thousand sons, the first human principle I would teach them should be to forswear thin potation, and to addict themselves to sack …

(4.3.85–124)

In this perspective, Hal, who plays the part of Falstaff's adoptive son (the phrase 'If I had a thousand sons' has here a bitterly ironic ring), uses the carnivalesque as a mask or as a cloud to hide his 'sun-like majesty' before he can rise in the full light of his glory and surprise the world with his sudden reformation in *Henry V*.[7] As a consummate actor, the Prince has understood all he could get out of his momentary eclipse from court in the 'anti-masque' of his underground life: this was a sure way of preparing his future metamorphosis and to mastermind the rebirth of the obscure changeling into a glorious sun-king, the apotheosis of the masque, where, after he has eliminated his rival Hotspur, he will keep the best role for himself.

In the last part of this essay, I shall focus on the importance of the ambivalent images of the body in the play. These serve to give a comic content to the punning association often made between carnival and cannibal.[8] This deep-seated ambivalence is part and parcel of the grotesque and it has been well analysed by Neil Rhodes in *Elizabethan Grotesque*: 'The Elizabethan grotesque derives from the unstable coalescence of contrary images of the flesh: indulged, abused, purged and damned.'[9] Indeed, at the beginning of *1 Henry IV* the king's description of the horrors of the intestine strife that tears apart the kingdom evokes images of cannibalism in its presentation of war as 'butchery':

> No more the thirsty entrance of this soil
> Shall daub her lips with her own children's blood.
>   ... those opposed eyes,
> Which, like the meteors of a troubled heaven,
> All of one nature, of one substance bred,
> Did lately meet in the intestine shock
> And furious close of civil butchery,
> Shall now ... be no more oppos'd.

(1.1.5–15)

Now, this pious wish is immediately opposed by Westmoreland's atrocious news from the Welsh front:

> the noble Mortimer ...
> Was by the rude hands of that Welshman taken
> A thousand of his people butchered,
> Upon whose dead corpse there was such misuse,

Such beastly shameless transformation
By those Welshwomen done, as may not be
Without much shame retold or spoken of.

(1.1.38–46)

Hence the second Henriad opens on these images of carnage, on the scandal of bodies shamefully mutilated by furious hags. The earth is here personalized in the pathetic fallacy of line 6, which turns it into an infanticidal and cannibalistic mother, a ghoul that drinks fresh blood. This image is reinforced by Hotspur's heroic stance when he says that he is ready to shed all the precious liquid in his veins: 'Yea, on his part I'll empty all these veins,/And shed my dear blood, drop by drop in the dust ...' (1.3.131–2). The grotesque is born out of the juxtaposition of this with the quantities of sherris-sack drunk by Falstaff all along the two parts of the play! The vampiric earth is as thirsty for blood as he is of wine!

This is also present in the subterranean network of imagery which associates Falstaff's cony-catching and carnival activities with hunting: it is indeed indirectly linked to the images of 'Diana's foresters' and to the name of the 'Boar's Head' in Eastcheap.[10] Furthermore, if one thinks that the battle described by Westmoreland takes place on Holy-rood Day (14 September), one can note that the date corresponds to the opening date of the hunting season in early modern England.[11]

In this light, it is clear that the game that is being hunted in the play is no other than Falstaff himself, the big boar that will have to be chased, thus creating the comic image of a predator losing part of his tallow in the sport: '... Falstaff sweats to death,/And lards the lean earth as he walks along' (2.2.103–4). This is a subliminal introduction to the famous theme of the hunted hunter – a theme also found in *The Merry Wives of Windsor*, when Falstaff, wearing the horns of the mythical hunter, is finally identified with a deer. This is because of the expected deer/dear pun in a love comedy and also a reference to the myth of Actaeon which is here rendered in its moralizing, bourgeois version of *Ovide moralisé*.[12]

The underlying motif of the hunt in *1 & 2 Henry IV* is itself an indirect metaphor of civil war under its double appellation of 'intestine shock' and 'civil butchery' in the king's speech. One is naturally tempted to equate the adjective 'intestine' with the obsession with Falstaff's belly or 'guts', which are part and parcel of the carnivalesque preoccupation with foodstuffs and tripe. Shrove

Tuesday was then regarded as the time for slaughtering cattle and Bruegel, in his 'Battle of Carnival and Lent', has painted King Carnival as a butcher straddling a wine barrel and brandishing a pike with a piglet on the spit.[13]

Shakespeare then brings carnival, tavern and hunting together on the battlefield scene when Falstaff simulates death in order to keep his body alive. The rhythm of Shrewsbury's battle is indeed quite intense and breathtaking. On the one hand we find the war tactics consisting in multiplying the images of the king (called 'counterfeits' or 'shadows') who has his arms worn by barons such as Blunt, thus giving the fiery Douglas the feeling that the king's body may grow again as fast as Hydra's heads (5.4.24). On the other hand, there is a double duel. The one opposes Hal and Hotspur and is ended by the death of the champion of a decaying chivalry while the other is a shadow combat between Douglas and Falstaff since the latter avoids the fight to fake death. This is the moment when the Prince, seeing him lying upon the earth, pronounces his death elegy:

> What, old acquaintance, could not all this flesh
> Keep in a little life? Poor Jack, farewell ...
> Death hath not struck so fat a deer today.
> Though many dearer, in this bloody fray.
> Embowell'd will I see thee by and by
> Till then in blood by noble Percy lie.
>
> (5.4.101–9)

Falstaff rises at once, indignant at the words he has just heard: 'Embowelled? If thou embowel me today, I'll give/you leave to powder me and eat me tomorrow' (5.4.110–11). On the one hand, we find war with its codes, tricks and honour, on the other the hunt and its ritual. Falstaff, like the deer before the quarry, must be embowelled. His body becomes food in the ironical anti-phrase, which he mentally addresses to the Prince as already suggested earlier in the burlesque scene of the bottle used as a pistol:

> Well, if Percy be alive, I'll pierce him. If he do come in my way, so: if he do not, if I come in his willingly, let him make a carbonado of me
>
> (5.3.56–8)

So, Falstaff is once again turned into the 'Manningtree ox with the pudding in his belly' (*1 Henry IV*, 2.1.446–7), fat carnival food to feast his friends. Besides those discrete allusions to cannibalism, echoed by Pistol's slip when he evokes in front of the Hostess and Bardolph 'Caesars and … Cannibals' instead of Hannibals (1.4.163), he becomes, in the phrase of Michael Bristol, 'a clownish paraphrase of the political doctrine of *dignitas non moritur*: the king's mystical identity or dignity never dies.'[14]

In the last analysis, whether it presents us with Douglas's frustration in his inability to kill the king during the battle, since he can only attack his make-believe counterparts ('counterfeits') or duplications of himself ('shadows'), or whether it is the question of Falstaff's fake death, the comedy of the grotesque lies in the multiplication of trompe-l'oeil images and in the physical impossibility of seizing the reality of the identity or of the state of the adversary's body (either alive or dead).

Parallel to these *ad infinitum* duplications, the tension between the macabre and the culinary or between horror and festivity remains the dominant factor. Before the battle, Falstaff had cynically called his lean and hungry troops 'food for powder' (*1 Henry IV*, 4.2.65–6). At the heroic level, Percy's last words before he dies are a real macabre exemplum, a form of *Vanitas* in which human flesh is nothing but food for worms:

Hotspur O, I could prophesy
   But that the earthly and cold hand of death
   Lies on my tongue: no, Percy thou art dust,
   And food for –[*Dies.*]
Prince For worms, brave Percy.

(*1 Henry IV*, 5.4.82–6)

At this juncture, we are made to understand the fundamental complementarity of tavern life and battleground, of Carnival exuberance and Lenten restriction or negativity: they are the two sides of the same coin. On the one hand, there is the slaughtering of cattle at Martinmas and the pigs butchered in Carnival time with vast amounts of wine or sherris sack being drunk to fill Falstaff's hungry belly and bottomless throat; on the other, we find the butchery of civil war that fattens the worms and offers fresh drink to a vampiric earth. The recurring images of molten grease or lard in the various Falstaff scenes are the grotesque counterpart of the blood shed by the victims of the war. The libations in honour of Bacchus and the price paid for sacrifices to the god of war, Mars, all look like almost reversible elements in the carnivalesque vision of body and body politic where battle and banquet, hunting party and hearty eating are progressively woven into one another's patterns in successive networks of analogies.

The world of appetite, as illustrated by Falstaff cynical sponging on the Hostess, leads to ruin as the latter bitterly complains to the Lord Chief Justice: 'He hath eaten me out of house and home, he hath put all my substance into that fat belly of his' (*2 Henry IV*, 2.1.72–3). The voracity of the carnivalesque body, emblematized by a gaping mouth and a swollen belly ('embossed', 'blown', etc.), provides an objective correlative of the idea of uncontrollable expense. It is also at the origin of a movement of expansion and excess illustrated by the puns on Falstaff's belt (see, for instance, the pun on 'waste' and 'waist' in *2 Henry IV* 2.2.39–42).[15] Falstaff is an apostle of extravagance like Lear with his hundred knights. This anticipates the whole trend of sickness imagery which announces both the end of carnival and of Falstaff himself. These become more and more important in *2 Henry IV*, so that Falstaff's banishment at the end can be read as a 'farewell to the flesh' or *Carni vale*, one of the supposed etymologies for the word carnival. At the beginning of *2 Henry IV*, Falstaff is anxious about the state of his urine, he complains of the various evils that plague him (gout and the pox) or of the weight of his belly ('my womb, my womb, my womb undoes me', 4.3.22–3). But these metaphors, as everything else in this play of mirrors and structural correspondences, overlap on the higher spheres, as Falstaff's diseases are also the symptom of the evil that is eating away into the body politic. Indeed, the king's body is itself being wasted by disease:

King Then you perceive the body of our kingdom
       How foul it is, what rank diseases grow,
       And with what danger, near the heart of it.

(*2 Henry IV*, 3.1.38–40)

In the Falstaff scenes of *1 & 2 Henry IV*, the battle of Carnival and Lent serves as a comic duplication of the opposition between the worlds of court and battle on the one hand, and of the festive life of the tavern on the other. The dominant patterns of imagery in these scenes find their justification and coherence in carnival and popular culture which pits the fat against the lean in a series of comic verbal assaults. There is a pendulum effect from one pole to the next which one may observe at work in the two Falstaff plays.

In this world of shadows, the more than substantial body of Falstaff becomes the metaphor of the avatars of the body heroic and politic in a world which, because of the crisis of traditional values, has now been possessed by a sense of relativity. In this murky world, the royal son/sun has been obscured by clouds and the heir to the throne, Prince Hal has decided to wear the mask of a reveller and boon companion, money and the body have become the yardsticks of all things. The size of Falstaff's body is certainly partly due to a capacity for caricatural and carnival enlargement and excess, but it also stands for the triumph of life at the expense of tragic sacrifice.

Carnival, like the king, never dies.

NOTES

All Shakespeare references are to the current Arden editions: *1 & 2 Henry IV*, ed. A.R. Humphreys; *Richard II*, ed. Peter Ure; and *The Merry Wives of Windsor*, ed. H.J. Oliver.

1. Mikhail Bakhtin, *Rabelais and His World* (1965), trans. Hélène Iswolsky (Bloomington: Indiana University Press, 1984).
2. See Marie-Christine Pouchelle, *Corps et chirurgie à l'apogée du Moyen Âge* (Paris: Flammarion, 1985).
3. *Sir Tophas* [a bragging soldier] ... love is a lord of misrule, and keepeth Christmas in my corps.
   Epithon [page to Sir Tophas] No doubt there is good chere: what dishes of delight doth his lordship feast you with withal?
   Top. First, with a great platter of plum-porridge of pleasure, wherein is stued the mutton of distrust.
   Ep. Excellent love lap.
   Top. Then commeth a pye of patience, a hen of honey, a goose of gall, a capon of care, and many other viands; some sweet, and some sowre.... (V.2)
   The Dramatic Works of John Lyly, ed. F.W. Fairholt, (2 vols, London, 1892) I, pp. 69–70
4. See my article 'La notion de "Misrule" à l'époque élisabéthaine: la fête comme monde à l'envers et comme contre-temps' in *L'image du monde renversé et ses représentations littéraires et para-littéraires de la fin du XVIe siècle au milieu du XVIIe*, ed. Jean Lafond et Augustin Redondo (Paris: Vrin, 1979), p. 167.

5. Indeed Falstaff says of Shallow 'a was the very genius of famine', *2 Henry IV*, 3.2.307–8.
6. *Rabelais*, p. 419. But the analysis of the concept is found earlier in the book: 'Praise and abuse are, so to speak, the two sides of the same coin. If the right side is praise, the wrong side is abuse, and vice versa. The billingsgate idiom is a two-faced Janus. The praise ... is ironic and ambivalent. It is on the brink of abuse; the one leads to the other, and it is impossible to draw the line between them' (p. 165).
7. See Kristen Poole, 'Saints Alive! Falstaff, Martin Marprelate, and the Staging of Puritanism', *Shakespeare Quarterly* 46 (Spring 1995), p. 73: '*Henry IV, Part I* ... is largely driven by Hal's flirtation ... with border between authority and subversion, orthodoxy and heresy. Like the anti-Martinists, Hal enters into the terms of carnival subversion, represented and embodied by Falstaff, while still maintaining his position of authority.'
8. In this connection, see Le Roy Ladurie's *Carnival in Romans*, p. 198 and my own comments on these analyses in *Shakespeare's Festive World* (Cambridge: Cambridge University Press, 1991, repr. 1994), p. 274.
9. *Elizabethan Grotesque* (London, Routledge & Kegan Paul, 1980), p. 4.
10. As P.E. Jones reminds us in his book *The Butchers of London* (London: Secker and Warburg, 1976), pp. 77–8, Eastcheap was the butchers' headquarters in London and a boar's head was the emblem of the Butchers' Guild of Saint Luke. I am grateful to Richard Wilson for calling my attention to this in his paper '''A Brute Part'': *Julius Caesar* and the Rites of Violence' (forthcoming in *Cahiers Élisabéthains*).
11. On this see Richard Marienstras's *Le proche et le lointain* (translated as *New Perspectives on the Shakespearean World*, Cambridge University Press, 1985), Paris, Éditions de Minuit, 1981, pp. 61–2. When reading this, we realize that the time which corresponds to the symbolic calendar of *1 & 2 Henry IV* follows closely the calendar of doe hunting which went from Holy-rood Day to Candlemas (2 February), i.e. to the first possible date before Shrove Tuesday (St Blaise's Day on 3 February).
12. See my article 'Ovidian Transformations and Folk Festivities in *A Midsummer Night's Dream, The Merry Wives of Windsor* and *As You Like It*', *Cahiers Élisabéthains* No. 25 (April 1984), pp. 27–9. Let us note, incidentally, that Falstaff, earlier on in this comedy, had expressed a feeling of nausea at the image of a 'barrow of butcher's offal' (*Merry Wives*, 3.5.5).
13. See Claude Gaignebet, 'Le combat de carnaval et de carême de P. Bruegel (1559)', *Annales*, No. 2, March/April 1972, p. 336.
14. *Carnival and Theater. Plebeian Culture and the Structure of Authority in Renaissance England* (New York & London, Methuen,1985), p. 183.
15. See Poole, p. 74: 'Within the plays themselves, Falstaff assumes a voice and role similar to that of Martin Marprelate, becoming a swelling carnival force that threatens to consume Hal's "princely privilege"....'

6

Facing Puritanism: Falstaff, Martin Marprelate and the Grotesque Puritan

Kristen Poole

The Lollard martyr Sir John Oldcastle is best known to literary scholars as the model for Shakespeare's Sir John Falstaff. The likeness between the militant religious leader and the irreverent, drunken knight is not, however, obvious. Oldcastle had become a prominent cultural figure in Elizabethan England, his trial and death recounted in Foxe's *Acts and Monuments*, Stowe's *Annales*, Holinshed's *Chronicles* and elsewhere.[1] For some, Oldcastle was a valiant, victimized martyr; for others, he was a devious, schismatic heretic and traitor, who betrayed his friend and king, Henry V.[2] Yet within Shakespeare's own time, audiences had no difficulty recognizing Falstaff as a caricature of Oldcastle. Falstaff appears to have been called 'Oldcastle' in early performances of *1 Henry IV*;[3] the name was subsequently changed in order to placate the outraged Lords Cobham, or to appease a disgruntled Protestant audience, who hailed Oldcastle as a hero, but even after 'Oldcastle' was re-dubbed 'Falstaff' extensive historical and literary evidence indicates that the public did not quickly forget the character's original and 'true' identity.[4] The name 'Oldcastle' was retained for private (including court) performances, and many seventeenth-century authors indicate that 'Falstaff' was widely understood as an alias for the Lollard martyr.[5]

The decision of recent prominent editors to reinstate Falstaff's original name in *1 Henry IV* has resulted in significant editorial debate, and has once again brought the Oldcastle connection into scholarly limelight.[6] While Falstaff's genealogy has sparked diverse critical discussions,[7] one of the simplest and most provocative questions has remained, however, largely unasked and unanswered: why, contrary to so many of the contemporary representations, did Shakespeare take the figure of this 'noble Christen warryour' (in John Bale's phrase[8]) and mould him into the Rabelaisian, gluttonous coward of the Henriad? Or, conversely, why did he deviate so far from the alternative tradition of depicting Oldcastle as a bellicose heretic, a serious military threat to king and state? Some critics maintain that 'Shakespeare simply blundered'[9] – that he more or less picked a name out of an historical hat, a name that happened to have unfortunate political consequences. Others assert (somewhat more plausibly) that Shakespeare intended to satirize the Elizabethan Lords Cobham, Sir William Brooke or his reputedly less competent son and successor, Henry, descendants by marriage of the original Oldcastle.[10] Neither of these answers seems satisfying. The notion of the playwright innocently and ignorantly choosing the name of a figure who had become hotly contested as a cultural icon by competing religious/political factions does not seem likely. And while Elizabethan and Jacobean gossips seem to have revelled in the Falstaffian portrayal of the Lord Cobhams' namesake, thus far scholars have established no clear motive for personal parody; rather, there were strong reasons to *avoid* conflict with William Brooke, then Lord Chamberlain and in control of the theatres (Scoufos, 1979, pp. 35–6).

Examining the Henriad in the greater context of Elizabethan polemical discourse reveals that Shakespeare's depiction of the Lollard Oldcastle was not a daring, radical or innovative departure from the stereotypical image of the Puritan, as critics have supposed. Nor is it, as J. Dover Wilson suggested, simply an ingenious modernization of the Vice character from earlier morality plays (although Falstaff's presentation is certainly indebted to this tradition).[11] Rather, this presentation of Oldcastle is fully in keeping with the tenor of late- sixteenth-century anti-Puritan literature, especially the anti-Marprelate tracts and the burlesque stage performances of the Marprelate controversy (1588–90), in which Puritans were frequently depicted as grotesque individuals living in carnivalesque communities. In many ways Falstaff epitomizes the image of the grotesque Puritan.[12] Shakespeare's representation of a prominent Lollard martyr does not depoliticize Falstaff, but transposes him into a register of religious/political language familiar to his Elizabethan audience. Harold Bloom has noted that Falstaff 'is given to parodying Puritan preachers'.[13] Falstaff does indeed parody such preachers, but not just as an overweight, ungodly knight making bar-room jokes about them; rather, the person of Falstaff is himself a parody of the sixteenth-century Puritan. Shakespeare's audiences would most likely have recognized Falstaff (whose very name, 'False staff', could be read as a parody of such Puritan names as More Fruit, Faint Not, Perseverance, Deliverance[14]) in the literary tradition of the grotesque Puritan begun by the Marprelate Tracts; Falstaff in turn becomes a foundational moment for a theatrical traditional of grotesque Puritans, which would continue with Jonson's Zeal-of-the-Land Busy and Middleton's Plumporridge.

The pamphlet warfare of 'Martin Marprelate' and his adversaries marks the entrance of the Puritan figure into popular literature. By the late 1580s, the Puritans' hopes of ecclesiastical reform had faded; 'popish' vestments and ceremonies remained an integral part of the English Church, and in 1583 the anti-Puritan John Whitgift had been appointed Archbishop of Canterbury. As the desired reforms became more illusory, Puritans such as the popular, 24-year-old preacher John Penry increasingly went underground, illegally publishing attacks on the bishops and non-preaching (often non-resident) clergy. The Church authorities felt the sting of these attacks and appointed John Bridges, Dean of Salisbury, as their spokesman. But his *Defense of the government established in the Church of Englande for ecclesiasticall matters* (1587), a large quarto volume containing 1,400 pages of 'lumbering orthodoxy', did little to stop the flow of anti-prelatical attacks.[15] Early in 1588 Penry sallied forth with the *Exhortation*, a scathing assault on the bishops, and in April of the same year the young John Udall challenged the episcopacy with *The State of the Church of England laide open*. The printer for many of these pamphlets was the Puritan sympathizer Robert Waldegrave, whose printing press was finally seized and destroyed in the spring of 1588.[16]

According to legend, during the chaos surrounding the destruction of his press Waldegrave managed to escape with a box of types hidden under his cloak.[17] Armed with these and a newly acquired press, Waldegrave was able to help launch the guerrilla pamphlet warfare of Martin Marprelate. In October of 1588, Martin's first clandestine tract, *The Epistle*, exploded onto the scene, quickly circulating in and around London. Intended as an introduction to *The Epitome* (a critical summary of John Bridges' work), *The Epistle* hailed the 'terrible priests' in a riotously irreverent and comic tone, a stark contrast to the stodgy pedantry of Bridges's *Defense*. Martin Marprelate (a pseudonym for one or more undetermined authors, most likely including Penry, Udall and Job Throkmorton[18]) informs his readers from the first that he must play the fool, since that is the appropriate response to Bridge's text: 'Because, I could not deal with his book commendably, according to order, unless I should be sometimes tediously duncical and absurd.'[19] He asks in *Hay any Worke for Cooper*, 'The Lord being the author both of mirth and gravity, is it not lawful in itself, for the truth to use either of these ways?' (*MT*, 239). Martin recognizes the public's apathy regarding ecclesiastical controversy, and seeks a means to attract their attention: 'perceiving the humours of men in these times ... to be given to mirth, I took that course' (*MT*, 239).

While the text bursts with laughter ('Ha ha ha!' 'So-ho!' 'Tse-tse-tse!' 'Wo-ho-ho!'), the attack on the bishops is ominously real: 'All our Lord Bishops, I say, are petty popes and usurping antichrists,' Martin writes in *The Epistle* (*MT* 28). Marprelate's chief weapon is rollicking ridicule. Rather than confute the biblical basis and authority of an episcopal church government (the standard approach of most Puritan pamphleteers), Martin endeavours to mar the prelates with personal insults. He asks Stephen Chatfield, the vicar of Kingston, 'And art thou not a monstrous atheist, a belly god, a carnal wicked wretch, and what not?' (*MT*, 75). The personal foibles of parish ministers are related with unmitigated zest and extensive poetic license; Martin promises, 'In this book I will note all their memorable pranks' (*MT*, 84).

Martin's charm comes from what Christopher Hill termed a 'witty, rumbustious, savage and extremely effective colloquial style'.[20] He writes in a vivid, informal first person; he is part-reporter, part-neighbour, part-preacher, part-gossip. Martin inflicts the greatest harm on the clergy simply by not taking them seriously; for him, nothing in the episcopacy is sacrosanct. He openly scoffs at Archbishop Whitgift (whom he hails with such names as 'John Cant', 'Dumb John' and 'Don John'), accusing him of playing 'the fool ... in the pulpit' (*MT*, 86). He mocks the bishop's mitre with parodic titles such as 'my horned Masters of the Convocation' (*MT*, 25), and provides them with helpful, moralistic 'true' stories:

> Old Doctor Turner ... had a dog full of good qualities. Doctor Turner, having invited a Bishop to his table, in dinner-while, called his dog, and told him that the Bishop did sweat. (You must

think he laboured hard over his trencher.) The dog flies at the Bishop and took off his corner-cap – he thought belike it had been a cheesecake – and so away goes the dog with it to his master. Truly, my masters of the Clergy, I would never wear corner-cap again, seeing dogs run away with them.

(MT, 86)

With this one tale, Martin inflicts more damage to the bishops' image than tomes of biblical exegesis could ever have accomplished. Now the bishops not only had egg on their faces, but cheesecake on their heads; who could take them seriously?

Judging by the official response, the Marprelate Tracts were enormously popular. Hill observes, 'Martin's rude, personalizing style appealed because it was subversive of degree, hierarchy and indeed the great chain of being itself. The shocking thing about his tracts was that their rollicking popular idiom, in addition to making intellectuals laugh, deliberately brought the Puritan cause into the market place' (Hill, p. 77).

The bishops were confronted with a new breed of ecclesiastical enemy: the Puritan wit. The Martin Marprelate author(s) – fiery young men such as Penry and Udall – were the Puritan counterpart to the London wits. Indeed, at least one critic maintains that Martin Marprelate originated the grotesque comic prose of the 1590s.[21] After futile attempts to take the Martinists by force, sermon or dense theological prose, the bishops finally hired mercenaries who could challenge Martin on his own ground: John Lyly, Robert Greene, Anthony Munday and the young Thomas Nashe (Penry's former schoolmate at Cambridge). These new arrivals studied Martin's style, learned to imitate it and, for the next six months pamphlets were furiously hurled back and forth. Colourful insults flew, and each side lampooned the other with zeal and relish. New personae entered the scene (Mar-Martine, Pasquill, Marphoreus, Cuthbert Curryknave, Plaine Percevall the Peace-maker) as the pamphlet warfare took on a plot of its own. Characters made personal challenges to other characters, formed alliances and at one point rumours filled London that Martin was dead. Martin was portrayed on the stage and became the target of broadsides; Marprelate was attacked by Mar-Martine, who in turn came under fire from Marre Mar-Martin. The controversy became so prominent that even Gabriel and Richard Harvey and Francis Bacon entered the fray, defending Martin against the anti-Martinists.[22]

The anti-Martinists changed the tenor of the controversy, amplifying the grotesque undertones of the Martinist tracts. Throughout Martin's writing, there are hints of the carnival grotesque; the prelates, those 'carnal and senseless beasts', 'monstrous and ungodly wretches', revel with their 'boosing mates' in a world of social madness and hierarchical inversion (where bishops become common labourers – 'coopers' – and Martin proclaims himself 'the great'). In *The Epistle* the bishops are 'swine, dumb dogs ... lewd livers ... adulterers, drunkards, cormorants, rascals ... [causing] monstrous corruptions in our Church'. Martin blasts, 'Horrible and blasphemous beasts, whither will your madness grow in a while, if ye be not restrained?'[23] In the anti-Martinist tracts, however, elements of the carnival grotesque become explicit and predominant; Martin's own rhetorical strategies are turned against him with full force. In *An Almond for a Parrat* (1589) Nashe asserts he will attack the Puritan 'Hipocrites' by 'imitating ... that merry man Rablays'.[24] Throughout the anti-Martinist literature, Martin becomes 'the ape, the dronke, and the madde':[25] he copulates, vomits, drinks, gorges himself and gives birth.

Martin becomes, then, the grotesque body *par excellence*, the archetype of Bakhtin's description; Martin's form 'transgresses its own limits' and 'discloses its essence as a principle of growth which exceeds its own limits only in copulation, pregnancy, childbirth, the throes of death, eating, drinking or defecation. This is the ever-unfinished, ever-creating body, the link in the chain of genetic development, or more correctly speaking, two links shown at the point where they enter into each other.'[26] Nashe and Lyly depict Martin and his 'neast' as a swarm of monstrous, intertwined beings; death, birth, sex and bodily functions are often simultaneous and inextricably coexistent. Witness Martin's very birth as described in *An Almond for a Parrat*: 'think that nature tooke a scouring purgation, when she voided all her imperfections in the birth of one *Martin*' (McKerrow 3: 355). In *A Countercuffe given to Martin Junior* (1589), the self-proclaimed cavalier Pasquill (Nashe?) responds to the rumours of Martin's death: 'If the Monster be deade, I mervaile not, for hee was but an error of Nature, not long liued: hatched in the heat of the sinnes of England ... The maine buffets that are given him in euery corner of this Realme, are euident tokens, that beeing thorow soust in so many showres, hee had no other refuge but to runne into a hole, and die as he liued, belching' (McKerrow 1: 59). Dying and hatching, belching at his death in the womblike recesses of a hole: the epitome of the grotesque, in which birth and death intersect. Again, consider Lyly's image of a birthing, dying Martin in *Pappe with an hatchet*:

I sawe through his paper coffen, that it was but a cosening corse ... drawing his mouth awrie, that could neuer speake right; goggling with his eyes that watred with strong wine; licking his lips, and gaping, as though he should loose his childes nose, if he had not his longing to swallowe Churches; and swelling in the paunch, as though he had been in labour of a little babie, no bigger than rebellion; but truth was at the Bishoppes trauaile: so that Martin was deliuered by sedition, which pulls the monster with yron from the beastes bowells. When I perceived that he masked in his rayling robes, I was so bolde as to pull off his shrowding sheete, that all the worlde might see the old foole daunce naked.[27]

A man in a coffin, feigning death yet childlike, giving birth through his bowels, masquing in a shrouding sheet: this, to many, was a late sixteenth-century image of the Puritan.

Such caricatures were soon translated onto the stage, much to the shock and disgust of the very bishops and city magistrates who had orchestrated the anti-Martinist attack. While texts for these theatrical entertainments have not survived (if they ever existed),[28] both Martin and his foes repeatedly and pervasively allude to the popular anti-Martinist lampoons.[29] Such performances appear to have been in the same vein as the prose tracts. Pasquill writes in *A Countercuffe* of 'the Anatomie latelie taken of [Martin], the blood and the humors that were taken from him, by launcing and worming him at London vpon the common Stage' (McKerrow 1: 59). In another performance mentioned in *The Returne of ... Pasquill*, a battered and scratched character named Divinity is brought forth 'holding of her hart as if she were sicke, because *Martin* would haue forced her' (McKerrow 1: 92). Unsuccessful in his rape attempts, Martin then 'poysoned her with a vomit which he ministred vnto her'. In other shows Martin was depicted as an ape (most likely adapted from the first anti-Martinist broadside, *A Whip for an Ape*) and as Maid Marian. As Charles Nicholl (p. 68) observes, the anti-Martinist productions 'were obviously coarse, sensational performances, full of violent antics'.

This theatrical entertainment was 'to the greate offence of the better sorte', as John Harte, Lord Mayor of London wrote to Lord

Burghley.[30] In 1589 Edmund Tilney, as Master of Revels, closed the theatres on account of the grotesque representations of Martin Marprelate. The Privy Council agreed with this move, and a letter was sent to the Archbishop of Canterbury, the Lord Mayor of London and the Master of the Revels requesting strict censorship of the theatre. The Council wrote to the Archbishop that 'there hathe growne some inconvenience by common playes and enterludes in & about the cyttie of London, in [that] the players take upon [them] to handle in their plaies certen matters of Divinytie and State, unfitt to be suffered.'[31] The anti-Puritan authorities thus quickly decided to contain the disruption they had orchestrated, much to the annoyance of Lyly, who complained that there were still anti-Martinist plays waiting to be performed.[32]

Even as the Bishops were suspending the hired pens of their own anti-Martinists, they finally succeeded in silencing Martin Marprelate himself. While printing the long-awaited *More work for the Cooper*, the Martinist press, now operated by John Hodgkins, was ambushed by the Earl of Derby's men; the press was seized, the tract destroyed and Hodgkins and his assistants were tortured. Penry and Throkmorton received news of the discovery and quickly produced a small, error-ridden Octavo (most likely printed hastily by these two themselves, inexperienced as they were with the printing press). *The Protestacyon* (mid-October 1589) was the last of the Marprelate Tracts; it expressed concern for the captive prisoners, and contained arguments against imprisonment and torture which verge on a plea for freedom of conscience. Soon after the suppression of anti-Martinist productions and the capture of the Martinist press, the Marprelate controversy fizzled out. Writing for or against Martin had become a politically dangerous gesture. Martin's hot-blooded challenger, the cavalier Pasquill, reappeared briefly in the summer of 1590 – but only to offer *Pasquills Apologie*, in which the tattered knight acrimoniously defends himself against the backlash against the anti-Martinists, his overzealous attacks on Puritanism having earned him accusations of being a Catholic.

One of the actors likely to have participated in the staging of Martin Marprelate was Will Kemp, who may also have been the first actor to play Falstaff.[33] The connection, though tenuous, is intriguing. The Marprelate controversy, which took place a mere six or seven years before the production of *1 Henry IV*, remained in the collective memory long after the silencing of the tracts and sensational stage manifestations.[34] Indeed, Martin Marprelate remained a vivid cultural figure for the next 50 years.[35] Shakespeare revived Martin, or at least relied on his legacy, when introducing his Oldcastle/Falstaff to the stage; the presence of Will Kemp would have served as a vivid, visual reminder of the Marprelate connection. Shakespeare's creation was not entirely a 'profoundly original ... representation' or a 'daring and provocative inspiration':[36] if Oldcastle was widely identified as an early Puritan, and stage Puritans were widely expected to be comically grotesque figures, then the depiction of Oldcastle as the grotesque Falstaff was not only natural, but even expected. Falstaff, I would argue, thus continues the burlesque representation of the Puritan established in the staging of the Marprelate Tracts.

This, of course, has not been the prevailing understanding of Falstaff, and such a reading may at first seem counterintuitive. Literary scholars have long been influenced by the pervasive post-Restoration image of the Puritan; this figure is dry, dour, Casaubon-like. Puritans and the carnival grotesque are considered not only distant, but even antithetical; this antithesis is fundamental to the ways in which literary historians have conceptualized and structured the early modern world. Falstaff's Puritan origins have thus been consistently resisted, even by critics uncovering and foregrounding those very origins; his Puritan speech patterns are routinely acknowledged and then quickly dismissed, often apologetically, as a bad joke, or his foundation as a prominent religious/cultural figure become channelled into discussion of topical satire on an elite Elizabethan family.

As we have seen, however, our current popular image of the Puritan was not the only one available to Shakespeare's Elizabethan audience. Certainly one predominant stereotype was the austere, rigid Puritan, such as Malvolio or Tribulation Wholesome. But a competing representation (and I would argue a more pervasive one) was the grotesque Puritan. It was this tradition, so graphically realized in the staging of Martin Marprelate, to which Shakespeare turned when depicting the Lollard Oldcastle. A history of critical prejudices and misconceptions has largely eclipsed popular religious culture from studies of the early modern theatre.[37] With an awareness of such polemical literature and performances, we are able to restore an important context influencing the ways in which Elizabethans recognized and reacted to Falstaff as a social representation.

Modern editions of the Henriad (such as the Arden, the 'New' Arden, the Riverside, the Folger, the New Variorum, the New

Shakespeare and the New Cambridge Shakespeare) all acknowledge Falstaff's theatrical origins in the character of Sir John Oldcastle from the *Famous Victories of Henry V*, and critics have often commented on Falstaff's 'Puritanical' characteristics and speech patterns. J. Dover Wilson noted that 'traces of Lollardry may still be detected in Falstaff's frequent resort to Scriptural phraseology and his affectation of an uneasy conscience', and that the passages on repentance, 'together with the habit of citing Scripture, may have their origin ... in the Puritan, psalm-singing temper of Falstaff's prototype'.[38] Alfred Ainger, one of the earliest twentieth-century critics to discuss the Falstaff–Oldcastle connection, similarly observed: 'What put it into Shakespeare's head to put this distinctly religious, not to say Scriptural phraseology into the mouth of Falstaff, but that the rough draft of the creation, as it came into his hands, was the decayed Puritan? For the Lollard of the fourteenth century was in this respect the Puritan of the sixteenth, that the one certain mark of his calling was this use of the language of Scripture, and that conventicle style which had been developed out of it.'[39] Falstaff does indeed quote extensively from Scripture; of the 54 biblical references identified in *1 Henry IV*, 26 come from Falstaff.[40] He quotes indirectly from Genesis, Exodus, 2 Samuel, Psalms, Proverbs, Matthew, Mark, Luke, 1 Corinthians, 2 Corinthians, and 1 Thessalonians (citing from the nonconformist Geneva Bible rather than the officially sanctioned Bishops' Bible).[41] The parables of Dives and Lazarus and the Prodigal Son in particular, as Ainger notes, 'seem to haunt him along his whole course' (Ainger, p. 142).

Editors and critics also note that Falstaff speaks in a 'parody of liturgical language'[42] and that his lengthy speeches often smack of the 'scriptural style of the sanctimonious Puritan'.[43] This rhetorical style, employed extensively by early modern Puritan preachers, is repetitive, pedagogic, laced with abundant biblical exegesis, and often incorporates a question-and-answer format. One example of Falstaff's use of this 'precise manner of one of the Covenanting preachers' (Ainger, p. 142) is his famous meditation on honour:

> What is honour? A word. What is in that word honour? What is that honour? Air. A trim reckoning! Who hath it? He that died a-Wednesday. Doth he feel it? No. Doth he hear it? No. 'Tis insensible, then? Yea, to the dead. But will it not live with the living?

No. Why? Detraction will not suffer it. Therefore I'll none of it.
Honour is a mere scutcheon – and so ends my catechism.

(1 Henry IV, 5.1.134–41)

In addition to biblical allusions and a rhetorical style typical of
Puritan preachers, Falstaff's speech is also rich in sixteenth-century
Puritan jargon. He compares himself to a 'saint', Puritan cant for
one of God's elect, being corrupted by the 'wicked' (*1 Henry IV*,
1.2.88–93). In both Parts 1 and 2, Falstaff makes references to psalm-
singing, a key element of the sixteenth-century Puritan stereotype.[44]
He wishes he 'were a weaver' so that he 'could sing psalms'
(*1 Henry IV*, 2.4.130) (weavers, who often sang at their work, being
particularly notorious for their Puritan psalmody), and later claims,
'for my voice, I have lost it with hallooing, and singing of anthems'
(*2 Henry IV*, 1.2.188–9). As Ainger notes, 'the Lollard and the
Puritan were alike famous for their habit of chanting and singing',
the root of 'Lollard' supposedly being the low-German *lollen*, to
sing, 'just as the Puritan form of religion in much later times has
impressed upon the vulgar mind as its most prominent association
that of *psalm-singing*'.[45] (Ainger points to the Puritan in *The Winter's
Tale* who 'sang Psalms to hornpipes', 4.3.44–5.) Critics have also
commented on Falstaff's repeated allusions to salvation by faith
alone and his death-bed reference to the Whore of Babylon, 'the
customary Puritan term for the Church of Rome'.[46]

Modern literary scholars are not the only ones to note these
Puritan allusions; Falstaff's companions also appear to identify him
– or mock him – as a man of religion. Hal, who prides himself on
his chameleon-like ability to speak to various social groups (such as
the drawers) in their own language, repeatedly uses biblical idiom
when speaking to Falstaff: since Falstaff (Oldcastle) is a famous
Puritan, Hal attempts to speak to him in the Lollards' own (biblical)
terms. The Prince teases Falstaff, whom he calls an 'elder' (a well-
known term referring to the presbyterian form of church government) with 'I see a good ammendment of life in thee, from praying
to purse-taking' (*2 Henry IV*, 2.4.256; *1 Henry IV*, 1.2.99–100);[47] later
Hal angrily challenges Falstaff's Calvinist assumptions: 'Is she of
the wicked? Is thine hostess here of the wicked? Or is thy boy of the
wicked? Or honest Bardolph, whose zeal burns in his nose, of the
wicked?' (*2 Henry IV*, 2.4.324–7). ('Zeal', of course, is another
Puritan byword.) The Puritan rhetoric is neither incidental nor a

moment of local humour, but constitutes one of the many discursive registers through which Falstaff is constructed.[48]

Falstaff's Puritan associations, then, are pervasive and unmistakable. Most critics noting Falstaff's tendency to speak in biblical idiom and Puritan jargon have assumed that such speech is intended as active mockery of the Puritans on Falstaff's part. They comment that Falstaff himself is a self-conscious satirist making 'jibes at the Puritans', that his part 'involves Puritan posturing', and that 'his "religiousness" is a joke at this stage of his life.'[49] Several editors have also held the opinion that Falstaff is repeatedly ridiculing Puritans. Samuel Hemingway, who edited *1 Henry IV* for the New Variorum Shakespeare, maintains that 'in mimicry of the Puritans Falstaff here uses one of their canting expressions' (a reference to his use of 'the wicked'), and that 'Falstaff here repeats in ridicule another Puritan shibboleth' (a reference to his use of 'vocation'), to cite two examples (pp. 36, 37, 38n). A.R. Humphreys, editor of the New Arden edition of the Henriad, also notes that Falstaff uses 'frequent Puritan idiom', 'mimics Puritan idiom' and devises 'Puritan parody'.[50]

But considering Falstaff as a straightforward satirist, or merely as a Vice figure mocking 'precisians,' neglects the complex ramifications of his own religious associations and identity. An audience would always 'see' not only Falstaff, but Oldcastle. As a multivalent, polyvocal entity, 'Falstaff', the epitome of the carnival grotesque, encompasses and embodies contradictions, rather than flattens them; Falstaff's religious language, like Jack Cade's political protest, is at once ridiculous and sincere. Further, to explain Falstaff's religious language as merely a parody of Puritan speech fails to take into account the legacy of the Marprelate Tracts, especially the stage lampoons of Martin Marprelate and the precedent established for grotesque representations of the Puritan. I believe an audience attuned to such representations, as well as Oldcastle's own history, would have laughed not only *with* Falstaff, but simultaneously *at* him: Falstaff does not simply satirize Puritans, but in many ways is in himself a sustained, satiric representation of a famous Lollard martyr.

On an obvious level, the discrepancy between Falstaff's gluttonous lifestyle and the more restrained and abstemious conduct expected of a reformist religious leader becomes a basis for satire that runs throughout both parts of *Henry IV*. Although Bale has Oldcastle admitting 'that in [his] frayle youthe [he] offended the

(lorde) most greuouslye in pryde, wrathe, and glottonye, in coue-
tousnesse and in lechere' (fol. 26^{r-v}), in his wiser maturity he aban-
doned such pursuits; Shakespeare, however, retains this aspect of
Oldcastle's personality even as he fills the Lollard's mouth with
reformist jargon. The discrepancy between the belligerent Lollard
leader of historical accounts and the coward of the Henriad is just
as obvious a source of satire. Before Falstaff can engage in Puritan
parody or function as a comic figure, he must be disenfranchised as
a serious martial threat. In virtually all histories of Oldcastle and
Henry V, this Lollard is a powerful figure, and often a dangerous
one.[51] As Holinshed and others report, Oldcastle intended to lead
an army consisting of thousands of commoners against Henry V;
the attack was averted, but the threat posed to the throne by
fifteenth-century Lollards was daunting. In Shakespeare's account,
however, Oldcastle's qualities as traitor and militant religious
leader are dispersed among other characters in the plays; the historical Oldcastle is dissected, his parts scattered, his subversive potential attached to other characters. It is the Archbishop of York, not
Oldcastle/Falstaff, who leads rebellion and 'turns insurrection to
religion' (*2 Henry IV*, 1.1.201). Similarly, Oldcastle/Falstaff is not
given the role of traitor. Holinshed and other chroniclers implicate
Oldcastle in the Scroop–Grey–Cambridge plot, a domestic conspiracy that hinged on competing claims to the throne (rather than on
personal greed and pay-offs from the French, as Shakespeare
portrays it). In *Henry V* Shakespeare completely removes
Oldcastle/Falstaff from this treacherous triad; indeed, we might
speculate that Falstaff's premature death is an effort to avoid the
awkwardness of the historical Oldcastle's alliance with these traitors. Oldcastle's position as militant and treacherous religious
leader is thus categorically evacuated, as the cowardly and incompetent Falstaff becomes a parody of the 'Christen knyght' described
by Bale, who 'in all adventerouse actes of wordlye manhode was ...
ever bolde, stronge, fortunate, doughtye, noble, & valeaunt' (fol. 4^v).

To an audience familiar with Foxe or Holinshed or *The Famous
Victories of Henry V*, Falstaff is easily recognizable as a satiric rendition of Oldcastle – but this is not to say that Falstaff does not also
assume the role of satirist. Even as he is disempowered as a religious and military figure, Falstaff becomes a powerful centre of carnival and articulates overtly subversive sentiments, freely
criticizing – even mocking – king and prince. Through his jests,
which respect neither rank, nor hierarchy, nor social order, Falstaff

assumes a voice similar to that of Martin Marprelate. Phyllis Rackin has noted that 'Falstaff's irrepressible, irreverent wit epitomizes the unruliness of present oral speech, which, unlike a written text, can never be fully subjugated to official censorship and authoritative control.'[52] While the Elizabethan political machinery kept a tight rein on the press, the Marprelate Tracts presented an important and, for sixteenth-century English men and women, highly visible exception to this rule: the Marprelate Tracts were unruly written texts which *did* evade censorship and authoritative control – at least for a time. Like the texts themselves, Martin's irreverent wit was irrepressible and unruly. Martin's manner of heckling the bishops and kicking away their pedestals (reducing Cooper to a cooper), enabled him to taunt them as equals; Martin explodes sanctioned hierarchies and pieties, and it is this levelling tendency that makes him so threatening – and so appealing.

Similarly, it is only through Falstaff that the audience comes to know the Prince familiarly as 'Hal'. Falstaff's insults to Henry are just as dismissive of social hierarchy as are those of Martin to the bishops. Falstaff's speech itself reverberates with Martin's own grotesque, carnivalesque tone; indeed, the banter between Falstaff and Hal resounds of the taunting exchanges between Marprelate and his textual opponents such as Cuthbert Curryknave or Pasquill.[53] Falstaff hails the Prince as his 'dog' (2 *Henry IV*, 1.2.144–5), hurls such colourful insults as 'you starveling, you eel-skin, you dried neat's-tongue, you bull's pizzle, you stock-fish' (1 *Henry IV*, 2.4.240–1), and tells Hal to 'hang thyself in thine own heir-apparent garters' (1 *Henry IV*, 2.2.42). In addition to mocking the Prince, Falstaff lacks all respect for the Lord Chief Justice and undermines the very code of chivalry ('honour is a mere scutcheon') which was to become so central to the way nostalgic Elizabethans viewed Henry V; at Shrewsbury, Sir John discredits the notion of chivalric honour, and in Part II he boisterously sings "When Arthur first in court' – Empty the jordan. – "And was a worthy king" – How now, Mistress Doll?' (2 *Henry IV*, 2.4.33–4), intermingling allusions to the paragon of chivalry with references to chamberpots and prostitutes. In Falstaff, as in Martin Marprelate, social and discursive order are undermined and overturned.

Falstaff thus plays the role of satirist even as he is the butt of satire. In this dual and contradictory position, Falstaff reproduces a fundamental dynamic of the staging of Martinism. These burlesque performances provided Shakespeare not only with a performative model for representing Puritans in terms of the grotesque, but also with a vivid example of the staging of satire and the use of the carnivalesque; Falstaff, like Martin, inhabits a pivotal, liminal position from which he is able to toy with the boundaries of orthodoxy and subversion. The duality as satirist and object of satire which lies at the heart of the Marprelate controversy is largely a function of the indeterminate social boundaries which Martin and his adversaries test and prod. In his irreverent attacks on the bishops, Martin challenged ecclesiastical hierarchy and organization, thus questioning the episcopal basis for church government. As Evelyn Tribble has recently noted, Martin's defiance of hierarchical social boundaries is mirrored in the tracts themselves, where Martin continually shifts his authorial position from the textual margins to the main body of the text. Tribble writes, 'In her proclamation [against "Schismatical Bookes"] Elizabeth characterizes the pamphlets as attacking the bishops and the church as a whole "in rayling sort and beyond the boundes of good humanitie." "Beyond the boundes": these words sum up the nature of the Marprelate threat. The pamphlets enact a grotesque breaking of the boundaries of the text and of conventional ecclesiastical discourse.'[54] The broken borders of the text were probably the least of the queen's immediate worries; the unlocatable, unstoppable production of the Marprelate Tracts revealed a very real breach in the authorities' ability to control discursive territories. The illegal pamphlets that continued to stream forth despite all attempts to stop them at their source became a graphic manifestation of permeable borders – borders as uncontrollable as those of Falstaff's own sack-filled paunch.

In commissioning the vicious anti-Martinist attacks, the city magistrates and church authorities made a desperate attempt to demonstrate their control over these social and discursive boundaries. The violent, grotesque stage lampoons concocted by the anti-Martinists can be seen as an attempt to reclaim the system of social borders which Martin threatened. Far from marking his exclusion from the community, however, the staging of Martinism demonstrated Marprelate's ability to draw others into of his own festive world. In a lampoon known as 'The Maygame of Martinism', Martin appears cross-dressed as Maid Marian with a cloth covering his beard; still the object of laughter, Martin becomes a participant in communal festival, the focal point of the festivities and a source of carnival energy, not a scapegoat of mob violence. Crossing into his territory has perilous political consequences, however: in a debate where laughter becomes the ammunition for attacking political targets, to laugh *with* Martin even as he is supposed to be laughed *at* suggests – or could lead to – sympathies with his anti-episcopal politics. In the roar of communal laughter, it becomes impossible to distinguish anti-Martinist from anti-prelatical sentiment. The same chuckle at Martin's stage antics could be simultaneously at and with Martin – or, what amounts to the same thing, at and with the city magistrates leading the attack.

Employing Martin's own carnivalesque terms, the anti-Martinists do not reassert a social boundary so much as they playfully test rhetorical bounds. The line demarcating orthodoxy from heresy, which these authors were hired to enforce, becomes dangerously thin; similarly, the distinction between a mob exacting punishment for subversive activities and a crowd revelling in the possibility of that subversion begins to fade or even disappear. 'The representation of disorder threatens to collapse into disorder itself,' writes Tribble (p. 119). The anti-Martinist authors themselves were aware of the boundaries they were dancing along – and aware of the dangers of slipping over them. Lyly 'goes to some pains to avoid a potential collapse of satirizer and satirized'; Bacon, urging the suppression of the anti-Martinists, also 'recognizes the tendency of the satirist and satirized to collapse' (Tribble, pp. 118, 121).

In one anti-Martinist pamphlet, where the anonymous author attempts to mock Marprelate and his readers by depicting the way in which his tracts were received, we can see the ambiguous, slippery terms of this satire. In this vignette, the reader is asked to visualize a riotous tavern scene with an illegal anti-episcopal Marprelate Tract (perhaps read out loud) providing the evening's entertainment:

> [Martin], together with his ribauldry, had some wit (though knavish) and woulde make some foolish women, and pot companions to laugh, when sitting on their Alebenches, they would tipple, and read it, seruing them in steede of a blinde Minstrell, when they could get none, to fiddle them foorth a fitte of mirth.[55]

The scene is intended as ridicule, but it is none the less attractive; who does not enjoy being fiddled forth into a fit of mirth? The conspiratorial, underground nature of the scenario is also appealing, conjuring images of clandestine camaraderie. The seduction of this scene overwhelms its satiric purpose; even as it ridicules Martin, the passage inadvertently illustrates and effects his popular appeal, drawing the reader into Martin's circle. The anti-Martinist authors themselves seem unable to avoid a sense of community with Martin even as they lambast his opinions and scoff at his prose style. Using Martin's own satiric terms, they are unable to convert him entirely into an object of ridicule or to maintain the distance required for hostile satire. 'Even as he attacks Martin,' Tribble writes, 'Lyly inadvertently implies a sort of fellowship with him; momentarily they become two ruffians drinking together' (p. 117). Despite his awareness of and resistance to the potential collapse of discursive – and ultimately political – boundaries, Lyly (like Nashe) cannot successfully maintain the distance between the satirist and the object of his satire.

The anti-Martinists thus played with, rather than policed, the boundaries they were assigned to defend. The tantalizing appeal of the Marprelate controversy is located along this quivering border between the authoritative and the subversive, the orthodox and the heretical. This same play at and with social boundaries infuses the Henriad with much of its dramatic energy. These plays, *1 Henry IV* in particular, are largely driven by Hal's flirtation precisely with this border between authority and subversion, orthodoxy and heresy. Like the anti-Martinists, Hal enters into the terms of carnival subversion, represented and embodied by Falstaff, while still maintaining his position of authority. The danger, however, is that the tension between these two positions might prove stronger than Hal's ability to control and define his own situation, that the boundary distinguishing the role of the Prince from that of the reveler could snap before Hal can orchestrate his glorious return to orthodoxy and filial duty. In Act 3, scene 2 of *1 Henry IV*, King Henry explicitly warns his son of the dangers of slipping over this line, advocating instead a strict division between community and king and lamenting that Hal 'hast lost [his] princely privilege/With vile participation' (ll. 86–7). Describing Richard II's fall and his own rise to power, Henry prides himself on not becoming 'stale and cheap to vulgar company'; he rather kept his 'person fresh and new … like a robe pontifical' (3.2.41, 55–6). By contrast Richard II, 'the skipping King' (l. 60) in Henry's version of events,

> Grew a companion to the common streets,
> Enfeoff'd himself to popularity,

That, being daily swallow'd by men's eyes …
He was but as the cuckoo is in June,
Heard, not regarded; seen, but with such eyes
As, sick and blunted with community,
Afford no extraordinary gaze …
Being with his presence glutted, gorg'd, and full.

(3.2.68–84)

By 'mingl[ing] his royalty with cap'ring fools' (as Henry says of Richard [l. 63]), Hal risks losing himself in the bowels of the common community, being absorbed and swallowed so that the distinction between the crowd and the Prince is no longer recognizable. This breakdown of hierarchical division is precisely what Oldcastle threatened by leading a mob against the king, and in part what Marprelate advocated by seeking to pull down 'robe[s] pontifical'. The ever 'glutted, gorg'd, and full' Falstaff thus seems almost to literalize this removal of social, hierarchical boundaries: Falstaff becomes the community which can, through jest, ingest its leaders. His rotund, expansive figure, though emblematic of carnivalesque festivity, potentially signifies absorption and loss of social distinction.

The Henriad thus dramatizes issues of discursive and political control presented by the Marprelate controversy. For a short time, the audience becomes Falstaff's 'pot companions', and they too are 'fiddled forth' into mirth – subversive laughter at the king's expense. It is this wit that draws the spectators into 'vile participation' with a figure who led an army against the king. From the position of the satirized, both Falstaff and Martin Marprelate entice the audience to join their carnival revelries. The spectators simultaneously laugh at and with subversive forces, are simultaneously disapproving and participating; this is the play of the play.

Recent critical incorporations of Bakhtin's study of the grotesque have tended to focus on binary structures and processes of inversion or transformation of these binaries. Bakhtin's distinction between the open, porous nature of the grotesque body and the closed, impermeable qualities of the classical body, for example, has provided a rich heuristic model for feminist critics; theorists of the body have also turned to the Bakhtinian idea of the grotesque body as a site where the 'high' human attributes (intellect, reason) become displaced and replaced by the lower bodily stratum, by the organs of reproduction, digestion, expulsion. Such a reversal of bodily hierarchies has an analogue in the reversal of political order which takes place in carnival; critics interested in the enforcement and reversal of authoritative structures have also found Bakhtin's theories invaluable.[56] Such binarisms necessary for a process of inversion and travesty – high/low, closed/open, dominant/dominated – figure prominently in Bakhtin's thought. But a competing structure at play in *Rabelais and His World* is not so much travesty and reversal as synthesis. While Bakhtin emphasizes that 'grotesque realism played with this double image, we might say with the top and bottom of the world' (p. 162), the primary means by which that 'play' between top and bottom took place was through integration. As Bakhtin continues,

> life and death, birth, excrement, and food are all drawn together and tied in one grotesque knot; this is the center of bodily topography in which the upper and lower stratum penetrate each other. The grotesque image was a favorite expression of the ambivalence of the material bodily lower stratum, which destroys and generates, swallows and is swallowed. The 'swing' of grotesque realism, the play of the upper with the lower sphere, is strikingly set into motion; the top and the bottom, heaven and earth, merge in that image.
>
> (p. 163)

Though Bakhtin speaks of a 'world inside out' (p. 11) and writes of a 'bodily hierarchy turned upside down' (p. 309), the image of coexistence and synthesis becomes equally prominent (even predominant) through his repeated emphasis on the pregnant-dying form: 'One body offers its death, the other its birth, but they are merged in a two-bodied image' (p. 322). In Bakhtin's definition of the grotesque, an 'indispensable trait is ambivalence. For in this image we find both poles of transformation, the old and the new, the dying and the procreating, the beginning and the end of the metamorphosis' (p. 24).

We have seen this two-bodied image in the dancing, shrouded, birthing Marprelate as he appeared on the stage. Falstaff, too, is a two-bodied image. As Valerie Traub has discussed, Falstaff functions as maternal figure;[57] this, however, is a mother who devours, 'a sow that hath overwhelm'd all her litter but one' (*2 Henry IV*, 1.2.11–12), a figure who at once exemplifies fertility and decay. And as a palimpsest upon the legend of Oldcastle, Falstaff is, narratively speaking, again a two-bodied image. The presence of Oldcastle creates an inescapable duality in Falstaff; not only does the audience see both the historical figure and Shakespeare's creation, but the ambiguous legacy of Oldcastle and the memory of the Marprelate tracts even allows for even further layering in this character. As a religious figure, Oldcastle–Falstaff is at once the leader of a defeated Lollard uprising, and a father of a Lollard movement identified by many as the genealogical origin of a native Protestant history. As a grotesque Puritan, he is at once staged in the same mode as Martin Marprelate, spokesman for a defeated organized presbyterian movement, and Martin Marprelate, enormously popular and irrepressible voice of a disseminated oppositional religious sentiment. 'Puritanism', as most historians of the period lament, is an essentially indefinable term; binary terms once used to clarify the dynamic of religious politics in the late sixteenth century no longer seem adequate. In a recent essay, 'The Theatre Constructs Puritanism', Patrick Collinson has discussed the ways in which the drama created an image and provided a language for discussing 'Puritanism'.[58] While Collinson locates the origin of the figure of the Puritan in the characters of Ben Jonson, I would argue that characters such as Zeal-of-the-Land Busy follow in the model of Falstaff, who himself follows the grotesquely portrayed Martin Marprelate. In a climate of undefined, transitional, ambiguous and metamorphosizing religious identities, the grotesque, with its incessant ambiguity and mergence of bodies, best articulated the emergence of popular Protestantism.

NOTES

1. The present essay is a modified version of 'Saints Alive! Falstaff, Martin Marprelate, and the Staging of Puritanism', *Shakespearean Quarterly*, 46 (1995), pp. 47–75. The most thorough catalogue of sixteenth-century references to Oldcastle can be found in Alice-Lyle Scoufos, *Shakespeare's Typological Satire: A Study of the Falstaff–Oldcastle Problem* (Athens, Ohio: Ohio University Press, 1979).
2. John Stowe's *Annales of England* (1592) describes Oldcastle as a 'strong ... [and] meetely good man of war, but [who] was a most perverse enimie to the state of the church at that time' (Scoufos, p. 65).
3. See Scoufos, chapter 2. See also Gary Taylor, 'The Fortunes of Oldcastle', *Shakespeare Survey* 38 (1985), p. 91.
4. The name-change is often attributed to complaints by William Brooke, Lord Cobham; see Robert J. Fehrenbach, 'When Lord

Cobham and Edmund Tilney "were at odds": Oldcastle, Falstaff, and the Date of *1 Henry IV'*, *Shakespeare Studies* 18 (1986), pp. 87–101. Thomas Pendleton argues convincingly that the switch resulted from 'the displeasure of a significant part of Shakespeare's audience at his treatment of a hero of their religion' (p. 68) in '"This is not the man": On calling Falstaff Falstaff', *Analytical and Enumerative Bibliography* 4 (1990).

5.   For evidence of court performances of *1 Henry IV* under the name of 'Oldcastle', see Taylor, 'Fortunes', pp. 90–1.

6.   Gary Taylor, Stanley Wells, John Jowett and William Montgomery changed the name of 'Falstaff' back to 'Oldcastle' in the Oxford edition of *William Shakespeare: The Complete Works* (Oxford: Clarendon Press, 1986). Taylor defends his decision in 'The Fortunes of Oldcastle'. For arguments against the Oxford edition name-change, see Jonathan Goldberg, 'The Commodity of Names: "Falstaff" and "Oldcastle" in *1 Henry IV'*, in *Reconfiguring the Renaissance: Essays in Critical Materialism*, ed. Jonathan Crew, *Bucknell Review* 35 (1992), pp. 76–88; David Scott Kastan, '"Killed With Hard Opinions": Oldcastle, Falstaff, and the Reformed Text of *1 Henry IV'*, in *Textual Formations and Reformations*, ed. Tom Berger and Laurie McGuire (Cambridge: Cambridge University Press, forthcoming). Thomas Pendleton further notes the flaws in the assumption that only the name was changed, without corresponding changes in the text (pp. 59–71). David Bevington, first to disagree with Taylor and Wells's decision, keeps the name of 'Falstaff' in the single volume *Henry IV, Part I* which he edited for *The Oxford Shakespeare* (Oxford, 1987).

7.   For a pointed summation of this issue, see John W. Velz, Review of *1 Henry IV*, ed. David Bevington, *Shakespeare Quarterly* 43 (1992), pp. 107–9.

8.   *Brefe Chronycle, concernynge the Examinacyon and death of the blessed martyr of Christ syr Johan Oldecastell the lorde Cobham* (Antwerp, 1544), fol. 4ᵛ.

9.   Fehrenbach, p. 92. Fehrenbach agrees with S. Schoenbaum, *Shakespeare: A Documentary Life* (Oxford: Clarendon Press, 1975) that the name was simply a mistake (p. 144).

10. These include E.A.J. Honigmann, 'Sir John Oldcastle: Shakespeare's Martyr', in *'Fanned and Winnowed Opinions': Shakespearean Essays Presented to Harold Jenkins*, ed. John W. Mahon and Thomas A. Pendleton (London and New York: Methuen, 1987), pp. 118–32; and Mark Dominik, *A Shakespearean Anomaly: Shakespeare's Hand in 'Sir John Oldcastle'* (Beaverton, Oregon: Alioth Press, 1991), p. 5.

11. *The Fortunes of Falstaff* (Cambridge: Cambridge University Press, 1953), ch. 2.

12. Elizabethan Puritans hailed Oldcastle as a proto-Puritan; as religious reformers traced the progress of their battle against the Antichrist, they frequently claimed Wyclif and his followers as the origin of their movement. Stephen Brachlow cites several examples of prominent Puritans who claimed a genealogy from the Lollards in *The*

Communion of Saints: Radical Puritan and Separatist Ecclesiology 1580–1625 (Oxford: Oxford University Press, 1988); see pp. 81, 89, 89n and 90. See also Anthony Milton, 'The Church of England, Rome, and the True Church: The Demise of a Jacobean Consensus', in *The Early Stuart Church,* ed. Kenneth Fincham (London: Macmillan, 1993), esp. pp. 191–2.

13. Harold Bloom, *Ruin the Sacred Truths* (Cambridge, Mass.: Harvard University Press, 1987), p. 84.

14. P.A. Scholes, *The Puritans and Music,* pp. 113–16 (cited in Patrick Collinson, *The Elizabethan Puritan Movement* [Oxford: Clarendon Press, 1967], p. 370). One of the anti-Marprelate tracts includes the line, 'Who trusts a broken staffe, we see, doe fall ere they be ware.' *Sir Martin Mar-People,* sig. A4^v.

15. See Charles Nicholl, *A Cup of News: The Life of Thomas Nashe* (London: Routledge and Kegan Paul, 1984), p. 64.

16. For a concise history of the Marprelate printings, as well as the related activities of Udall, Penry, Waldegrave, and Throkmorton, see Collinson, *Elizabethan Puritan Movement,* pp. 390–6.

17. William Pierce, *An Historical Introduction to the Marprelate Tracts* (London: Archibald Constable, 1908), p. 152.

18. See Leland H. Carlson, *Martin Marprelate, Gentleman: Master Job Throkmorton Laid Open in his Colors* (San Marino: The Huntington Library, printed by Kingsport Press, 1981). Whether or not Throkmorton was the direct author of some (or even all) of the Tracts, he was involved in their production, and his own writings have been deemed 'para-Martinist' (Collinson, *Elizabethan Puritan movement,* p. 395). J. Dover Wilson also advanced his own theory of authorship for the Marprelate tracts, suggesting that Martin was Sir Roger Williams; see *Martin Marprelate and Shakespeare's Fluellen: A New Theory of the Authorship of the Marprelate Tracts* (London: Alexander Moring Limited, 1912).

19. This and all references to the Marprelate tracts come from William Pierce, ed., *The Marprelate Tracts 1588, 1589* (London: James Clarke & Co., 1911). I shall be using the abbreviation *MT* in citations; here, *MT* 17.

20. *The Collected Essays of Christopher Hill, Volume One: Writing and Revolution in 17th Century England* (Amherst: The University of Massachusetts, Press, 1985), p. 76.

21. Neil Rhodes, *Elizabethan Grotesque* (London: Routledge & Kegan Paul, 1980), p. 4. Rhodes discusses Shakespeare's debt to the 'Nasheian grotesque', in *1 & 2 Henry IV* (p. 5), but as Nicholl writes, 'Of all the anti-Martinists it was Nashe who took most readily to Martin's polemic "vein," caught its effervescence and bite, revelled in its ranging freedom' (p. 76). The 'Nasheian grotesque' was thus indirectly inherited from Marprelate himself.

22. Nicholl, pp. 74–5. C.L. Barber discusses the ways in which those entering the Marprelate fray styled themselves as joining Martin's May game; *Shakespeare's Festive Comedy* (New York: Meridian Books, 1963), p. 55.

23. *MT* 71, 78, 248, 262, and 279.
24. Ronald B. McKerrow, ed., *The Works of Thomas Nashe*, Vols 1 and 3 (Oxford: Basil Blackwell, 1958) Vol. 3; here, 3: 342 and 374. McKerrow lists *The Almond* under 'Doubtful Works', but Nicholl describes this text as 'the one anti-Martinist pamphlet accepted as entirely his', while establishing a collaborative relationship with Robert Greene for the authorship of the Pasquill tracts, with Nashe as the 'news-hound' and Greene as the author (pp. 71–3, esp. p. 72).
25. *Martins months minde*, sig. A1^r.
26. Mikhail Bakhtin, *Rabelais and His World*, trans. Hélène Iswolsky (Bloomington: Indiana University Press, 1984), p. 26.
27. *Pappe with an Hatchet*, 1589. Reprint by Puritan Discipline Tracts (London: John Petheram, 1844), p. 37.
28. Mary Grace Muse Adkins argues that *A Knack to Know a Knave* is a surviving anti-Martinist play in 'The Genesis of Dramatic Satire Against the Puritan, as illustrated in *A Knack to Know a Knave*', *Review of English Studies* 22 (86) (1946), pp. 81–5. While this play probably emanates from the Marprelate controversy, it is both too late (1592) and too formally constructed to be one of the grotesque anti-Puritan interludes referred to in the tracts themselves.
29. According to *Pappe with an hatchet*, Marprelate was mocked at St Paul's by the choir children; at the Theatre, a playhouse near Finsbury; and at Thomas a Waterings in Southwark; Pierce, *Historical Introduction*, p. 222.
30. Nicholl, p. 68. The letter is quoted in full in the notes to *Pappe with an Hatchet*, p. 48.
31. The letter to the Archbishop is also recorded in *Pappe with an Hatchet*, p. 49.
32. 'Would those Comedies might be allowed to be plaid that are pend, and then I am sure he would be decyphered, and so perhaps discouraged' (*Pappe with an Hatchet*, p. 32).
33. Nicholl writes: 'Will Kemp may also have contributed his famous comic talents: a later Martinist tract mentions a "Kemp" among the "haggling and profane" detractors of Martin, and Nashe dedicated his own effort, *An Almond for a Parrat*, to Kemp. Both [John] Lanham and Kemp were old members of Leicester's troupe, which had dispersed on the death of its patron in 1588 and joined ranks with Lord Strange's Men. The latter company was specifically mentioned by Lord Mayor Hart in November 1589, when the authorities were moving to suppress the unseemly plays they had originally encouraged. It seems probable that Strange's Men, including Kemp and Lanham, were responsible for some of these gruesome travesties of Martin' (p. 68). Martin Holmes persuasively argues for Kemp's role as Falstaff in *Shakespeare and His Players* (New York: Charles Scribner's Sons, 1972), pp. 47–50.
34. See Nicholl, pp. 112–115.
35. Hill, *Collected Essays*, p. 78.

36. Bloom, *Sacred Truths*, p. 86. Taylor states that Shakespeare's 'decision to conflate the historical Oldcastle with the theatrical Vice' (J. Dover Wilson's reading) was a radical innovation ('Fortunes', p. 96).

37. Neil Rhodes is one critic who does examine such pamphlet literature, locating the origins of the English grotesque in the Marprelate controversy and exploring its subsequent evolution, largely in the writings of Thomas Nashe. He positions *Henry IV* in the context of the Marprelate tracts and discusses the influence of Nashe on Shakespeare's earlier writing, but does not claim the same direct connection for Falstaff, perhaps because he seems unaware of Falstaff's Lollard origins (pp. 89–99).

38. *Fortunes* 16, 33.

39. *Lectures and Essays*, Vol. 1 (London: Macmillan and Co., Limited, 1905), pp. 141–2. J. Dover Wilson quotes this essay as his primary reference for comments of Falstaff's Puritanism (*Fortunes*, pp. 16, 21).

40. Naseeb Shaheen, *Biblical Reference in Shakespeare's History Plays* (Newark: University of Delaware Press, 1989), p. 137.

41. The Arden edition quoted here notes that Falstaff's advice, 'watch tonight, pray tomorrow' (*1 Henry IV*, 2.4.273), not only echoes Matthew 26: 41, but perhaps refers to the page heading of 'Watch & Pray' which appears in the Genevan version above Luke 22. Later Falstaff refers to 'tattered prodigals lately come from swine-keeping, from eating draff and husks' (*1 Henry IV*, 4.2.34–6). According to the New Arden, 'Shakespeare recollects the Geneva Bible's "huskes" (Luke, 25:16) rather than the Bishops' or Great Bible's "coddes"' (p. 130n).

42. S.L. Bethell, 'The Comic Elements in Shakespeare's Histories', *Anglia* 71 (1952), p. 99.

43. *Henry The Fourth Part 1*, ed. Samuel Burnett Hemingway, New Variorum Shakespeare (Philadelphia and London: J.B. Lippincott, 1936), cited in Humpreys, p. 15n.

44. Puritans set psalms to music in order to make them easier to memorize, part of their educational agenda to encourage learned Christians (Collinson, *Elizabethan Puritan Movement*, pp. 356–71).

45. Ainger, p. 145. Giorgio Melchiori, the editor of *The Second Part of King Henry 4* for *The New Cambridge Shakespeare* (Cambridge University Press, 1989), also notes that 'Falstaff's hymn-singing is ... possibly a survival of the caricature of the original Oldcastle, a Lollard, equated by the Elizabethans with the Puritans' (p. 76).

46. H. Mutschmann and K. Wentersdorf *Shakespeare and Catholicism* (New York: Sheed and Ward, 1952), p. 347; see pp. 345–9 for a discussion of Falstaff's status as a Puritan. Bethell also discusses Falstaff's 'Puritan' dialogue (pp. 94, 98–9).

47. 'Amendment of life' echoes Luke 15: 7, Matt. 3: 8 and Acts 26: 20 (Humphreys, p. 16n).

48. In this I would disagree with Graham Holderness, who, in a discussion of Falstaff's origins in the historical Oldcastle, writes: 'Falstaff's Puritan parody and his anti-Puritan satire would have ... [the] function ... of inviting the audience to enjoy a burlesque on the popular

butts of Elizabethan and Jacobean stage satire (cf. Ben Jonson's *The Alchemist* and *Bartholomew Fair*), with perhaps a concealed jibe at Puritan interference with the theatre. Falstaff's sorties into this are not, like Jonson's, sustained exercises in social and religious satire: they show a character simply 'dropping into' a style of comic performance familiar to the audience … *for the sake of the performance alone'; Shakespeare Recycled: The Making of Historical Drama* (New York: Harvester Wheatsheaf, 1992), p. 158 (original italics).

49. Christopher Baker, 'The Christian Context of Falstaff's "Finer End"', *Explorations in Renaissance Culture* 12 (1986), pp. 72, 76; Goldberg, p. 77; Honigmann, p. 127.

50. The notes to Humphreys' edition provide fascinating examples of the editorial tunnel vision that results from this denial of Falstaff's associations with Puritanism and his origins in a famous reformist religious leader. One instance of editorial inconsistency is the definition given for the terms 'not-pated' and 'knotty-pated'. In a moment of anger, Hal calls Falstaff 'thou knotty-pated fool' (*1 Henry IV*, 2.4.222). The Arden footnote for this line glosses 'knotty-pated' as 'block-headed' (p. 68n). The term 'not-pated', however, which the Prince hurls at the unfortunate Francis in a similar tirade (*1 Henry IV*, 2.4.69), is defined as a reference to short hair, 'common among the lower and middle classes, and the Puritans got the nickname of roundheads because they for the most part belonged to these ranks' (pp. 59–60n). Similarly, in *Part II* 'smooth-pates' is defined as 'city (Puritan) tradesmen who, despising long locks of fashion, cropped their hair short; known later as Roundheads' (p. 21n). Hal could also be using the term 'knotty-headed' with Puritan connotations when he speaks to Falstaff.

In *Part II* Falstaff is associated with 'Ephesians … of the old church' (2.2.142), which the New Arden glosses as follows: 'The allusion is perhaps to the unregenerate Ephesians, with the sensual faults St Paul warns them against (particularly indulgence in wine: *Ephes.*, 5. 18) before they "put off the old man" and put on the new … The Page hardly seems to allude (unless ironically, and the irony would be lost on the stage) to "the prime church of the Ephesians", whose conditions St Paul laid down, and which was the Puritan court of appeal for purity of life' (p. 57n). This gloss, with its blanket refusal to consider the possibility of Puritan overtones ('the Page *hardly* seems to allude'), pre-empts the valid possibility of irony even as it provides an ironic reading of the (otherwise gratuitous) line. In Falstaff's case, the irony of the phrase – an irony that would have been glaringly obvious to an audience aware of both Falstaff's Lollard origins and his bacchanalian behaviour on stage – stems from the coexistence of these diametrically opposed social models in the person of Falstaff.

51. The bland Oldcastle in *The Famous Victories of Henry V* is a rare exception. The neutrality of this figure perhaps indicates another playwright's uneasiness with Oldcastle, and the difficulties of presenting him on the stage in Elizabethan England.

52. *Stages of History: Shakespeare's English Chronicles* (Ithaca, NY: Cornell University Press, 1990), p. 238.

53. For Nasheian allusions, see Rhodes, pp. 92, 93–5; J. Dover Wilson, *The First Part of the History of Henry IV* (Cambridge: Cambridge University Press, 1946), pp. 191–6.

54. Evelyn Tribble, *Margins and Marginality: The Printed Page in Early Modern England* (Charlottsville and London: University Press of Virginia, 1993), p. 109.

55. *Martins Months Minde*, sig. D^v.

56. Peter Stallybrass and Allon White, *The Politics and Poetics of Transgression* (Ithaca, NY: Cornell University Press, 1986) has been especially influential in its brilliant analyses of the symbolic power of the poles of 'high' and 'low'.

57. Valerie Traub, *Desire and Anxiety: Circulations of Sexuality in Shakespearean Drama* (London: Routledge, 1992), pp. 53–8.

58. Patrick Collinson, 'The Theatre Constructs Puritanism', in *The Theatrical City: Culture, Theatre, and Politics in London*, ed. David L. Smith, Richard Strier, and David Bevington (Cambridge: Cambridge University Press, 1995).

7

The Evacuations of Falstaff (*The Merry Wives of Windsor*)

Jonathan Hall

Counterfeit? I lie, I am no counterfeit. To die is to be a counterfeit, or he is but the counterfeit of a man who hath not the life of a man. But to counterfeit dying when a man thereby liveth is to be no counterfeit, but the true and perfect image of life indeed.

(Falstaff)[1]

Laughter is essentially not an external but an interior form of truth; it cannot be transformed into seriousness without destroying and distorting the very contents of the truth which it unveils. Laughter liberates not only from external censorship but first of all from the great interior censor ...

(Bakhtin)[2]

Falstaff's language in *1 & 2 Henry IV* is inseparable from the much discussed 'polymorphous perversity' which it expresses. Its historical resistance to the Crown's centralizing 'Lenten civil policy', as Michael Bristol has called it,[3] remains to this day essential to the kind of pleasure which it affords to the audience. In the wake of Mikhail Bakhtin's reading of Rabelais, the concept of popular or festive laughter (which C.L. Barber had already established as a major and productive approach in Shakespearean criticism) has been extended to embrace the difficult but useful idea of a 'language of the grotesque body'. Common sense tells us that the idea is paradoxical, since it appears that the body, if considered as an entity distinct from the mind, cannot be said to have a language. Deconstruction of this old Cartesian dualism, apart from being tedious and perhaps a bit too predictable, is not necessarily very persuasive. A more pragmatic approach would be to point out that, whether it can be said to have a language or not, it can certainly be made to signify. This can be put more strongly. The body cannot escape from signification, even from the standpoint of the person spontaneously performing a gesture or bodily function. This is so even if the function in question is labelled 'natural', for that too is to place it within, or in relation to, an order of meaning. There is no gesture that escapes from social meaning (that is, from having the quality of a sign), and there is no bodily movement or impulse that is free from interpretation as gesture. But any sign can be the site of contestation, as Bakhtin and Voloshinov have argued. And in the conflict between the monological impulse and the dialogical con-testation, the monological must attempt to mark the site of its victory by a negation of the conflict itself.

Following this line of thought with an example in terms of a lan-guage of the body, it can usefully be argued that the aesthetics of ballet arose from the long history of the disciplining of the 'grotesque body' by European court society, and culminated in its almost absolute negation, in the Freudian sense, by the Absolutist French court of the seventeenth century. At that point, the court dance entirely loses its participatory quality, and is transformed into spectacle. To say this is not to limit its potential for further development by tying it to its origins. For my purposes, however, the usefulness of this is that it highlights the 'inner dialogism' in Bakhtin's own use of the term, 'the grotesque body'. For, although he often writes of the 'grotesque body' as a collective reality histor-ically prior to the establishment of the idealizing forms of the cen-tralizing, and ultimately bourgeois nation-state, it is clear that his use of the term 'grotesque' is taken from the lexicon of the scorn-fully dismissive representatives of that idealization, in order to be given a reversed valorization. (It is not just a neutral term bor-rowed from the history of pictorial art.) What emerges from his account of centralism and its monologizing discourses, as it attempts to assert itself over and above the polyglossia of the popular, is that it produces its antagonist *as grotesque* by the same moves that it monologically idealize itself.[4] European court society's tendency towards the spectacular, in order to impose both inward psychological and outward social distancing in the place of acknowledged interdependence, is inherent to its mono-logical cultural politics. My example of the still participatory court dance culminating in the more distanced spectacle of the ballet illustrates the point that the cultivation of ethereal lightness, 'natural' poise, and delicacy of line, is actually the product of an iron discipline in which the body of apertures, protuberances, sweat and real weight, is not really suppressed (go backstage to confirm this), but is negated and labelled 'grotesque', 'ungraceful', 'ugly' or whatever in order to banish it from the spectacle of the idealized, sublimated body. The distancing of spectacle enables this effect of banishment, but what is banished still persists, known about but disregarded.

And yet my own term 'iron discipline', with its connotations of a purely external repression, can be misleading too. The *corps de ballet* is not exactly the same as the regimentation which the rationalizing practices of centralism imposed onto the bodies of undisciplined warriors (again, 'undisciplined' only from the standpoint of the emergent order), in order to produce a more rational use of force abstracted from the individual body and its characteristics. None the less, it *is* part of the same cultural development; and, after all, regimentation went on to produce its own non-rational aesthetics of precision in military display, for which there are still more spell-bound enthusiasts (at Horseguards Parade or on the Champs Elysées, for example) than there have ever been for ballet. The transformed body of the ballet dancer, however, is not merely discip-lined in this machinic sense. The discipline takes the form of a countering and controlling energy which negates and overcomes the potential disaster of the 'grotesque', and whose source is also the dancer's own body. Discipline here does not mean the curbing or restraint of energy but its redeployment in a controlled way. To see discipline as internalized countering energy is to come very close to Freud's account of the ego, but instead of repression here, we might wish to have recourse to a more Foucauldian notion of the *production* of a new body, to be perceived, identified with, desired as an ideal model. A 'discourse' of the body, then, which means more than a set of ideas *about* the body. A discourse in Foucault's sense is lived. It re-orders perception and self-perception. So, reinterpreted as discursive production, the concept of a language of the body loses the merely paradoxical quality that Saussurean or other rationalist ideas of language as a conceptual system makes unavoidable.

And yet Foucault's concept of a discourse and the discursive production of the subject is too holistic to deal with Bakhtin's idea

of the 'language of the grotesque body'. This is particularly so
when Foucault posits it as a preferable alternative to Freud's
'repressive hypothesis' in volume one of his *History of Sexuality*.[5]
What is lost here is precisely the history of a repression, which is
what Bakhtin's argument about the disappearance of the language
of the carnival's 'grotesque body' invites us to investigate.
Stallybrass and White in their *Politics and Poetics of Transgression*
have made the important point that although empirically minded
historians have accurately charted the suppression of carnival practices by the centralizing state, they are mistaken to describe this as
achieving a total disappearance. The two authors argue that, on the
contrary, what takes place is the transfer of the formerly collective
'language of the grotesque body' into a privatized, silenced, inner
psychological space. It returns as the repressed of the
bourgeoisified individual.[6] In this connection they write of the
extreme relief of writers like Marie Cardenal in her *Words to Say It*
and Jean Rhys in her diary[7] when they rediscover the public language of the carnival, which is once again adequate to the organs
and impulses of the lower body. Anguish turns back to a laughter
of recognition and indentification.

This surely suggests a wider reconnection for us too in the language of the major carnival Fat Man of the English stage, Sir John
Falstaff. But the problem here, which I have hinted at in my reference to the pleasures of the ballet, is that in *1 & 2 Henry IV* the language of the lower body finds its most powerful expression in a
play which deals with its enforced disappearance at the hands of a
determined Prince Hal. And it is Prince Hal who throughout the
two plays stresses mockingly the 'grotesque' nature of that which is
to be made to disappear. When he finally becomes king, of course,
he completes this distancing mockery by banishing the bearer of the
'grotesque body' from his presence altogether, on pain of death. He
also publicly makes his own subjective independence from Falstaff
the very condition for the rule of law and the perpetual banishment
of chaos and riot from the realm of England. In terms of the mould-
ing of audience response, this is the crux of the matter. The language of the 'grotesque body' in this play is made to appear as an
agent of potential chaos and civil war. Furthermore, in so far as
Prince Hal has consorted with Falstaff, he is also open to the suspicion of parricidal desire, so that the repeated repudiations of such a
rumour, and finally their public denial as the new king submits to
the Chief Justice as a 'father' (i.e. to the law rather than Falstaff),

become, like Freud's reading of the repression of Oedipal desire and the formation of the complex, the wished-for cornerstone of social order and peace. Thus the casting-off of Falstaff, which is correlative to the stern policies of the centralizing state, are also intensely desired. Deleuze and Guattari write in their *Anti-Œdipus* that the object of their 'schizo-analysis' is to 'show how desire can be brought to desire its own repression even in the desiring subject'.[8] There could be no more striking example of the discursive production of the modern subject than this play which deals with the repression of desire in the service of desire.[9] The language of the carnival yields to the scornful mockery which labels it 'grotesque', and even 'monstrous', as part of a strategy of misrecognition leading to recoil and repression. In Freudian terms, but not those of Freud's argument, the id is constructed *as* rebellious and 'lower' by an ego which can be understood as a historical formation.[10]

My epigraph from a famous speech by Falstaff concerning the truth of lies, occurs when he rises from a feigned death on the heroic battlefield. He asserts that the life of the body is the only truth, and that to call his 'counterfeit' a falsehood is itself a falsehood, produced out of the empty rhetoric of heroism. What is appealing here is not merely the verbal play, though the verbal control of wit is important, but what Bakhtin would identify as the resistance against a dominant ideology by the verbal expression of a counter-truth. But here the discussion gets difficult. In an obvious sense such counter-truths remain identifiable as lies and simple fakery. Prince Hal is constantly on hand to call him a liar (though his own unifying project is more duplicitous than Falstaff could ever be). Certainly Sir John is no ideal monological spokesman for a suppressed class. If he is indeed a vehicle for the expression of counter-truths, that consists in his very perversity and mobility rather than in his propositions. His verbal dexterity thus serves and addresses the audience's desire to elude the social discipline and its discourses of truth, as Foucault would put it, which are none the less also desired. Yet all of this, to come to the forefront of attention, requires the constant witty mockery of the Prince. This mockery also occasions laughter, though it always tends to the exposure of Falstaff as fraud and liar. Furthermore, to pick up Bakhtin's language here, the Prince is the one who describes and denounces Sir John's body as 'grotesque' and doubly grotesque because it is old. The Prince's wit, then, is the verbal instrument of a social discipline that must engage dialogically with its other, in order to negate it ultimately. When he finally replaces this monologizing mockery with an act of banishment, separating his controlling self from the grotesque old body, he is denying something in himself. But the final act of banishment is not only the fulfilment of the project of distance and separation which he announces to the audience in soliloquy in Part 1 (*1 Henry IV*, 1.2.192–214), it is also implicit in his unmasking mockery throughout. The most intense dialogue in the comic scenes in these plays is marked by this difference in intention and power between the two speakers. The emergence of monologism and separation from the 'grotesque body' is already foreshadowed in the inner conflict of the two régimes of pleasure offered to the audience. But it should be emphasized that Bakhtin's use of the term 'grotesque' runs a necessary risk. For it is only from the standpoint of the esthetics of the culture of centralism that the popular, lower, fleshly has been made to appear 'grotesque' in the negative sense. In other words, the 'grotesque' is as much a product of the culture of the centralizing state as the sublime creations, like the ballet for example, which come into being to leave it behind. It is the underside of the production of the controlling form, which Nietzsche calls Apollonian in his own revalorization of the Dionysian,[11] in the sense that it is a strategy of misrecognition, which can even lead to horror, imposed upon the so-called 'lower' body by the practices of distancing and mockery. (I shall return to this horror later.) Bakhtin writes at the beginning of his book on Rabelais that the essential 'difficulty' of this author for us is that we can no longer think within the language of the 'grotesque body' which prevailed before the rationalizing and moralistic concept of laughter came to dominance in the seventeenth century:

> Rabelais is the most difficult classical author of world literature. To be understood he requires an essential reconstruction of our entire artistic and ideological perception, the renunciation of many deeply rooted demands of literary taste, and the revision of may concepts. Above all, he requires an exploration in depth of a sphere as yet little and superficially studied, the tradition of folk humor.[12]

Bakhtin argues throughout the first two chapters of his book on Rabelais, that with the advent of the culture of centralism, laughter itself changes in quality, as it assumes a satirical, rationalistic purposiveness. I am arguing for a further corollary: that this involves a

misrecognition of the languages of the body, and their corresponding reproduction as precisely 'grotesque'. Actually, Bakhtin himself
sets out why the term 'grotesque' acquired its negative sense, when
he explains why Rabelais became not only 'incomprehensible' but
also 'monstrous' for the neoclassical critic La Bruyère. This seventeenth-century critic had written:

> Rabelais above all is incomprehensible: his book is a mystery, a
> mere chimera; it has a lovely woman's face with the feet and tail of
> a serpent or of some more hideous animal. It is a monstrous jumble
> of delicate and ingenious morality and of filthy depravation.[13]

Bakhtin comments very aptly:

> The chimera is grotesque; in classical aesthetics there was no
> place for it. The combination of human and animal forms is one
> of the most ancient images, but it is completely alien to La
> Bruyère, the faithful spokesman of his time. He is used to con-
> ceive being as something finished, stable, completed, clear, and
> firm. He draws a dividing line between all bodies and objects.
> Even the moderate grotesque image of Melusine in popular
> legends appears to him a monstrous mixture.[14]

This discussion is extremely significant, because it shows how
the monologizing aesthetics of centralism paranoiacally *produces*
the 'grotesque' body as its monstrous other. The narrowing perspective of rationalist aesthetics reveals its own horror of all
unboundedness which it transforms into the monstrous. What is
important, however, is not the presence or absence of a particular
image or representation. After all, Boileau had written before La
Bruyère: 'Il n'est point de serpent, ni de monstre odieux/Qui, par
l'art imité, ne puisse plaire aux yeux.'[15] ('There is no serpent or
odious monster who, when imitated by art cannot please the eye'.)
    The importance of the gaze to the aesthetics of the transformation
of the monstrous to a controlling clear perception is there in Boileau
too. What matters, as Bakhtin says, is the presence of a demarcation,
the 'dividing line between all bodies and objects'. When this control
fails, the 'grotesque' object of the distancing or satirical gaze easily
tips over into the monstrous, and the other face of the mockery can
easily turn into a repression in those who are led to negate their own
lower bodily functions, as Stallybrass and White have written.

Now, none of Shakespeare's comedies is predominantly satirical, but the emergence of a purposive and narrowing laughter, focalized through the mockery of Prince Hal, is very central to the thematic concerns of *1 & 2 Henry IV*. Whether in the composition of *The Merry Wives of Windsor* Shakespeare did or did not answer a royal command to recall Falstaff and depict him in love, there is no doubt that he is indeed recalled into a world where he is diminished already, a world where bourgeois values predominate, and where the historical conflicts of the *1 & 2 Henry IV* are over. Moreover, he is recalled only to be expelled again, at least from the domestic interiors which are the main setting. (Later I shall argue that the final humiliating public integration in the park is not as distinct as it may seem.) Yet, though the decisive historical conflicts are over, there is a definite socio-historical dimension to this comedy. Shakespeare does not merely rewrite, but moves on to explore the consequences for the discourse of the 'grotesque body', and for its antagonists, in the emergent bourgeois order. It should be understood that the chronology of composition is not the main issue. *Merry Wives* actually may have been composed before *2 Henry IV*, but it is concerned none the less with the stabilized bourgeois world that succeeded historically to the history cycle.

There is a diminution in the carnival Fat Man. In *1 & 2 Henry IV* he has the stature of a challenging counter-culture, which the projects of centralism necessarily represent as a threat, and one which has to be reckoned with as much as with the feudal divisiveness of a Hotspur, but with a far greater verbal cunning than is reserved for the other, noble 'traitors'. In the later carnival play *Twelfth Night* Sir Toby Belch is reduced to the level of a dependent relative of the ruling Lady, whom he none the less loyally defends against the concealed upwardly mobile desires of the apparently Lenten Malvolio. In *Merry Wives*, the old Fat Man appears as an external threat to households and ladies alike, but not quite as external as these defenders of propriety affirm. These defenders are the so-called 'merry' wives (the term is Mistress Page's), and the pleasures of laughter afforded by the play are largely, though certainly not exclusively, organized by them. Like Prince Hal, they too organize the plot, though this no longer has the dimensions of national history.

Mistress Ford asks angrily: 'What tempest, I trow, threw this whale with so many tuns of oil in his belly, ashore at Windsor?' (2.1.61) This could almost be Prince Hal elaborating on the

'Manningtree ox', though it is more short-winded. And there are many such examples of the persistence of the old rhetoric dwelling on fatness and oldness, not least in the self-defending and aggrandizing language of Falstaff himself. Yet it is characteristic that Mistress Ford cuts short her own verbal play with the more self-righteous 'How shall I be revenged on him? I think the best way were to entertain him with hope, till the wicked fire of lust have melted him in his own grease. Did you ever hear the like?' (2.1.65). 'Revenge' is a constant refrain in the mouths of both of the wives, and it is always doubled with self-justifying motives of moral punishment and reform. Virtuous or not, plotters are always duplicitous in their manipulation of others' desires, and here the constant renewal of Falstaff's lust through the lure of hope is legitimated by the desire to make the vice manifest and hence punishable. However, the psychological motivation that engenders the virtuous desire for revenge in the two 'merry' wives is not the same, even though they share their anger and reinforce it in each other.

The preoccupation with revenge against the invasive 'grotesque' body, that is with a personal desire to control and correct the carnivalesque, is significantly supported by a language of domestic cleansing. Mistress Page's strategem for punishing Falstaff and expelling him from the house in the comic guise of saving him, is also in her own joking words a cleansing procedure:

> Look, here is a basket. If he be of any reasonable stature, he may creep in here; and throw foul linen upon him as if it were going to bucking. Or – it is whiting time – send him by your two men to Datchet Mead.
>
> (3.3.121–4)

And Mistress Ford later echoes this linkage of correction to washing: 'I am half afraid he will have need of washing, so throwing him into the water will do him a benefit' (3.3.172–4). However, simply casting the dirty object into the Thames (Falstaff's actual fate) is a good deal milder than the operation which Mistress Page names and would probably like to perform. Buck-washing was a process of boiling foul linen in alkaline lye (buck), then beating it, and finally rinsing it in clear water. Falstaff is lucky that Mistress Page's violence remains purely verbal! But, in this same scene it is also striking how Ford in his monomania puns on the word 'buck', and unknowingly foretells the end of the play:

Mistress Ford: Why, what have you to do whither they bear it [the basket]? You were best meddle with buck-washing!
Ford: Buck? I wish I could wash myself of the buck! Buck, buck, buck? Ay, buck, I warrant you, buck. And of the season too, it shall appear.

(3.3.148–52)

This pun transforms the cleansing agent ('buck') back into the carnivalesque horned animal which Ford fears to become (a cuckold) and which Falstaff will become (as Herne the hunter who becomes the hunted):

Mistress Ford: Mistress Page is come with me, sweetheart.
Sir John: Divide me like a bribed buck, each a haunch. I will keep my sides to myself, my shoulders for the fellow of this walk, and my horns I bequeath your husbands.

(5.5.22–5)

Ford's pun, which far surpasses his understanding (indeed *he* may not be punning at all), runs through the play, confounding the cleansing remedy with the ill, the invasive dirty body which has to be cast out.

The starting point for this action is the 'merry' wives' reception of Falstaff's rather transparently crude love letter. At first, neither knows that it is identical to the letter sent to the other, so their initial response is to the letter itself, rather than to the fact of its duplication, which comes later. Mistress Ford's response is the simpler, more direct one. Her opening jest moves quickly to an open statement of anger:

Mistress Ford: Perceive how I might be knighted. [*Mistress Page reads*]
I shall think the worse of fat men as long as I have an eye to make the difference of men's liking. And yet he would not swear, praised women's modesty, and gave such orderly and well-behaved reproof to all uncomeliness that I would have sworn his disposition would have gone to the truth of his words. But they no more adhere and keep place together than the hundred and fifty psalms to the tune of 'Greensleeves'. What tempest, I trow, threw this whale … ashore at Windsor?

(2.1.53–62)

It is worth commenting on the way in which this serious speech emerges from within the 'merry' joking, thereby suggesting its motivation. Mistress Ford accuses Falstaff of a smooth and convincing hypocrisy, that is, an apparent conformity with the rules of social decorum. We as audience never witness such a polite performance, which would require an internalized self-control entirely alien to the exuberant enthusiastic liar that we in fact have. We may just accept the existence of this more duplicitous Falstaff in the imagined offstage world, or we may feel that Mistress Ford is so simple that she has been taken in by a display that would fool nobody else. (Master Ford's notorious jealousy would have some basis in that case.) If so, her subsequent anger is a reaction to being made a fool of. Eric Auerbach's comments on Tartuffe, the most famous hypocrite in European comedy, seem helpful here. He partly agrees with Molière's contemporary, La Bruyère, who wrote that real hypocrites are not as transparent as Molière's grotesquely gluttonous and lascivious hero.[16] Auerbach agrees with the statement about real hypocrites, but says that the comic stage demands the broad effects of transparency, so that the appetites constantly burst through the appearance of decorum and religiosity. If comedy depends on this artificial visibility, it is simply irrelevant to invoke any standards of realism. One should think within the norms of comedy. But Auerbach is too good a critic himself to remain content with a concept of closed form. He contradicts himself, but enriches our view of comedy as exploration of unconscious desire, when he takes the next step in his argument. Although the canons of neoclassical probability would seem to make Tartuffe's success impossible, in view of his grotesque transparency (which is what La Bruyère objects to), he actually succeeds because he addresses the desires and fantasies of those whom he fools. So Molière is a realist, after all. This move by Auerbach re-establishes comic realism on the basis of a psychology of desire, rather than on contemporary neoclassical ideas of probability. Only those are fooled who want the deceptive image which they are offered. Similarly, Mistress Ford's construction of the image of Falstaff which fooled her and is now broken, seems to tell us more about her than it does about Falstaff. Her anger is at a betrayal which his gross declaration of appetite brings about, but which she seems to have encouraged in its non-declared polite form. This casts a revealing light upon her joking attack on Falstaff's fat and old body. This familiar motif, from *1 & 2 Henry IV* and from the carnival tradition in general, acquires a reaccentuation in her utterances. Her anger expresses and instals a desire for distance and a repudiation of an attention that has until recently been acceptable, on condition of its decorous guise. In itself this may appear to be an over-interpretation. More needs to be said about the function of the wives' anger and desire for revenge in the overall structure of the play. But first I would like to consider Mistress Page's anger, whose motivation is distinct but, I think, complementary to Mistress Ford's.

It is in fact Mistress Page who opens this scene (2.1) with a reading of Falstaff's fatuous letter, interspersed with her own mocking retorts. Having finished it, she gives vent to her feelings:

> What a Herod of Jewry this is! O, wicked, wicked world! One that is well-nigh worn to pieces with age, to show himself a young gallant! What an unweighed behaviour hath this Flemish drunkard picked, i' th' devil's name, out of my conversation, that he dares in this manner assay me?
>
> (2.1.19–24)

As in Mistress Ford's case, Falstaff's inappropriate age is turned into a case of indecency. But the indecency that outrages her is the thought that Falstaff must have picked something innocent out of her conversation and misconstrued it. In her case this immediately develops into a general hostility to men, virtually a refrain with her, unlike Mistress Ford:

> Why, I'll exhibit a bill in the Parliament for the putting down of men. O God, that I knew how to be revenged on him! For revenged I will be, as sure as his guts are made of puddings.
>
> (2.1.26–30)

The same response is repeated when she scornfully talks of Falstaff's producing multiple copies of the same letter: 'Well, I will find you twenty lascivious turtles ere one chaste man' (2.1.77). In the light of the constancy of this response, Page's assurance that Falstaff will get nothing but sharp words from her, which seems foolishly over-confident to Ford, appears to be less the product of his principles or his character, and more of an experience of his wife's tongue. But there is more here. In her case too, the excessive anger suggests something in her motivation, just as it does in the case of Mistress Ford. But here, what is suggested is that the anger is an over-compensation for uncertainty. Even in the speech quoted above there is at least a potential self-reproach for some act of 'unweighed behaviour' giving Falstaff an opening, however unintended. Now when Mistress Ford goes on to utter their shared concern for his misconstruing of their characters: 'What doth he think of us?', Mistress Page replies:

> Nay, I know not. It makes me almost ready to wrangle with mine own honesty. I'll entertain myself like one that I am not acquainted withal; for sure, unless he know some strain in me that I know not myself, he would never have boarded me in this fury.
>
> (2.1.80–5)

As is so often the case in Shakespearean comedy, the controlled language none the less deals with a divided speaking subject and his or her barely maintained control. Mistress Page here concedes, if only in a curious rhetoric whose main intention is denial, that Falstaff's misconstrual may be the accurate construal of another self which he has detected but which she does not know. And, of course, Falstaff was indeed first incited by what he was looking for in the wives' display of normal hospitality, in the form of glances rather than words, which he interprets in line with his desires. In this process, gestures are 'construed', that is translated into the English language. Of Mistress Ford he says:

> I spy entertainment in her. She discourses, she carves, she gives the leer of invitation. I can construe the action of her familiar style; and the hardest voice of her behaviour, to be English'd rightly, is 'I am Sir John Falstaff's'.
>
> (1.3.39–43)

And 'construing' Mistress Page similarly, he says: '[she] even now gave me good eyes too, examined my parts with judicious oeil-lades; sometimes the beam of her view gilded my foot, sometimes my portly belly' (1.3.52–5). Clearly the comic effect here depends upon his self-flattering misconstrual of the women's innocent gestures and looks. But as the play explores the motivation for their anger and desire for revenge, simple misunderstanding is left behind. It is not at all that Sir John turns out to be right. It is rather that, at least in Mistress Page's case, she is angry at the very thought that he may be partly right, even though she can find no evidence for it. What is involved is the power of speech-acts. It is as though Falstaff's fictional constructions have at least sufficient force to result in angry denial. In this, Page's confidence in his wife is reconfirmed, since she is so internally vigilant as to expel a desire that she does not even think that she has. Such close self-policing makes the jealous surveillance of a Ford totally unnecessary. She is the very epitome of a self-assertive bourgeois cleanliness, for which even the suspicion of impropriety is itself a contamination and provocation to anger. In short, Mistress Ford finds a hypocritical duplicity in Falstaff, whereas Mistress Page, the more complex and perhaps more modern of the two, suspects and negates an unwilled complicity in herself. For both, Falstaff is an invasive force. When Mistress Page utters those ambiguous words 'for sure, unless he knew some strain in me that I know not myself, he would never have boarded me in this fury', Mistress Ford channels this unintentional confessional note back into a joke, by elaborating the metaphor of naval warfare. It is a case of what Freud calls displacement, and it enables Mistress Page to recover herself:

Mistress Ford: Boarding you call it? I'll be sure to keep him above deck.
Mistress Page: So will I. If he come under my hatches, I'll never to sea again. Let's be revenged on him.

(2.1.86–9)

She then proposes a strategy of 'fine baited delay' that would ruin Falstaff economically, but Mistress Ford rejects such a 'villainy' that would 'sully the chariness of our honesty'. Mistress Pages's anger testifies to the fact that something has got partly under the hatches and has to be repelled. But it is certainly not a question of a secret attraction to Falstaff which she is virtuously lying about. Clearly the wives do not feel seriously threatened by Falstaff himself. On the contrary, they are extremely aware that they have the upper hand, since they can control him through manipulating his lust, and they demonstrate that power through controlling the plot, no less than Prince Hal in *1 & 2 Henry IV*. So what is the provocation to anger and revenge? The real issue here is: what has happened to the discourse of the 'grotesque body' and its open acknowledgement in the public realm? What form of banishment is the angry mockery helping to instal?

Falstaff's opening speech in 2 *Henry IV* begins:

Men of all sorts take a pride to gird at me. The brain of this foolish-compounded clay, man, is not able to invent anything that tends to laughter more than I invent, or is invented on me. I am not only witty in myself, but the cause that wit is in other men.

(1.2.6–10)

As usual, everything is miraculously ego-syntonic for Falstaff! But there is a truth in this statement too. We do not just laugh at him, but *with* him too. As Leo Salingar has noted, his 'inexhaustible resilience' makes us aware of 'the multiplicity or deep duplicity in the causes of laughter'.[17] And this statement remains true of *Merry Wives*. But the kind of wit that he engenders in others in this play is much more that of a mockery which distances and objectifies him. The mockery is still recognizably carnivalesque in this play. But it is psychologically motivated, and carries a desire to expel him, from the self or from the bourgeois household, by representing him as an unclean invader from the outset. That is why there is an unremarked slippage in both of the wives' discourse, by which their moral condemnation of Falstaff's lechery finds ambiguous support in a physical revulsion for his body. The unasked, but occasionally glanced at question is whether moral outrage would be so strong if the tempter were to be recognized as attractive. But Mistress Page's excess of anger against Falstaff points to a more general defensive hostility in the maintenance of her virtue. Thus she repeatedly takes his grotesque attempts at seduction as typifying the lust of men in general, for it is really this generalized lust that she is resisting. Thus, however diminished he is in this play, Falstaff still stands for something wider than his own individuality, and that is what underlies the desire for his expulsion. The 'merry' wives organize the plot which achieves this, culminating in the collective taunting at the end, but the ironic question of virtue in relation to the 'grotesque body' is still there:

Mistress Page: Why, Sir John, do you think, though we would have thrust virtue out of our hearts by the head and shoulders, and have given ourselves without scruple to hell, that ever the devil could have made you our delight?
Ford: What, a hodge-pudding, a bag of flax?

Mistress Page: A puffed man?
Page: Old, cold, withered, and of intolerable entrails?
Ford: And one that is as slanderous as Satan?
Page: And poor as Job?
Ford: And as wicked as his wife?
Evans: And given to fornications, and to taverns, and sack, and
wine, and metheglins; and to drinkings and swearings, and star-
ings, pribbles and prabbles?

(5.5.145–58)

Although this scene of vengeful taunting is still funny, it is close to
self-righteousness. Evans' comic summarization of Falstaff's faults
at the end serves to blunt the edge of this fleering, and to ensure
that something of the carnival pleasure still remains. But my main
point is that, even in the wives' discourse, the dialogism of carnival
is not really left behind when the 'grotesque body' is constructed as
an alien disgusting other. What happens is that the old dialogism is
negated, and the site of its disappearance is taken over by scorn,
distance and anger. But the anger, through its very excess leaves a
revealing trace of what has been made to disappear.

Now, *2 Henry IV* also deals with the expulsion of Falstaff, plotted
and anticipated in Part 1, by Prince Hal who, on becoming king,
both denies access to Falstaff and, more psychologically, negates
the former relationship, by transforming it into a dream:

I know thee not, old man. Fall to thy prayers...
I have long dreamt of such a kind of man,
So surfeit-swelled, so old and so profane;
But being awake I do despise my dream.
Make less thy body hence, and more thy grace.
Leave gormandizing. ...

(5.5.47–53)

In a very real sense *Merry Wives* repeats this action, but the realm
that is being defended is the bourgeois household. In the narrower
confines of this domestic comedy, the order is already pre-
established. There is none of the pathos or the grandeur afforded by
the drama of its historical establishment, and hence relatively little
scope for the Falstaffian voice beyond its construal as the language of
lies and of a disgusting monstrosity seeking to invade from outside.

The importance of the domestic interior as a space liable to invasion is not new in comedy. It is important in some of the comedies by Plautus, for example, and also in Shakespeare's early Plautine comedy, *The Comedy of Errors*. There too, the liminality and the metonymic linking of the house with its open or shut doors to the bodies of wife and mistress is quite explicit. Access to one is entry to the other. In *Merry Wives*, the domestic space is even more charged with significance than in the Roman and Italian tradition, though the theme of erotic invasion is often there too. (In later bourgeois comedy, the domestic setting is less erotically charged with liminality and transgression, since it appears as a more established, or 'natural' setting for the whole action.) A clear pattern in this earlier influential tradition is that the house is normally guarded by an angry *senex* figure and that the desiring young male from outside is usually a welcome and desired deliverer from domestic tyranny. In the case of Falstaff, of course, the invasion is not by graceful young love, opposed by the *senex*, but of a 'grotesque' old lust opposed by everyone. And yet, there is a doubling of plots, familiar in the structure of Shakespearean comedies, with a corresponding contrast of styles. This contrast is also a hierarchization here. The Italianate plot is taken over by Fenton's courtship of Anne Page. It doubles and parallels the 'grotesque' failed courtship of Falstaff, and it leads to the final integrative conclusion of the whole play. In style it is not unlike the courtship of Bianca plot in *The Taming of The Shrew*, which contrasts with the vigorous, farcical, bodily and 'English' humour of Petruchio's courtship of Kate. The contrast of styles is of major importance because it is also a contrast of contents. In the case of *Merry Wives*, to see what the 'higher', refined and ultimately successful love plot shares with its 'lower' parodic double is to grasp why they both converge, from opposing polarities of social style so to speak, to represent an invasive threat to the bourgeois household. The key is obvious enough, as it dominates the whole play. It is Master Page's money, which is threatened from above and from below.

This linking of love and money is sounded from the outset, when Evans equates Anne Page's 'pretty virginity' with her 700 pounds inheritance and pushes the reluctant and incompetent Slender into her pursuit. With regard to Falstaff, money is much more the goal of his pursuit than in *1 & 2 Henry IV*. There his attempted robbery at Gad's Hill, or the later corrupt abusing of the king's press, appear, like his ambition on Hal's succession, more as aspects of revelry and living beyond the law for the body and satisfaction of appetite than as calculated stratagem. In *Merry Wives*, the fact that both Mistresses Ford and Page are keepers of their husbands' purse plays a major role in firing his desire for their bodies. His penetration of the house is aimed at the treasure within, in both senses. His verbal bombast where he articulates this intention borrows extensively from the language of contemporary mercantile and colonizing adventure capitalism. For example:

> She is a region in Guiana, all gold and bounty. I will be cheaters to them both, and they shall be exchequers to me. They shall be my East and West Indies, and I will trade to them both.
>
> (1.3.61–5)

Now, in itself, the association of women with the desirability of money and property is not new in Shakespearean comedy. It plays a central role in Petruchio's motivation in *Shrew* and in Bassanio's enterprise in *The Merchant of Venice*, and Shakespeare certainly exploits the potential doubleness of motive. This in turn is open to reaccentuation in productions, and some critics make a lot of it in interpretation, which is itself a form of production of the text. René Girard, for example, makes it the basis of his reading of Bassanio as representative of a 'Venetian' (i.e. early capitalist) hypocrisy shared by Antonio.[18] Such readings constitute a perfectly valid but empirically unprovable hermeneutics of suspicion, since they articulate what the text does not say. These readings are unprovable, but also undeniable, since the textual doubleness is certainly there, and to valorize it in a production or an interpretation is not only permissible but a valuable expansion of possibilities.[19] But what is textual potential in *Shrew* and *Merchant* is explicitly articulated in this slightly later play, set more firmly in contemporary England. Master Page may well occupy the slot of the traditional *senex*, but his motives for blocking access to young Fenton are clearly stated in contemporary social terms. Fenton is of the upper aristocracy and, far from making him a desirable match, this makes him no less a danger to accumulated bourgeois money than Falstaff's profligacy. For the bourgeois these are closely linked threats. Fenton himself explains to Anne that his status and and conduct appear to Page as a threat to both property and, interestingly, true love:

> He doth object that I am of too great birth,
> And that, my state being galled with my expense,

I seek to heal it only by his wealth.
Besides these, other bars he lays before me –
My riots past, my wild societies;
And tells me 'tis a thing impossible
I should love thee but as property.

(3.4.4–10)

Page, like his wife, may be besotted with an unsuitable suitor in a manner more typical of Molière's tyrannical fathers than Shakespeare's, but his motives for mistrusting Fenton are very sober. Furthermore, he explicitly links Fenton to Falstaff by bringing up the former revelries with Prince Hal. Page is not confident that this historical epoch is over:

He kept company with the wild Prince and Poins. He is of too high a region; he knows too much. He shall not knit a knot in his fortunes with the finger of my substance. If he take her, let him take her simply [i.e. without dowry]; the wealth I have waits on my consent, and my consent goes not that way.

(3.2.66–71)

Fenton does not simply say that Page is wrong in his assessment of him. But, challenged by Anne: 'Maybe he tells you true', he replies:

No, heaven so speed me in my time to come!
Albeit I will confess thy father's wealth
Was the first motive that I wooed thee, Anne,
Yet, wooing thee, I found thee of more value
Than stamps in gold or sums in sealèd bags;
And 'tis the very riches of thyself
That now I aim at.

(3.4.12–8)

Fenton actually confirms that Anne's father was right. He goes on to claim that love has transformed him but, of course, he could still be pretending. Therefore, only the elopement without the prospect of a dowry, can validate his words by deed. Without this, he would not be above suspicion. Accordingly, a comic norm reappears here in a slightly altered guise. The comic norm in question is that the ultimately providential transgression by the suitor against the will of the father figure actually enables the necessary and desirable transmission of the daughter from the father to the son-in-law. This underlying pattern of countless comedies breaks the potentially incestuous possession of the heroine by the father; it permits exogamy without challenging the structures of patriarchy. Psychoanalytical theorists like Charles Mauron argue that it stages the avoidance of Oedipal conflict which tragedy represents.[20] Basically this is the same argument as the anthropological formulation. The challenge to the tyrannical father is permitted by comedy so that patriarchy can avoid a competitive primal chaos, ending in the murder of the father. But, although this ancient comic pattern may be said to persist and to provide harmonious closure through the integration of Fenton, the linking of Fenton as aristocratic profligate reformed through love and Falstaff as a dangerous profligate from the same pre-bourgeois world is certainly a radically new inflection of the old structure. Falstaff, of course, cannot be reformed through the sublimating love that redeems Fenton. He has to be corrected in order to be integrated. This is somewhat like the 'grotesque' Caliban, who is also misrepresented through an imperial discourse, as 'monster', 'lying slave' and rightly despoiled son of a 'witch'. (Shakespeare's text, however, gives Caliban a right of reply, even if it has been taken until recently as the voice of mere resentment.) The 'merry' wives' anger can be understood in the same way as Prospero's, exercised in defence of the decencies of 'civilisation'.

From the bourgeois point of view, in resisting Fenton, Page is defending the same thing as his wife in resisting Falstaff, namely his, or her, purse. (This begins to acquire some of the same connotations that Freud notoriously constructs for Dora,[21] with a metaphorical and offensive 'lowness' worthy of Falstaff himself.) Page and his wife share a resistance to aristocratic profligacy trying to break into their ordered domesticity. Ultimately, this is providentially resolved in the case of Fenton. But Falstaff's conflation of monetary and sexual desire is something else. It threatens the very possibility of domestic order. Mistress Page's anger at his monstrous body, whether it is as external as she claims or something that produces a troubling disquiet in herself, as I have argued, is the emphatic defence of a newly established but not quite confident set of values, struggling still to leave the world of *1 & 2 Henry IV* truly behind.

Fenton is integrated, and so, in a sense, is Falstaff, but only after a series of shamings. The first two take the form of expulsions from the domestic space, and the last is public. The reinvention of a theatricalized and thoroughly controlled carnival in a public space for this last shaming is important. It is a carnival memory, with its old connotations of fertility now reduced to mere foolishness or baseless fear. And it is conjured up out of this folk celebration and fear by Mistress Page herself for her more narrow moralizing purpose. It confirms again Bakhtin's words on the fate of carnival laughter when it is yoked to a narrow rational purposiveness. Bakhtin's view on the narrowing of laughter, which I have cited and discussed already, closely resembles Max Weber's arguments on the 'disenchantment of the world' under the influence of the rational instrumentality of modernity.[22] In such a changed world, the carnival becomes a pastiche, or sentimental evocation of that which has disappeared. And indeed Weber's 'disenchantment' is palpable in this play if one compares it, for example, to the troubling ambiguities of *A Midsummer Night's Dream*, which do not completely disappear at the end.[23] Falstaff himself is never so completely uncrowned as at the end of *Merry Wives*, when he too mingles demystification with the morality that has finally and successfully been thrust upon him:

> And are these not fairies? By the Lord, I was three or four times in the thought they were not fairies, and yet the guiltiness of my mind, the sudden surprise of my powers, drove the grossness of the foppery into a received belief – in spite of all rhyme and reason – that they were fairies. See now how wit may be made a Jack-a-Lent when 'tis upon ill employment!
>
> (5.5.120–7)

This triumph of the prose of the world, where error is also equated with moral deviance, is the very antithesis of carnival. And it is the final achievement of the 'merry' wives, confirmed in the public domain.

The previous two shamings take the form of an expulsion of the 'grotesque body' from the domestic interior, first, as a reduction to the level of excrement amidst the dirty clothes in the buck-basket which is then emptied into the river, and second, in the form of a transformation into the body of a 'witch' who is angrily beaten out by Ford. But neither of these expulsions or evacuations of Falstaff is complete, since the secretive nature of the wives' 'revenge' is dictated by the setting in the bourgeois interior and the precarious position of the women's guardianship of it. After the second humiliation of Falstaff, the third and last is prepared differently. The wives decide to tell their husbands, to come clean with them, as we say nowadays. There are two reasons for this change. The first is to try to cure Ford of his jealousy, by presenting him with his wife's honesty. The second is that it will then be up to the men to decide whether 'the poor, unvirtuous, fat knight shall be further afflicted' (4.2.203–4). The men will be put back in control of a plot not of their making, so that they can make the final judgement. As in the case of all of Shakespeare's comedies with active heroines, the restoration of patriarchy is their goal and justification, though it is never free from contrivance. In this case, if the men decide on further punishment, 'we two will be their ministers' (4.2.204–5), which is a finely ironic reference to subordinates in the service of God. The point is that to put the ceremonial conclusion into the men's hands is also to be able to put it irrevocably into the public domain. Up till now the women have had to operate covertly themselves, and this has meant that the unmasking could not be completed. Now, Mistress Ford makes the point that the shame will put an end to all ambiguity, that is to the language of jesting itself.

Mistress Ford: I'll warrant they'll have him publicly shamed, and methinks there would be no period to the jest should he not be publicly shamed.

And Mistress Page is eager to forge this end of merriment:

Mistress Page: Come to the forge with it, then shape it. I would not have things cool.

                                                                    (4.2.206–10)

Public shaming was traditionally one of the possible functions of the carnival, and it was often aimed at women. Here it is contrived by women, acting for their husbands, and it puts an end to the jesting and the threat of the 'grotesque body'. It stabilizes the new community, and it ends equivocation together with the secrecy of plotting, as the husbands are put back in control. The conclusion is one of a transparency of motive which leaves behind the furtiveness inseparable from even virtuous plotting.

I have read this comedy in socio-historical terms as a successor to *2 Henry IV*. Many critics have been sensitive to the sense of loss that the banishment of Falstaff entails at the end of that play. Given the reading of Falstaff's body as the locus of 'polymorphous perversity', the ending of 2 *Henry IV* has been seen as an address to a common feeling of loss which we all experience, and then forget experiencing, as it were, upon entry into social and psychological order. In Lacanian terms, Falstaff's body becomes the lost object of desire, which brings desire itself into being through entry into the symbolic order under the sway of the law of the father. Hal's career repeats a primal pattern, but he becomes the master of himself and the realm, whereas the audience is more ambiguously divided, and registers a loss too. Thus Falstaff's ambiguous body has been equated with the lost body of the mother. Such readings, however contrary to the critical rationality of many critics suspicious of psychoanalytical categories, are not to be lightly dismissed when it is, after all, a question of analysing the *kinds of pleasure* that the play engenders in the audience. But primal separation from the mother's body has a kind of pathos which seems weak in the case of a play where women play a leading role in the expulsion, even if this is ultimately in the service of a patriarchal social order. Julia Kristeva's development of the concept of the loss of the maternal body into the more violent psychic process of 'abjection', in which the body is constantly preserved from the ultimate threat of filth and decay by vomiting and excreting aspects of itself that are found to be alien and monstrous, seems much more appropriate to the transformation of the carnivalesque body (for her, still basically the maternal body) into an object of revulsion.[24] This is less a narrative of simple loss through separation than of angry hurling out, even if it is repeated in a witty and 'merry' form. Bakhtin's argument on the narrowing effect of satiric laughter needs to be supplemented by such a theory of the negation of the presence of the alien other within this unstable would-be monological self. Kristeva relies on the anthropology of Mary Douglas to make the claim that the process of 'abjection' is a common feature of all societies.[25] This may have a certain truth, but the main part of her book *The Powers of Horror* uses this anthropology-cum-psychoanalysis to explain the furiously anti-Semitic but also self-evacuating loathing of the twentieth-century, paradoxically anarcho-fascist writer, Louis-Ferdinand Céline. Is this a social normality? Or is it the exaggeration of culmination of the anti-carnivalesque in bourgeois culture, because, in an inverted form, Céline is none the less the most carnivalesque of twentieth century writers? Significantly Céline also saw himself as the direct inheritor of Rabelais in French literature, which he considered to be mired in the rationalism of the intervening centuries. In this he is quite close to Bakhtin's reading of Rabelais. Céline identifies his own extraordinary and explosive anarchic argot with that suppressed counter-discourse of the body in French culture. Of Rabelais' 'failed' project, he wrote that it was democratic and fundamentally opposed to the ruling orders of discourse which later congealed around Cartesianism:

> What he wanted to create was a language for everyone, a real language. He wanted to democratize it, and that meant war. He was against the Sorbonne, the professors, and all that. But he lost. The winner was Amyot, the translator of Plutarch. In the centuries after that, Amyot had much more success than Rabelais. Even today, he is the one whose language we live by ... That's where Rabelais failed: Amyot is our heritage. Real shit. As I say, Rabelais wanted an extraordinary, rich language. But the rest of them castrated it. They flattened it. Nowadays, to write well you are supposed to write like Amyot, but that kind of language is nothing but a translation. ... The critic Lanson said, 'The French are not very artistic'. There's no poetry in France. Everything's too Cartesian. And, of course, he's right. Amyot was a pre-Cartesian.[26]

And, as though echoing Bakhtin on the 'difficulty' of understanding Rabelais after three centuries of triumphant rationalism and its reduction of language, he says:

> No, the French can no longer understand Rabelais. They have become too precious. The terrible thing is that it could have all turned out quite differently. Rabelais' language could have become the French language.[27]

But it must be added that, as Kristeva notes, the 'grotesque body' in Céline's writing is engaged in a delirious frenzy of vomiting. At the personal level, this is partly a result of close acquaintance with the very real fragmentation of bodies in the trenches in the First World War, and partly connected with his work as a doctor with the abused bodies at Ford's in Detroit and with the working class in Paris. In the famous delirium of Céline's style, there is a return of the repressed with a vengeance. He rediscovers everywhere the 'filth' which bourgeois culture failed to evaculate and tries to hide, and in a frenzy of denunciation he hurls it out again. In this denun-

ciation of filth there is a paradoxical loyalty to an absent cleanliness, which was so important to fascism and its dream of armoured
bodies[28] (but which Céline, as both pacifist and delirious writer,
also denounces). It is probably significant that it is in the name of
his mother, Céline, that Destouches, the bearer of the paternal name
and decorated war hero, becomes the delirious (perhaps hysteri-
cal?) writer of the lower body and its counter-truths. But these are
now distorted and fragmented, not celebrated. Céline's fragmented
but energetic style gives the possiblity of utterance to this broken
body. It is also remarkable that Céline's rewriting of the Rabelaisian
'grotesque' body is doubled by an enthusiasm for the dynamic and
'elastic' bodies of ballet dancers, which escape from the modern
condition of generalized degradation. Thus he too repeats, in his
own way, the history which I invoked at the beginning of this
essay, namely the formative dissociation of the 'grotesque' body
from its etherealized counterpart.[29] Now, of course, there is no
direct affinity, and certainly no literary affiliation, between
Shakespeare's *1 & 2 Henry IV* and *Merry Wives* on the one hand,
and Céline on the other. Such a connection defies common sense, as
well as established historical periodization. But the buried history
of the negated, but not truly abolished 'grotesque body' of the carnival, still remains to be written. Rather than read the plays in
terms of a psychological constant of laughter or of negation (which
still remains a possibility), I have tried to suggest that they should
be placed within a historical narrative of this disturbed and dis-
turbing underside of the modern subject in formation.

And yet, the pathological excess of Céline remains none the less
an abnormality. While the expulsion of whatever counts as dirt or
pollution is arguably true of all societies, there are big differences in
how violently acts of exclusion take place, and on what grounds
obsessive phobias are formed. The control over dirt, and the polic-
ing of the liminal area of the domestic space or the body may
indeed involve unconscious repressions as well, but it is not always
licit to interpret repression as a synonym for oppression or the
scapegoating of others. The problem is that they are not easily separated either. Socially necessary or salutary repressions are easily
translatable into socially oppressive and alienating forms via the
all-too-familiar metaphors of cleansing, maintenance of purity,
removal of social cankers, expulsion of alien filth. And the corresponding political bad faith in the imaginary construction of a
purity taken to be really in place and under threat (whether radical,

ethnic, national, religious or doctrinal) often borrows extensively from the horror discussed above, namely the abjected processes of the 'grotesque body' itself. The carnivalesque element in laughter (as distinct from the mockery of satire and distancing) remains important in this respect, because it is still capable of restoring a recognition of the dialogical implication of self and other, and of a relativizing acceptance of a shared participation in crude or 'lower' body existence. By contrast, all idealizing discourses of purity, which are by definition always under siege and always demanding vigorous defence, turn the processes and properties of the lower body into pathological symptoms of putrefaction or terrifying invasive otherness. At times this can lead to social violence, and at others to a loss of sense of boundaries, and even to a schizoid fragmentation of the isolated self.

Shakespeare's *Merry Wives*, perhaps because it is the most bourgeois of his comedies, clearly belongs to the more normal tradition of social control. My reading against the grain of this normality to show its participation in the more buried history of the modern subject, leading in literary terms from Rabelais to Céline, or in political terms from the formation of the rationalized but still hierarchical bourgeois nation state to the reactive obsessions of modern fascism, is bound to strike some readers as perverse. Be that as it may, there is a more normal history of modern domestic cleansing, strangely similar to the evacuations of Falstaff, which goes back to the same decade and the same Rabelaisian discourse.

In the years shortly before 1591, the Queen's godson, Sir John Harington, had been banished from the court (less seriously than Falstaff, admittedly) for translating the scurrilous book 28 of Ariosto's *Orlando Furioso* to amuse the ladies-in-waiting. His 'penance' was the fine translation of the whole epic, which appeared in 1591 and is still widely appreciated. His other main creation at the time was the invention of the flushing toilet, which was installed on his own estate and later at the Queen's palace at Richmond. It might well be said that this creation is far more widely appreciated today, but is not often talked about except in the language of the 'grotesque body' or else in the totally different discourse of technical installation or hygienic social administration. But in Harington's own writing on this invention, these discourses are not separate, and they combine with an extensive and witty erudition, as well as with a range of contemporary social commentary and covert satire. Harington uses the language of witty humanist learning to challenge all conventional decencies and pieties, which commentators have rightly called 'Rabelaisian', though it is more aristocratic in tone. He himself amusingly mounts an argument for putting 'Rabbles' in pride of place in the philosophical pantheon, perhaps recognizing in this spelling a connection between the lower body and the troublesome lower part of the social body.[30] One of the striking points about this *New Discourse of a Stale Subject, Called the Metamorphosis of Ajax* (i.e. A. Jakes) is that, despite the Rabelaisian joking (or more properly, by means of it), a serious claim is made for his invention to save the increasingly large city from its pollution. In humanist style the modern is addressed by reference to classical models. Roman legislation in particular, is laughingly but also seriously invoked, to show that the ancient city and empire paid honour to the deities of the cloaca, and that enlightened city founders, like Romulus or Trajan, ensured the provision of money and material for grandiose public works to keep the city clean. There is also a lot of witty biblical reference, aimed at inverting the received spiritual hierarchization of thought which would deny intellectual dignity both to his own invention in particular and to its importance in religious and secular culture in general. Harington's book is full of jokes and satirical comment on other matters too, much of which eludes modern commentators. But there is a serious argument concerning modernity's need to emulate this ancient wisdom, and to surpass it with his own invention for the cleanliness of the private, though implicitly still aristocratic, household. His book fits into the humanist tradition of learning in employing examples from the past, linked to Rabelaisian laughter, to address the needs of the present and the future. This also involves the practical, plumber's manual aspect of the text, with his instructions on how to make and install the apparatus. Such a mixture of discourses on a plane of playful equality is indeed both 'grotesque' and difficult for the modern reader to make sense of.

As a text, then, contemporaneous with *Merry Wives*, Harington's *Metamorphosis* faces both the past and the future. In actual fact, his Rabelaisian language will not outlast, except in debased forms, the future that he is arguing for, and for which his invention will indeed be indispensable. There is, of course, no sense in simply denoucing his machine as part of the repressive apparatus directed at the elimination of the 'gay relativity' of the lower 'grotesque body'. In the developing city culture it increasingly becomes a social necessity, even if at first, and for a long time, it forms part of a social differentiation between clean bourgeois and filthy slum dwellers. But newly developed social needs may also involve new kinds of repression, and the development of a machine to do impersonally and privately what used to be done by servants and porters, certainly reinforces the construction of a *cordon sanitaire* between the sayable and the unsayable about the self. To say this is simply to acknowledge that repressions are indeed socially constructed and always accompany new social needs. This is not necessarily disastrous, although it can produce disastrous results. The example of Céline makes us aware that the private psychic disaster can assume major social proportions when the repressed contents are projected upon an elusive other. In our social imaginary, this other is always seeking entry, and is sometimes actually uncovered, with astonishment and outrage, in the fortress of the self, the domestic stronghold, or the citadel of our never sufficiently policed nation-based order. The 'abnormal' phobias shadow the perfectly 'normal' administration of historically changing daily needs. A comprehensive cultural history needs to articulate the connections between the two.

NOTES

1. *1 Henry IV*, 5.4.112–18. All quotations are from *William Shakespeare: The Complete Works*, ed. S. Wells and G. Taylor (Oxford: Clarendon, 1986). However I have retained the name of Falstaff for *1 Henry IV*, rather than adopting their restoration of Oldcastle. This is because I am concerned with the question of the continuity and shifts in the representation of the carnival Fat Man figure.
2. Mikhail Bakhtin, *Rabelais and His World* (Cambridge, Mass: MIT, 1968), p. 94.
3. Michael Bristol, *Carnival and Theater: Plebian Culture and the Structure of Authority in Renaissance England* (New York and London: Methuen, 1985).
4. See also J. Hall, 'Unachievable Monologism and the Production of the Monster', in D. Shepherd (ed.), *Bakhtin: Carnival and Other Subjects* (Amsterdam: Rodopi, 1993); and *Anxious Pleasures: Shakespearean Comedy and the Nation State* (New Jersey: Fairleigh Dickinson, Associated University Presses, 1995), pp. 197–214.
5. M. Foucault, *Histoire de la Sexualité 1: la Volonté de Savoir* (Paris: Gallimard, 1976).
6. P. Stallybrass and A. White, *The Politics and Poetics of Transgression* (New York: Cornell, 1986), p. 180.

7.   Stallybrass and White, *Transgression*, pp. 181–3.
8.   G. Deleuze and F. Guattari, *L'Anti-Œdipe: Capitalisme et Schizophrénie* (Paris: Minuit, 1972), pp. 124–5.
9.   See Hall, *Anxious Pleasures*, pp. 215–34.
10. See R. Lichtman, *The Production of Desire: The Integration of Psychoanalysis into Marxist Theory* (New York and London: Macmillan, 1982), pp. 178–81.
11. F. Nietzsche, *The Birth of Tragedy* [1872] (Garden City: Doubleday, 1956).
12. *Rabelais*, p. 3.
13. *Ibid.*, p. 108.
14. *Ibid.*, p. 109.
15. N.D. Boileau, *Art Poétique*, III, 1–2 (Paris: Gallimard, 1966), p. 169.
16. E. Auerbach, *Mimesis: The Representation of Reality in Western Literature* (New York: Anchor, 1957), pp. 317–18.
17. L. Salingar, *Dramatic Form in Shakespeare and the Jacobeans* (Cambridge: Cambridge University Press, 1986), p. 34.
18. R. Girard, '"To Entrap the Wisest": a reading of the *Merchant of Venice*', E. Said (ed.), *Literature and Society: Selected Papers from the English Institute, 1978* (Baltimore and London: Johns Hopkins, 1980).
19. See also Hall, *Anxious Pleasures*, pp. 57–67.
20. C. Mauron, *Psychocritique de Genre Comique* (Paris: Corti, 1985), p. 58.
21. S. Freud, 'Fragment of an Analysis of a Case of Hysteria', *The Complete Psychological Works of Sigmund Freud* (London: Hogarth, 1953) vol. 7, pp. 1–122.
22. M. Weber, 'Science as Vocation' [1917], H.H. Gerth and C.W. Mills (eds), *From Max Weber*, (New York: Oxford University Press, 1946).
23. Hall, *Anxious Pleasures*, pp. 113–15.
24. J. Kristeva, *Pouvoirs de l'Horreur: Essai sur l'Abjection* (Paris: Seuil, 1980).
25. M. Douglas, *Purity and Danger: an Analysis of Concepts of Pollution and Taboo* (Harmondsworth: Penguin, 1970).
26. L.F. Céline, 'Rabelais, il a raté son coup', undated interview, *Cahiers de l'Herne 5* (Paris: Minard, 1965), pp. 19–20.
27. Céline, *L'Herne 5*, p. 20; author's translation.
28. See K. Theweleit, *Male Fantasies* (Minneapolis: Minnesota, 1987); and H. Foster, 'Armor Fou', *October, vol. 56*, 1991, pp. 64–97.
29. For an excellent discussion of the contrast between the ballet dancer's body and the putrefying grotesque one in Céline, see M. Beaujour, 'Temps et Substance dans *Voyage au Bout de la Nuit*', *L'Herne 5*, pp. 173–88.
30. J. Harington, *A New Discourse of a Stale Subject, called the Metamorphosis of Ajax* [1596], ed. E.S. Donno (London: Routledge, Kegan Paul, 1962), p. 68.

8

Towards a Theory of Play and the Carnivalesque in *Hamlet*

Phyllis Gorfain

In his history and theory of carnivalesque laughter in European culture, Bakhtin frequently praises what he considers a brilliant Shakespearean appropriation of the carnivalesque.[1] Yet few specific citations to particular plays or scenes illustrate Bakhtin's admiration for Shakespeare's dramatic methods. Bakhtin's most elaborate discussion of Shakespeare's carnivalesque methods is more provocative than probing; this typical passage among the 15 references he makes to Shakespeare exemplifies the large scope of his suggestive insights and the slender specifics:

> The analysis we have applied to Rabelais would also help us to discover the essential carnival element in the organization of Shakespeare's drama. This does not merely concern the secondary, clowning motives of his plays. The logic of crownings and uncrownings, in direct or indirect form, organizes the serious elements also. And first of all this 'belief in the possibility of a complete exit from the present order of this life' determines Shakespeare's fearless, sober (yet not cynical) realism and absence of dogmatism. This pathos of radical changes and renewals is the essence of Shakespeare's world consciousness. It made him see the great epoch-making changes taking place around him and yet recognize their limitations.

Furthermore, Bakhtin's comparisons of Shakespeare with Rabelais and the other Renaissance writers applies mainly to the festive comedies, the Falstaffian realm of exaggeration, gluttony, abuse

152

and defiance to which Bakhtin parallels the Rabelaisian world of celebration and scurrility.[2]

Far less typically does Bakhtin discuss the carnivalesque in Shakespearean tragedy, but when he does so, he emphasizes the integration of seriousness and laughter in Shakespeare's grotesque realism:

> In world literature there are certain works in which the two aspects, seriousness and laughter, coexist and reflect each other, and are indeed whole aspects, not separate serious and comic images as in the usual modern drama. A striking example is Euripides' *Alcestis* in which tragedy is combined with the satyric drama (which apparently becomes the fourth drama). But the most important works in this category are, of course, Shakespeare's tragedies.
>
> (p. 122)

In noting the way Shakespeare mixes genres and includes fools and grotesque images into a classically austere form, Bakhtin traces Shakespeare's tragic method to both ancient models from Hippocrates and Lucian as well as to a native tradition of medieval grotesque folk humour. Both traditions connect indecorous elements in which contrasting voices and styles do not simply complement each other, but essentially bond together in the fundamental organization of the work.

As Bakhtin outlines his history of a carnivalesque mode in culture and literature, he implicitly invites us to develop further his theory of the carnivalesque in dramatic tragedy. In this form, Bakhtin believes, carnivalesque elements help institute a form of the grotesque, one peculiar to the Renaissance. Examining Shakespeare's tragedies more carefully, then, offers an immediate way to try to explain this dissonant mixture in tragedy. More particularly, *Hamlet* – whose source provided Shakespeare with a carnivalesque amalgam of genres and voices in its riddling tests, tricky deceptions, grotesque revenges, and cyclical saga of deaths, near-deaths and returns – emerges as Shakespeare's most ludic and metatheatrical tragedy.[3] Among Shakespeare's tragic works, *Hamlet* also is the most fully centred in a Renaissance court, with its elaborate aristocratic play and performance. Taken together, these elements make *Hamlet* the most performance-centred of the tragedies, the only one with a full-scale play-within-the-play, a trickster hero and an elaborate series of other ludic performances, including the player's speech, the verbal gaming of the gravedigger scene and the fraudulent fencing match.[4] Regarding these inserted genres and mixed modes as typical of 'carnivalized literature', the rich tradition of dialogic forms which Bakhtin outlines and explains in his work on Dostoevsky, helps explain the odd tragic force of *Hamlet*.[5] In these terms, we can discuss more fully how the carnivalesque is more than an ingredient, digression or relief, but is a kind of attitude, a history of languages and practices, which functions as a structural and ideological method in this most ludic of Shakespeare's tragedies, yet one which is consistent with the double vision of all Shakespearean tragedy.[6]

In *Hamlet*, just as it does in any larger cultural context, the carnivalesque functions in a cultural ensemble of other forms of playing. Moreover, this spectrum of playing in *Hamlet* operates within a reflexivity which dramatically comments on carnival performance and other forms of play. *Hamlet* considers its own ludic content and methods by enclosing within itself numerous performances, foremost of which is the inner play which both mirrors and recasts the performance we watch. Yet this inner play connects to a series of other ludic forms: punning, other word-plays, role-playing, games, gambles, storytelling, songs, proverbs and riddling. Further, depictions of madness, ritual and parodies of ritualized routines establish a continuum of licensed genres in this drama. These forms reflect on one another to interrogate the methods and ends of formal performances. Comparing carnivalesque terms and structures to other forms of playing in *Hamlet* can exemplify a Bakhtinian theory of the carnivalesque and of carnivalized literature in terms of other theories of play, parody, and ritualized disorder.[7] Theories of play, riddling, performance and ritual, in turn, gain in cogency when placed within Bakhtin's complex view of the social and strategic meanings of carnival.

Bakhtin's history of the carnivalesque also helps us place *Hamlet* beyond inadequate genre-bound categories. Carnival parodies and mixes discordant genres and conventions for it blurs genre differences along with obscuring the other discriminations we use to purify the borderlines between life and death, the body and what surrounds it. Bakhtin's account of carnival thus helps us to appreciate *Hamlet*'s continuity with folk forms, marketplace and street performances.

TRAGIC INEVITABILITY AND CARNIVALESQUE CYCLICALITY

Just as Bakhtin treats carnival not as a safety-valve or inversion, but as a form which clarifies and enacts a cultural system, the carnivalesque in *Hamlet* intensifies its complex tragic mode. The folk view of a cyclical and double-bodied time in carnival opposes the unilinear trajectory of death and loss in formal tragedy, graphically represented in the image of the fall.[8] Organic imagery of death and life processes express the bodily focus of the carnivalesque vision; these processes also frequently express themselves in spatial figures:

> the people do not perceive a static image of their unity ... but instead the uninterrupted continuity of their becoming and growth ... For all these images have a dual body ... (p. 256). Not the ascent of the individual soul into the higher sphere but the movement forward of all mankind, along the horizontal of historic time, becomes the criterion of all evaluations. Having done its part upon earth, the individual soul fades and dies together with the individual body; but the body of the people and of mankind, fertilized by the dead, is eternally renewed and moves forever forward along the historic path of progress.
>
> (p. 404)

The irreversible and vertical movement of tragic form joins to the reversible and horizontal continuum of carnival in *Hamlet* to produce the double vision which one postmodern critic characterizes as not 'to be or not to be', but as 'to be and not to be'.[9] The play as a whole ultimately unites an Aristotelian logic of mutual exclusivity with the paradoxes of pluralism.

Throughout *Hamlet*, Shakespeare merges this ludic carnivalesque mode with a strictly Aristotelian drive toward tragic finality.[10] Many vectors push the action towards a linear and irreversible process of causal consequence. We hear the ghostly call for revenge and watch Hamlet's filial dedication to undertake it; that basic system is repeated and complicated in a lineage of other revenges as other sons undertake violent retaliations for murdered family members. We watch the manipulations of a regicidal usurper who acts through others to keep his crown and queen. Yet intermediary letters and partly unknowing third parties undermine these accelerating intrigues. A pattern in which 'indirections find directions out'

(2.1.63)[11] entangles the linear course of inevitable revenge in a system of deferred actions and interrupted forms.[12]

This recurrent pattern of momentum and interruption assaults orthodox order.[13] The pattern in *Hamlet* is not unique to Shakespearean tragedy; it is however, more exaggerated and interpretable. A remarkable blend of repetition and revision does not deny the consequences of events, but it does reinterpret reality through representation.[14] Through stories, role-playing, parodying discourses of others, performing a play (including a dumb show) and a speech extracted from a play, songs and other prefabricated forms of speaking, citational texts and scripts, characters find speech and performance genres with which to express, displace and reshape their angers, griefs, social criticisms, subversions and containments of others.[15] Through play, both intriguers and oppressed find the expressive and instrumental means to meet the system of denials and indirections erected by a manipulative patriarchal culture.[16]

The uses of play can be manipulative, death-centred and deceptive, or they can be liberating, life-asserting and revelatory; as they do in life, at the end of the dramatic action both model the heroic freedom of Hamlet's courage and commitment to open-ended play and action and, opposing that, the degenerate conniving of Claudius' cheating and manipulation of game and ritual coexist and compete as systems for asserting meaning and power. The patriarchal system of revenge leaves a stage of slain bodies for Fortinbras to manage and a responsibility for Horatio to tell Hamlet's story. We are the mute audience aware that the deaths suddenly ending this history are only represented within the world of fiction. In the realms of play we may learn that from such catastrophes emerge the works of art like *Hamlet*. In its celebration of imagination and its critique of manipulation, we can find the framework with which to re-evaluate and interpret the fictive events we have watched. For example, we see that the significance of revenge itself can be transformed in a series of nested stories about revenge. These stories, told over and over and within each other, seem to defy the ending that revenge seeks but cannot attain.

We first witness the ghost's story of his own fratricidal death, a story which becomes an injunction for Hamlet to remember and revenge; we next see a mimed version of a similar murder in the dumb show prologue to *The Murder of Gonzago*; in the full-scale enactment, we see and hear the fuller version of that poisoning;

later, we hear that Hamlet has told the Ghost's story to Horatio in an offstage action; finally, we become the audience for Horatio's summary digest of these same events for Fortinbras; Horatio's synopsis promises a longer account later. So we may imagine a possible offstage version of the story, to whose recital Fortinbras calls the 'noblest to the audience' (5.2.387). If Fortinbras speaks of that audience while looking out at us in the theatre, might we suppose that we have become, through this experience, 'the noblest' audience, who will soon hear this unperformed but imaginable report? Or do we subtly assume we are not that elite audience, but that we are, however like the court audience, also addressed by Hamlet, chance witnesses to a history which has suddenly become art? We may also fancy, in this confusion of present, past and future, that the subjunctive offstage narrative would have become the telling which has led to the very play we now watch. This kind of self-reflexive play with the boundaries between event and representation, past and present, subjunctive and actual, audience and performers defines and dissolves the differences between the world of the play and the world of the theatre. But these paradoxes differ from the interpenetration of performance and action in carnival. That exchangeability becomes more prominent in other sections of the play, such as the gravedigger scene.

Through many allusions to other works of art which depict assassinations, recounting revenge stories creates a pattern of recursiveness in *Hamlet*. 'To tell' is to count as well as to relate a story. Storytelling in Hamlet then replaces revenge; the law of talion (which counts the exchange of 'an eye for an eye and tooth for a tooth') is cancelled in the retelling of fictions – which 'don't count'. At the same time, we can hear in Hamlet's word-play some of his ambivalence about recollection or representation replacing revenge. Just before the performance of the play within the play, Hamlet induces Polonius to recall his university role in *Julius Caesar*. The old courtier relates that he played the part of Caesar and was killed in the Capitol by Brutus. Hamlet then puns mercilessly on Polonius's brief recollection: 'It was a brute part of him to kill so capital a calf there' (3.2.105–6). The anaphoric repetition calls attention to the re-callings in punning and in representations of the past. As Hamlet trifles with repeated sounds, he mocks memory in both nostalgia and history. In this parody on brutal repetitions at the phonological, theatrical and historical levels, Hamlet may also delicately allude to his own vow to join this lineage of regicides for he has promised the Ghost he will 'remember' through revenge. To please the Ghost, Hamlet must himself repeat the brute part of Claudius, who is the present player-king in Denmark's capital. In addition, the theatrical metaphors in Hamlet's punning further underscore the ironic differences between the representational reality of this event for Polonius as actor and the actual brutal event for Caesar as victim.

Earlier, Hamlet and the First Player together executed a highly stylized epic speech about the slaughter of King Priam.[17] Their elaborate presentation removed the speech from its context in a fictive play (never performed) and the two recitations then construct several levels of performance. First, Hamlet recites the speech as an elaborate cue or reminder for the actor; Hamlet also interrupts himself when he makes a false start in the speech and then revises his own brief performance-as-cue. The First Player next interrupts the Prince to continue the speech in a professional rendition. During that recitation, Polonius and Hamlet make intervening comments. Finally the First Player's speech breaks down when he dissolves in tears, and when the actor in the theatre can make the Actor produce real tears some very odd questions occur.[18] The tears seem to chastise Hamlet, who berates himself with his own inaction, which he invidiously compares to the actor's passion for an only imagined loss, 'What's Hecuba to him, or he to [Hecuba]' (2.2.559). (Both Q1 and F read: '... or he to Hecuba'; Q2 reads' or he to her'. Choosing an authoritative text lies beyond my scope here; I simply note important variations in the early printed texts.)

The actor's tears stopped the actor's act. In a sense, the tears, which define the edge of reality and fiction, lead Hamlet into profound questions about motives. Do stories prompt actions as well as do events? And if we hear a theatrical play, are we the audience to a story or participants in an experience? What kind of experience is a theatrical performance? The nesting of story within theatre, and of story within story, creates intricate stories which really tell stories about stories. This kind of self-enclosure comments on the relationships between deferring actions, revising actions through representation, and the making of 'deferred' meaning. The repeated narrations of revenge in the intervals and interludes in *Hamlet* can thereby upset our certainties of consequence and can strengthen the carnivalesque vision of renewal and returns.[19]

The alliance of linear consequence with cyclical carnivalesque reversibility becomes most evident in the final act of *Hamlet*. On one level, *Hamlet* concludes with a carnivalesque fearlessness and freedom as Hamlet decides to engage in an open-ended fencing match. If it were legitimate, it would be a game whose precise outcome, like the providential timing of a sparrow's fall, cannot be predicted. For both, however, the ending '[will] come' (5.2.222).[20] While the apparent game of the fencing match should lead to an outcome free of pre-knowledge or predetermination, Hamlet also fears something ominous. His new spirit of resolute play, however, impels him to 'defy augury' (5.2.219), that is, to renounce both trying to read and control endings. As a result, the Prince even more emphatically defends his choice to play with his newly won ludic philosophy, one learned, in part, with the carnivalesque clowns in 5.1. We thus hear a new note in his simple aphorisms: 'a man's life's no more than to say "one"' (5.2.74) and 'the readiness is all' (5.2.222). On another level, Hamlet also concludes with a devastating finality when the cheating and intrigue of Claudius defeat this ludic spirit.

This consolidation of irreversible history and reversible art matches other patterns of assertion and denial in the play. We learn that if we cannot annul or avenge consequences, we can reinterpret the meanings of mistakes. We can master mischance in the temporary submission to chance and dizziness offered by games of fortune and vertigo.[21] Most especially, we can take control of disorder in the deliberate mistakes of punning.[22]

The gravedigger scene shows most forcefully this carnivalesque gaming with words. The word-play (punning, witty literalism, clownish malapropism, word corruptions, nonsense) in the gravedigger scene displays control over one's own mistakes and others' manipulations. Yet puns convert understanding only by arresting the instrumental uses of speech. Puns block any straightforward movement of meaning by turning language into a playground of mimicry and revolution. The interruptions of punning then transform the syntagmatic discourse of assertion into a paradigmatic self-commentary on the making of meaning. For instance, in the first clown's word-play, Hamlet confronts both the inevitable consequences of death and a cyclical reformulation of it.

That prose interval, however, gives way to the measures of blank verse and the ritual of the apparently orthodox procession. Yet Hamlet also identifies that orderly form as 'maimed rites' (5.1.219) and Laertes complains to the 'churlish priest' by repeating: 'What ceremony else?' (5.1.223–5).[23] This language about Ophelia's truncated funeral may remind us of other 'maimed rites' through-out the action, which keeps erecting formal structures only to rupture or deny them. When the 'funeral bak'd meats/Did coldly furnish forth the marriage tables' (1.2.180–1), Hamlet's separation from the court deepens: Ophelia madly sings of cold burial cere-monies, and stage tradition frequently has her mime an unsatisfac-tory funeral for her father; Laertes' fury over his father's unpunished murder and inadequate mortuary rituals leads him to foment a rebellion. Stunted rituals and broken forms reproduce other forms of disorder and dissonance repeatedly in *Hamlet*.

Ophelia's reduced rite itself abridges the clowns' games, which interrupted their own gravedigging. Their work itself enacted various forms of 'fine revolution' (5.1.90) as Hamlet punningly characterizes the casual way they overturn graves, bones and class difference. The First Clown, who has doubtless been working centre-stage, becomes a side-stage witness or leaves, Hamlet assumes the position of voyeur until Laertes further interrupts the ritual by embracing Ophelia and possibly leaping in the grave (a stage direction in Q1 and F, but not in Q2). Hamlet himself inter-venes into that fraternal display of hyperbolic grief, and the ensuing skirmish, in turn, must be broken off by the more decorous funeral participants. The abbreviated funeral leaves Laertes and Claudius alone on stage to reconfirm their conspiratorial plan, a scheme which returns us to the linear plot of revenge.

The final scheme employs the formal artifices and rules of a game as a coverup for illegitimate poisonous assaults. But when Hamlet and Laertes fatally wound each other, Laertes three times calls attention to the ironic plots which have turned against their own makers. Hamlet calls attention to the ironic unions of subject and object when he asks the King, 'Is thy [union] here?' (5.2.326)[24] as he forces Claudius to drink the potion he concocted for the Prince, but which has divorced life from his own Queen. Playful transforma-tions or ruptures of continuity repeatedly suspend rule-bound pro-cedures. Punning and other figures of speech then encapsulate the patterns of both cyclicality and broken linear forms which together constitute *Hamlet*'s carnivalesque modes and tragic form.

LICENCE, CARNIVAL, THEATRE AND PLAYING

Carnival and play both use metacommunicative doubling. In asso-ciating carnival with playing in terms of metacommunication, I use the theories of Gregory Bateson and his followers in anthropology and folklore.[25]

They view play as an alternative mode of interpretation; in so defining play we treat play not as a catalogue of framed acts but as a process of playing, a way or reformulating the meaning of actions. In an account of playing as process, we inquire into how we take an event as playful, not into what actions can be defined as play. This view of playing as a process proposes that when we take a sign as play, we treat it as if it were framed by a message about how to take it, a metamessage which says, 'This is play.' For example, Bateson explains how, for chimps at play, the 'nip' signifies that it does not mean what a bite would mean.[26] So Hamlet reassures Claudius that the dramatic poisoning in the inner play commits 'no offense i' th' world' that it is but 'poison in jest' (3.2.234).

Bateson also points out that, while showing it is a 'not-bite', the nip also points to 'the bite', not necessarily to a particular bite. In similar fashion, Hamlet, punning on 'offense' can figuratively claim that the play-murder commits no specific offence. He implicitly denies that the performance refers to or recreates any actual recent Danish murder. At the same time, however, even as he disclaims the play can offend, Hamlet may also thereby indict Claudius' truly offensive poisoning as well as the opaque lies of Claudius' offensive cover-up. Play does not offend, for it transparently admits its fictionality and its alternative meanings. But deceit does offend for it secretly manipulates meaning. Playing and dramatic plays openly betray their subversions of meaning by proclaiming however subtly, 'this is play'. Hamlet also puns on the title of the inner play when he cryptically tells the king what it is called: '"The Mouse-trap". Marry, how? tropically' (3.2.237–8).[27] Here Hamlet's word-play claims a trope is only figuratively a trap. Paradoxically, however, this disclaimer admits, as did his earlier denials of offence, that the framed images of playing may 'work'. Moreover, as a trope about tropes as traps, this trope is also a trap which says, figuratively, it is not one literally. The endless cycle of self-referential denial and assertion in that kind of word-play is further replicated by the enclosed play, which mirrors the main play. So might we not also recognize the play we watch as another trope and trap?

A metacommunicative account of play helps explain how playing uses impunity both to evade responsibility and to enact figurative meanings. The licence of playing as a metacommunication also helps explain the licence of carnival. In both processes, a play frame disclaims liability for the normal consequences or meanings of the performed events. For instance, the nip says, 'this is a not-bite, so don't bite back'. Fools, madmen, poets, carnival maskers and players gain immunity, for the ludic frame licenses speech as inconsequential; in these frameworks, speakers are not taken as responsible for their own meanings. Through his 'antic disposition', Hamlet exploits this kind of 'insanity plea'.[28] While Hamlet can play mad, Ophelia must go mad.[29] She lacks Hamlet's mastery over reflexive role-playing because she is inhibited, in part, by gender restrictions about appropriate female role-playing.[30] To gain Hamlet's freedom to speak, which he gains through the symbolic role of fool in the licence of his 'antic disposition', Ophelia must speak in the licensed voice of the symbolic madman.[31] She further employs the alternate and marked voice of song, flower lore and other folk sayings to wield a speech not her own, but that of others. Ophelia acts out the Other into which Hamlet's misogyny places her, but she serves, in her authentic madness, as the paradigm of the Otherness into which theatre, fools, carnival and other forms of licence also fit. She is a paradigm of the Female Grotesque, a double-bodied figure of exuberant excess and mortality which dominates carnivalesque texts; the female figures created in carnival celebrations embody ambivalence as they are frequently depicted as pregnant, disorderly or mad – a threat to male order and a licentious release from it; their decaying and fertile bodies are associated with the duality of the grave itself, the fecund source of life and its fatal destination.[32] Ophelia's chaste bawdiness, her reticence and outbursts, her non-recognitions and discontinuous forms expose the hidden body of desire, death and knowledge while she also displaces her own subversive and revelatory comments by appropriating traditional songs, sententiae, blessings, greetings, farewells and other speech genres to speak the languages of others – and thereby comment on those languages. Through these devices, she achieves the same detachment of meaning from identity as does Hamlet's deliberate playing and seeming madness. But her easily 'prettified' attacks on court masks do not pose, for the court, the same danger as do Hamlet's indeterminate meanings.[33]

Although Ophelia's songs and enactments of feminine disintegration present repeated versions of linear tragedies, and while she parodies the same genres of court assault as were mounted by Hamlet's playing, her versions of these ludic forms only call attention to the differences between her powerless performances and Hamlet's reflexive ones. Her gender and a lack of self-consciousness in her double discourse displace her revelatory anger, grief, recognition and criticism so that while she may pose a threat – to Claudius' shaky power (notice that she is feared as able to engender suspicions and disorder through the ambiguities of her indeterminate utterances in 4.5.7–15), she is not openly pursued as is Hamlet.[34] Her passive madness poses less obvious danger than do Hamlet's more self-conscious strategies. Yet she, like the violently dangerous Hamlet and Laertes, is to be watched and followed, a signal that productions of the play which relegate the actress to play out Ophelia's mad utterances as merely feminine forms of victimized self-destruction miss in the force of her enactments as a carnivalesque critique of court order and tragic forms. Indeed the inexplicably detailed account Gertrude provides of her watery death could be played in a way that would suggest Ophelia's death was not wholly accidental. The Queen's performance can suggest how much and what kind of threat Ophelia seemed to pose for the court, and Gertrude may sentimentally and unselfconsciously narrate her death as a kind of passive, unknowing suicide – 'incapable of her own distress' (4.7.178), or the Queen may use the narration to deflect and deceive a Laertes who himself is prone to such a romanticized interpretation of Ophelia's performances. Perhaps the Queen here projects her own unreflexive condition onto Ophelia, a condition which also ends in her own – possibly knowing, possibly passive suicide; or perhaps Gertrude's longest speech in the play, a performed narration filled with purple passages and itself a long interruption of the conspiracy to kill Hamlet, is a dramatic signal that the actress should 'overact' this story. In this case, Gertrude occupies a different position in relation to the tragic feminine narrative she obviously fabricates, and her performance of deliberate deception stands in stark contrast to Ophelia's uncontrolled madness.

Viewing madness through the lens of metacommunication links it with playing and other forms of licence. Like ludic expressions, actions which are taken as 'mad' are placed within a reinterpretative framework. Functionally similar to the message, ' this is play', the framing metacommunication, 'this is mad', tells interpreters that such framed communications are to be taken not to mean what they would mean were they not so framed. Mad persons are not held responsible for the consequences of what they do because they

are believed to be unconscious of the social consequences or their
actions. Hamlet claims this kind of exemption when he asks
Laertes's pardon before the fencing match begins. The Prince's
apology proposes, in the paradoxical logic of play and madness,
that his madness has placed him beside himself. The real Hamlet
has not done (been responsible for) what the mad Hamlet
('Hamlet's madness') did:

> ... What I have done
> That might your nature, honor, and exception
> Roughly awake, I here proclaim was madness.
> Was't Hamlet wrong'd Laertes? Never Hamlet!
> If Hamlet from himself be ta'en away,
> And when he's not himself does wrong Laertes,
> Then Hamlet does it not, Hamlet denies it.
> Who does it then? His madness. If't be so,
> Hamlet is of the faction that is wrong'd,
> His madness is poor Hamlet's enemy.

(5.2.230–9)

The licence of carnival, playing, theatre and ritual depend on
similar metacommunicative frames. Hamlet compares the operations of this varied range of licensed representation as it explores
the paradoxes of consequence and inconsequentiality in institution-
alized foolishness, madness, carnival and theatre.

COURTLY ENTERTAINMENT AND CARNIVAL

Hamlet links these strategies of playing, theatre and carnival in a
succinct metaphor. In Act 2, Rosencrantz characterizes Hamlet's
apparent despair as a 'Lenten' attitude. He warns the Prince his
attitude will not provide the welcome 'entertainment' owing to the
itinerant players. At that moment, when Rosencrantz informs the
Prince that the Tragedians of the city are on the way to the palace,
Hamlet has been articulating a linear view of the fallen human condition. His speech characterizes man, a 'piece of work' no matter
how 'noble in reason, how infinite in faculties', as ultimately falling
into nothing more than a 'quintessence of dust'. Then Hamlet
breaks off this devolutionary view to acknowledge that
Rosencrantz's smile mocks his meanings. Like the metamessage,

'this is play', Hamlet suggests Rosencrantz's smile reframes his words as a play on words:

Ham. ... what is this quintessence of dust? Man delights not me – nor woman neither, though by your smiling you seem to say so.
Ros. My lord, there was no such stuff in my thoughts.
Ham. Why did ye laugh then, when I said 'Man delights not me'?
Ros. To think, my lord, if you delight not in man, what lenten entertainment the players shall receive from you ...

(2.2.308–17)

Rosencrantz's metaphor encloses an elaborate argument: since men themselves delight him not, Hamlet will serve, with Lenten entertainment, those who *play* men. One who delighted in man, Rosencrantz implies, would provide the players of men with a playful entertainment like their own. Such service would not be Lenten, but carnivalesque.

As Rosencrantz's metaphor constructs an implicit analogy between laughter and despair, carnival and Lent, theatrical interlude and philosophic argument, his figure of speech theorizes that the theatrical function (if not its content) resembles that of carnival. The players introduce into the linear tragic mode of *Hamlet* a cyclical and rupturing carnivalesque system. Symbolically, they set the reversibility of representation against the irreversible plots of lethal court.

The novel theatrical performances furnish a ludic alternative to the political play of the Claudian court even as Hamlet quickly appropriates playing for political ends.[35] Indeed, early modern peasants and aristocrats exploited carnival and other forms of ritualized disorder, such as charivari, for real protest and suppression, respectively.[36] Hamlet's contrastive uses of playing and performance accurately reflect the politics of theatricality in Elizabethan and Italian Renaissance courts. Personal performance did not function in a carnivalesque or ludic way in sixteenth-century courts, however; at court, performance had to accomplish serious work – making claims to status through the rhetoric or wit, flattery, insult, and artistic display.[37] In the theatrical world of the Claudian court, however, the presence of itinerant, displaced professional players and their ludic performances insert into Elsinore and the play itself not only an alternative to, but a mirror of, the political uses of play.

THE GRAVEDIGGER SCENE

Carnival offers a similar alternative to the official, doctrinal and monologic generic mode of classical genres. Carnivalesque play dissolves separations of audience and performer as well as hierarchies of privilege and subordination, and the gravedigger scene offers a superb example of such a dissolution. Performance routines in the gravedigger scene specifically challenge the suspect order of work, Church law, rulings on suicide, meditations on eternity and notions of possession. The clowns question what constitutes truth and what counts for a lie; they decompose the differences of gender and class with the radical relativity of death.

While the exchanges of the clowns assail differences, they also form a series of identifiable and different speech genres: parodic arguments, riddles, puns and songs. In its rhythm and juxtaposition this set of performances shapes into an almost vaudevillian chain of gags. In the February 1986 Wisdom Bridge production of *Hamlet* in Chicago, director Robert Falls brought on two young black men in bowler hats, colourful scarves and black silk waistcoats; they performed their routines in the style of a New Orleans funeral march. In this stylistic performance of death, the Wisdom Bridge gravediggers employed the licence and modes of Mardi Gras. Although Shakespeare could not have anticipated this New World folk idiom, it derives from the same European carnival sources as do Shakespeare's clowns and their routines. New Orleans funerals and Shakespeare's gravediggers share the same ancestry: they both employ the modes of carnival to joke with the complexities of death and to mock the establishment rituals which try to order it. That festive tradition does not distinguish between theatre and life, court and laity, Church and burial ground, or performers and audiences. To explain how Ophelia, a suicide, is permitted Christian burial, the clowns argue about a series of seemingly fundamental but doubtful differences. They demonstrate the comic likeness between seeking salvation and damnation, and they mock the slim distinction between choice and passivity in suicide. But they finally identify the one difference that matters: 'Will you ha' the truth an't? If this had not been a gentlewoman, she should have been buried out a' Christian burial' (5.1.23–5). This spotlight on the artifice of class difference leads directly into two riddles about Adam being a gentleman (he had arms to dig) and about who builds the strongest houses (the gravedigger, whose houses last until doomsday). The riddles tersely encompass the most extreme issues framing human experience. The first clown thus directs the other, through the indirection of riddling, in circles which pass from the beginning to the end of time and from their own lowliest occupations to the highest ranks of class. The riddling dialogue begins with a formal riddle, one which is not preceded by a formula or stated as a question. The clown poses a seeming contradiction (in effect, he asserts that Adam was a gentleman), and once he pronounces the solution, which relies on a pun, we recognize the clever reply as the answer to a riddle;

1. *Clo.* ... Come my spade. There is no ancient gentleman but gard'ners, ditchers, and grave-makers; they hold up Adam's profession.
2. *Clo.* Was he a gentleman?
1. *Clo.* 'A was the first that ever bore arms.
2. *Clo.* Why, he had none.
1. *Clo.* What, art a heathen? How dost thou understand the Scripture? The Scripture says Adam digg'd; could he dig without arms?

(5.1.29–37)[38]

The game of riddling becomes even clearer when the clown introduces the next riddle more formally. The second enigma elaborates the metaphors of digging; these metaphors characterize the action of searching for the answer as well as the actions of digging described in the riddle propositions and answers;

1. *Clo.* I'll put another question to thee. If thou answerest me not to the purpose, confess thyself –
2. *Clo.* Go to.
1. *Clo.* What is he that builds stronger than either the mason, the shipwright, or the carpenter?
2. *Clo.* The gallows-maker, for that outlives a thousand tenants.
1. *Clo.* I like thy wit well, in good faith, the gallows does well; but how does it well? It does well to those that do ill. Now thou dost ill to say the gallows is built stronger than the church; argal, the gallows may do well to thee. To't again, come.
2. *Clo.* Who builds stronger than a mason, a shipwright, or a carpenter?

1 *Col.* Ay, tell me that, and unyoke.

2. *Clo.* Marry, now I can tell.

1. *Clo.* To't.

2. *Clo.* Mass, I cannot tell.

1. *Clo.* Cudgel thy brains no more about it, for your dull ass will not
    mend his pace with beating. And when you are ask'd this ques-
    tion next, say 'A gravemaker'; the houses he makes lasts till
    doomsday.

                                                          (5.1.37–59)

The second gravedigger, earlier addressed as 'my spade', is now
comforted that he need no longer 'cudgel [his] brains' to excavate
an answer. As he encounters these fundamental questions, the
answerless worker learns that his riddling and gravedigging repli-
cate the labours of Adam. Baffled at first and then educated by
playing, the clown thus typifies the ways to reconstruct fallen
knowledge, just as his digging makes the hollow houses that will
last until doomsday. In such paradoxes are 'nothings' – games,
punnings, naughty puns, notings. Carnivalesque denial and profu-
sion in these riddling paradoxes structurally imitate the opposite
processes of living and dying, the polarities of Genesis and doomsday, the interchanges of questions and answers, the exchanges of
subjects and objects in all the answers; as diggers, they are Adam,
all gentlemen who have arms, and, of course, the gravemakers,
who build the strongest houses. Digging, riddling and gravemaking become substitutes for one another, performance can help show
us that this grave-making is a carnivalesque activity that gravely
riddles with beginnings and endings. Correspondingly, *Hamlet*, as
playmaking, then encloses both kinds of gravemaking in its own
grave carnivalesque play with death and meaning.

The on-stage house, the trapdoor, in which the gravediggers so
indecorously joke may also represent a carnivalesque trope;
perhaps the punning on traps and tropes can, in performance,
deconstruct the theatrical convention that the trap is a grave. If so,
we may see the visual pun about puns in this doubly carnivalesque
grave. Its open orifice holds a gravedigger whose mockeries repeatedly confuse and unite basic antitheses. When the work of
gravedigging and the game of riddling become themselves inter-
changeable at this carnivalesque juncture, then this scene enacts the
present as a middle reality between the genesis of work in Adam's
delving and the consummation of all work at the moment of

doomsday. That cycle is then mimed by the cycle of turns taken in the formal exchanges of the riddling dialogue and by the cycles of life, work, death and leisure in the substance of the riddle answers.

Riddling also represents a model for the exchange of power and knowledge in its dialogic structure of challenge and answer, confusion and clarification. In the social relationships of riddler and riddlee, in the grammar of interrogative and answer, and in the content and method of a particular riddle, riddling plays with the power of interrogation and the exchange of knowledge.[39] Bakhtin notes the significance of riddling as a popular folk genre in the literature of the early modern period:

> Riddles are extremely characteristic of the artistic and ideological conception of that time. The sad and terrifying, the serious and important are transposed into a gay and light key, from the minor key to the major. Everything leads to a merry solution. Instead of being gloomy and terrifying, the world's mystery and future finally appear as something gay and carefree.
>
> (p. 233)

Certainly the clowns' riddling parodies and celebrates the cosmic mysteries as it condenses them into a familiar folk game.

Word-play also confronts serious problems when a series of punning/literal exchanges about 'lie' and 'quick' quickly pass between Hamlet and the 'lying' gravedigger:

Ham. ... Whose grave's this, sirrah?
1. Clo. Mine, sir,
    '[O], a pit of clay for to be made
    [For such a guest is meet]'
Ham. I think it thine indeed, for thou liest in't.
1. Clo. You lie out on't sir, and therefore 'tis not yours; for my part, I
    do not lie in't, yet it is mine.
Ham. Thou dost lie in't, to be in't and say it is thine. 'Tis for the
    dead, not for the quick, therefore thou liest.
1. Clo. 'Tis a quick lie, sir, 'twill away again from me to you.

(5.1.117–29)

When language and death blur boundaries, word-play gains antic mastery over the loss of distinctive meanings, distinctive possessions, distinctive identities, distinctive classes, occupations and distinctive genders:

Ham. What man dost thou dig it for?
1. Clo. For no man, sir.
Ham. What woman then?
1. Clo. For none neither.
Ham. Who is to be buried in't?
1. Clo. One that was a woman, sir, but rest her soul, she's dead.

(5.1.130–6)

The gravedigger's dead literalism refuses to restrict interpretations to fit singular intentions. He thereby exposes the vanity in our fashionings of meaning. Like the stubborn soil and the irremediable fact of death, the material humour of the clown buries differences in a gay sameness which obliterates fine distinctions. The lower realm of the grave triumphs over the privileged level of meanings and social power, uncrowning its differences. As the gravedigger makes the body the fundamental site for the unmaking of absolute and relative meanings, so his word-play overturns any absolute sense, making the materiality of sound the fundamental problem in the making of meaning.

In such a context, Hamlet himself begins to play with a skull, after having earlier noted, perhaps indignantly in performance, that the gravedigger seems to 'play at loggats' (5.1.91–2) with the bones he 'jowls' (5.1.76) to the ground. With the same grotesque freedom granted the gravedigger by his intimate knowledge of death, Hamlet holds the skull and speaks to it, domesticating death differently than he did when he taunted the midnight ghost as an 'old mole' (1.5.162). Now a daylight grave opens to belch up its bones and a gravedigger now serves as Hamlet's ludic guide to the underworld. The circularity and carnivalesque logic of the clown reiterates Hamlet's words to refresh language and meaning in a very different fashion than did the revengeful values of echoing ghost.

Hamlet's punning in this scene further encapsulates carnival's double-bodied truths by using the body of sound to assault the authority of semantics; conversely, his meditations use wit to refashion obdurate fact. Like wordplay, puns operate on a double plane. On one level, these ludic strategies work as referential communications; they also use a second level of communication, the metacommunicative level, which says, 'this is play'. Puns thus behave as words that say something and as words which also say something about how words mean. By subverting singular signification, puns comment on their own play with meaning. These condensed dramas enact little contests of dialogic speech – languages calling attention to its own complexity, history and warfare of meaning.[40] As puns multiply simultaneous references, they target words and language, turning speech into a parodic text.

Hamlet's first pun in this scene, for instance, takes up the term 'fine' to refine its meanings. Hamlet meditates on how death has overcome a man he imagines may have been in his time a great buyer of land, 'with his statutes, his recognizances, his fines, his double vouchers, his recoveries' (5.1.104–6). Considering this imaginary man's real skull, Hamlet wonders, 'is this the fine of his fines, and the recovery of his recoveries, to have his fine pate full of fine dirt?'[41] Each time Hamlet pronounces 'fine', its sense should be univocal, for each sounding is a different lexeme. But the repetition of the identical sound defeats separating different meanings. Each vocalization echoes and puns on the others. The syntagmatic linearity of language collides with the paradigmatic 'recovery' of punning cyclicality. These monotonously repeating puns depend on recursive play; it refuses to move forward at the same time that it does so. Piling up difficulties like a gravedigger's shovel, Hamlet's puns compound confusions just as final death defies all our fine vanities. As the gravediggers pile fine dirt over all distinctions of gender and refinement, the repetition of pure sound buries and yearns for distinctive semantic sense.

CONCLUSION

We learn about the meaning of beginnings and endings through playing with them in this carnivalesque form of tragedy. In historical time, performances take place at particular moments. In fictive time, at the site of meaning, *Hamlet* is never complete. The reflexive play includes us with itself, as its eternal audience, but also projects us out of the play as ourselves, located at a precise moment in history, living witnesses at the very verge of performance and responsibility. As carnival obscures the differences between performers and audience, blending us all in a comedic vision of performed culture, so *Hamlet* uses its reflexive ending to make us observers of our own observing, objects of our own subjective knowledge, inheritors of the playful knowledge of paradox. The story is over, but the play reaches beyond the fiction and language to something real, or so it seems.

Bakhtin characterizes Renaissance literary realism thus: 'The evergrowing, inexhaustible, ever-laughing principle which uncrowns and renews is combined with its opposite: the petty inert "material principle" of the class society.'[42] *Hamlet* embodies this principle. Refining Bakhtin's literary history with theories of play can explain more precisely how such material aspects of meaning are reinterpreted through laughter and how such laughter enters into a carnivalesque tragedy such as *Hamlet*.

NOTES

This essay first appeared in *Hamlet Studies* 13, nos. 1–2 (1991): pp. 25–49.

1. See Mikhail Bakhtin, *Rabelais and His World* (Cambridge, Mass: MIT. Press, 1968).
2. *Rabelais*, pp. 11, 72, 275.
3. Frederic Amory, 'The Medieval Hamlet: a lesson in the use and abuse of a myth', *Deutsche Vierteljahrschrift für Literaturwissenschaft und Geistesgeschichte* 51 (1977), pp. 357–95; Sir Israel Gollancz, ed. *The Sources of 'Hamlet' with an Essay on the Legend* (London: H. Milford, Oxford University Press, 1926); William F. Hansen, *Saxo Grammaticus and the Life of Hamlet. A Translation, History and Commentary* (Lincoln and London: University of Nebraska Press, 1983). H. Sperber, 'The Conundrums in Saxo's Hamlet Episode', PMLA 64 (1949), p. 865.
4. I do not mention Ophelia's performances of songs and other broken and parodic forms, which certainly amplify the spectrum of performed genres, because her interludes seem close to the performances of a mad Lear, of his Fool and of Poor Tom; while Antony and Cleopatra refer often to games and play, we see very few of their masquerades, and Cleopatra's play-death is, in fact, only reported to a despairing Antony.
5. See the discussions of carnival and carnivalized literature in Bakhtin's *Problems of Dostoevsky's Poetics*, ed. and trans. Caryl Emerson (Minneapolis: University of Minnesota Press, 1984).
6. Norman Rabkin, *Shakespeare and the Common Understanding* (New York: Macmillan, 1967), and *Shakespeare and the Problem of Meaning* (Chicago: University of Chicago Press, 1981). Emphasizing the complex method of the carnivalesque in Shakespearean tragedy, a form which Bakhtin mentions but does not discuss, may avoid the criticism of Linda Woodbridge about the inappropriate uses of Bakhtin's notions of carnival when discussing the festive comedies: see, '"Fire-in-your-heart-and-brimstone-in-your-liver"; Towards a Unsaturnalian *Twelfth Night*', *Southern Review*, 17.3 (1984), pp. 270–91.

7.   Johann Huizinga, *Homo Ludens: A Study of the Play Element in Human Culture* (1938; Boston: Beacon Press, 1950).

8.   See especially *Rabelais* chapters 5 and 6 on 'The Grotesque Image of the Body and its Sources' and ' Images of the Material Bodily Lower Stratum'.

9.   James Calderwood, *To Be and Not to Be: Negation and Metadrama in 'Hamlet'* (New York: Columbia University Press, 1983).

10. Leon Golden, '*Othello, Hamlet*, and Aristotelian Tragedy', *Shakespeare Quarterly* 35.2 (Summer, 1984), pp. 142–56.

11. This and all subsequent quotations are from *The Riverside Shakespeare*, ed. G. Blakemore Evans (Boston: Houghton Mifflin, 1974).

12. See A. Lynne Magnuson, ' Interruption in *The Tempest*', *Shakespeare Quarterly* 37.1 (Spring, 1986), pp. 52–65, and David J. McDonald, '*Hamlet* and the Mimesis of Absence: A Post-Structuralist Analysis', *Education Theatre Journal* 30 (1978), pp. 36–53.

13. On rupture and meaning see Erving Goffman, *Frame Analysis: An Essay on the Organization of Experience* (New York: Harper, 1974), and Roland Barthes, *The Pleasure of the Text*, trans. Richard Miller (New York: Farrar, Straus and Giroux, 1974).

14. Terence Hawkes, 'Telmah', *Shakespeare and the Question of Theory*, eds. Patricia Parker and Geoffrey Hartman (London and New York: Methuen, 1985), pp. 310–32.

15. Harry Herger, 'Bodies and Texts', *Representations* 17 (Winter, 1987), pp. 144–66, defines 'citational texts' as those performed genres which use traditional and culturally established forms, patterns, discourses, and the like, through performances involving the presence of the body and its naturalistic powers. Barbara Herrnstein Smith, *On the Margins of Discourse* (Chicago: University of Chicago Press, 1978), pp. 57–64, defines and discusses 'prefabricated discourse' as those traditional forms, such as proverbs, which we appropriate into our natural and fictive discourses.

16. Kirby Farrell, *Shakespeare's Creation: The Language of Magic and Play* (Amherst, Mass.: University of Massachusetts Press, 1977), and David Leverenz, 'The Woman in *Hamlet*: An Interpersonal view', *Signs* 4.2 (1978), pp. 291–310, both discuss the ways the fathers and father figures (Ghost, Polonius, Claudius and the King of Norway) manipulate children and women to abdicate their own subjectivity and identity to act out patriarchal prescriptions. Anne Wilson Schaef, *When Society Becomes an Addict* (San Francisco: Harper and Row, 1987), analyses our present patriarchal culture as an addictive system of denial and indirection; for me, her analysis illuminates the same tragic patterns of action between parents and children and between genders in *Hamlet*.

17. Robert R. Wilson, 'Narratives, Narrators and Narratees in *Hamlet*', *Hamlet Studies* 6.1–2 (1984), pp. 30–40.

18. The actor, Jim Beard, produced real tears in a production of *Hamlet* directed by Lindsay Anderson in March 1984 for the Shakespeare Theatre at the Folger Library.

19. Jan Kott, '*The Tempest*, or Repetition: I. Plantation on a Mythical island. II. The Three Hours of Purgatory', *Mosaic* 10.3 (1977),

pp. 9–36, and John T. Irwin, *Doubling and Incest, Repetition and Revenge: a Speculative Reading of Faulkner* (Baltimore: Johns Hopkins University Press, 1975) connect repeated stories, embedded stories and revenge.

20. F reads 'will' and Q2 reads 'well'.
21. Roger Caillois, *Man, Play, and Games*, trans. Mayer Barash (1958; New York: Schocken, 1979), pp. 14–22, 17–19, 23–6.
22. Susan U. Philips, 'Teasing, Punning; and Putting People On', *Working Papers in Sociolinguistics*, No. 28 (Austin, Texas: Southwest Educational Development Laboratory, 1975).
23. Michael McDonald, 'Ophelia's Rites', *Shakespeare Quarterly* 37.3 (1986), pp. 309–17, takes issue with Roland Mushat Frye's interpretation of the offensiveness of Ophelia's funeral in *The Renaissance Hamlet: Issues and Responses in 1600* (Princeton, NJ: Princeton University Press, 1984); see also Michael Neill, '"Exeunt with a Dead March": Funeral pageantry on the Shakespearean stage', *Pageantry in Shakespeare*, ed. David Bergeron (Athens: University of Georgia Press, 1985), pp. 153–93.
24. As in Q1 and F; Q2 reads 'the Onixe' instead of 'thy union'.
25. Bateson's 'A Theory of Play and Fantasy', *A.P.A. Psychiatric Research Reports*, 2 (1955); reprinted in *Steps to an Ecology of Mind* (New York: Ballantine, 1972), pp. 177–93; 'The Message "This is Play"', *Conferences on Group Processes*, ed. Bertram Schaffner (New York; Columbia University Press, 1955), pp. 145–51; 'Play and Paradigm', *Play: Anthropological Perspectives*, ed. Michael Salter (Westport, NY: Leisure Press), pp. 7–16; and 'The Position of Humor in Human Communication', *Motivation in Humor*, ed. Jacob Levine (New York: Atherton, 1969), pp. 159–66. A helpful overview of the studies of play and literature may be found in James A.G. Marino, 'An Annotated Bibliography of Play and Literature', *Canadian Review of Comparative Literature* 12.2 (June 1985), pp. 306–58. Other theories of play which influence this discussion do not derive from Bateson; they include Roger Caillois, n. 21, above; Clifford Geere, 'Deep Play: Notes on the Balinese Cockfight', *The Interpretation of Cultures* (New York: Harper, 1973), pp. 412–53; Victor W. Turner, *From Ritual to Theatre: The Human Seriousness of Play* (New York: Performing Arts Journal Publications, 1982) and *The Ritual Process: Structure and Anti-Structure* (Chicago: The Aldine Press, 1969).
26. 'A Theory of Play and Fantasy', pp. 179–80.
27. Q1 reads ' how trapically:'; Q2, 'how tropically', F, 'how? Tropically.'
28. Carol Neely, 'Madness, Gender, and Ritual in Shakespeare', Seminar on Elizabethan Ritual in Shakespeare, Annual Meeting of the Shakespeare Association of America, Seattle, Washington, 3 April 1987. See also Michael MacDonald, *Mystical Bedlam: Madness, Anxiety, and Healing in Seventeenth-Century England* (Cambridge: Cambridge University Press, 1981), pp. 132–7.
29. Leverenz, p. 310.
30. On gender and double binds in play and madness, see Anna K. Nardo, 'Hamlet, "a man to double business bound"', *Shakespeare*

Quarterly 34.2 (Summer, 1983), pp. 188–92, and my essays, '*Hamlet* and the Play of Knowing: an excursion into interpretative anthropology', *The Anthropology of Experience*, ed. Victor Turner and Edward M. Bruner (Urbana: University of Illinois Press, 1986), pp. 207–38, and 'Hamlet and the Tragedy of Ludic Revenge', *The World of Play*, ed. Frank Manning (Westport, NY: The Leisure Press, 1983), pp. 111–24.

31. Don Handelman and Bruce Kapferer, 'Symbolic Types and the Transformation of Ritual Context: Sinhalese Demons and Tewa Clowns', *Semiotica* 30, 1–2 (1980), pp. 41–71.

32. For a review of attitudes of and about Bakhtin, see Mary Russo, 'Female Grotesques: Carnival and Theory', *Feminist Studies: Critical Studies*, ed. Teresa de Lauretis (Bloomington: Indiana University Press, 1986), pp. 213–29.

33. Elaine Showalter, 'Representing Ophelia: Women, Madness, and the Responsibilities of Feminist Criticism', *Shakespeare and the Question of Theory*, pp. 77–94. (See note 14 above.)

34. The passage is divided between the Queen, A Gentleman, and Horatio in Q2, but in the Folio the gentleman is cut, and the Queen, rather than Horatio, decides that Ophelia should be contained by the court rulers, Steven Urkowitz, '"Well-Sayd olde Mole": Burying three *Hamlets* in modern editions', *Shakespeare Study Today*, ed. Georgianne Zeigler (New York: AMS Press, 1986), pp. 37–70, and 'Five Women Eleven Ways: Changing images of Shakespearian characters in the earliest texts', unpublished paper presented at the World Shakespeare Congress, Berlin, April 1986, pp. 4–5, discusses the consistently increased power of Gertrude in the Folio, in just these changes.

35. Also see discussions of *Hamlet* in these terms in Kirby Farrell, n. 16, above, and Michael Holstein, 'Actions that a Man Might Play: dirty tricks at Elsinore and the politics of play', *Philological Quarterly* 55 (1976), pp. 323–37.

36. Natalie Zemon Davis, *Society and History in Early Modern Europe* (Stanford: Stanford University Press, 1975); Emmanuel Le Roy Ladurie, *Carnival in Romans*, trans. Mary Feeny (New York: George Braziller, 1978); Keith Thomas, 'The Place of Laughter in Tudor and Stuart England', *The Times Literary Supplement* (January 21, 1977), pp. 77–81; Edward P. Thompson, 'Patrician Society, Plebian Culture', *Journal of Social History* 7 (Summer, 1974), pp. 382–405.

37. Stephen Greenblatt, *Renaissance Self-Fashioning: From More to Shakespeare* (Chicago: University of Chicago Press, 1980); Frank Whigham, *Ambition and Privilege: The Social Tropes of Elizabethan Courtesy Theory* (Berkeley: University of California Press, 1984); Wayne Rebhorn, *Courtly Performances: Masking and Festivity In Castiglione's 'Book of the Courtier'* (Detroit: Wayne State University Press, 1978); and Gary Schmidgall, *Shakespeare and the Courtly Aesthetic* (Berkeley: University of California Press, 1981).

38. F presents the full riddle; Q2 has the first clown answer the question 'was he a gentleman?' directly with 'A was the first that ever bore

Armes'. No further riddling exegesis is given by the first gravedigger, who then continues, 'I'll put another question to thee ...'
39.   John Roberts and Michael R. Forman, 'Riddles: Expressive models of
      interrogation', *Directions in Sociolinguistics. The Ethnography of
      Communication*, ed. John J. Gumperz and Dell Hymes (New York:
      Holt, Rinehart, and Winston, 1972), pp. 180–210; and Phyllis Gorfain
      and Jack Glazier, 'Ambiguity and Exchange: the double dimension of
      Mbeere riddling', *American Folklore* 89 (1976), pp. 189–238.
40.   Bakhtin, *The Dialogic Imagination*, ed. Michael Holquist, trans. M.
      Holquist and Caryl Emerson (Austin: University of Texas Press,
      1981).
41.   Roland Mushat Frye discusses in detail the appearances of real skulls
      on stages, in studies, and in iconographic tradition.
42.   *Rabelais*, p. 24.

9

Shakespeare, Carnival and the Sacred: *The Winter's Tale* and *Measure for Measure*

Anthony Gash

In spite of the wide-scale adoption of Mikhail Bakhtin's term 'carnival' by Anglo-American criticism, two aspects of Bakhtin's theory tend to be suppressed in the process of paraphrase. The first is his interest in the development of the language of festivity by a specific literary tradition with its roots in antiquity which he sometimes calls 'Menippean' and the second is the convergence of Christian theology with the terms in which Bakhtin describes the logic of carnival. Both these suppressions amount to a dehistoricization of Bakhtin's work, and this essay will reintroduce these issues into a discussion of Shakespeare's relationship to the 'Carnival' concept in *The Winter's Tale* and *Measure for Measure* principally. The intention is less to apply a Bakhtinian model to Shakespeare than to investigate the relation of each to a common tradition, particularly the way in which Bakhtin's syncretist enterprise resembles that of Erasmus whose writings had a vast and immediate impact on Elizabethan education, politics and religion. Informing both Erasmus and Bakhtin are St Paul and Plato.

BAKHTIN AND THE PAULINE BODY

One of the things which has changed our initial relation to Bakhtin's book on Rabelais[1] is the discovery that in the 1920s Bakhtin was associated with religious and philosophical groups who wanted to keep theological and spiritual knowledge alive in post-revolutionary Russia.[2] One of the charges on which he was arrested in 1929 was of being a member of one such group, the brotherhood of St Seraphim. We also know that the first version of the Rabelais book was written in the late 1930s at the height of the Stalinist show-trials, and that it was submitted as a dissertation to the Gorki Institute in 1940.[3] It now looks as if in describing the official medieval Church as monolithic, monoglot and dogmatic, and as ruling through fear and addicted to anathematizing dissenters, Bakhtin was equivocally indicting the Stalinist empire, its purges and the official literary doctrine of socialist realism. But by invoking a progressive and plebeian medieval counter-culture, he was able simultaneously to conform to many of the criteria which the Marxist-Leninist examiners required of their candidates – namely a condemnation of 'idealism' and religion, in the name of dialectical materialism, a championing of the people and an expression of historical optimism. In this way he let those that had ears to hear infer that he regarded the Stalinist regime as a betrayal of popular traditions rather than their fulfilment, as evidenced by the proliferation of ironies, jokes and Aesopic allegories devised by way of protest. But this does not mean that he was covertly acknowledging the medieval Catholic Church or even the pre-revolutionary Orthodox Church as the sole repositories of truth. He could genuinely have thought that the Church's gloomy persecution of heresy was a mirror of the Stalinist state. What he does not say, but liberally hints at, is that Church organization, as Humanist reformers like Erasmus had also maintained, betrayed the Christian Gospel – for example, its communist and pacifist ideals, which he alludes to by calling the alternative festive world 'utopian', and by distinguishing the isolating ideology of the official Church which provoked a constant fear of damnation, from the people's celebration of 'the collective ancestral body of the people',[4] a term which recalls Paul's teaching of the egalitarian community of believers in the body of Christ.

Just as the concept of the collective body of folk culture is, for Bakhtin, the metaphor which unites festivities, parodic literature and marketplace oaths, so, as an eminent theologian has argued: 'the body forms the cornerstone of Paul's theology. In its closely connected meanings the word Soma [Body] knits together all the great themes.'[5] Moreover, Paul's conception of the Christian's 'membership' of the body of Christ (1 Corinthians 12.27) still retained an almost shocking physicality which subsequent metaphorical uses of the terms 'body' and 'members' to describe a social organization tend to obscure. The Church is literally the resurrected body of Christ. And as Bakhtin's grotesque body of the people is opposed to the official repressive order, so Paul's body of Christ is opposed to the body or kingdom of sin, death and law, in which the individual has become a chattel to a slave-owner (e.g. Romans 5.14; 6.14; 7.14). Like the grotesque body, the body of Christ which is the invisible Church, transgresses boundaries of class, gender and nationality, and reverses hierarchies of honour and shame. The first point is expressed by Galatians 3.28: 'There is neither Jew nor Greek, there is neither bond nor free: for ye are all one in Christ Jesus', and the second in a text which has remarkable affinities with the rhetorical tradition of the paradoxical encomium, Galatians 3.28: 'And those members of the body which we think to be less honourable, upon those we bestow more abundant honour; and our uncomely parts have more abundant comeliness.' Moreover, by insisting that carnivalesque parodies 'bring down to earth' what was abstracted and 'turn their subject into flesh',[6] and by describing the 'ambivalent' logic of carnivalesque rituals in terms of 'crowning and uncrowning', 'burying and reviving',[7] Bakhtin is also describing the Christian paradoxes of incarnation, passion and resurrection. In his book on Dostoevsky's poetics, he had already remarked that the basic narrative genres of early Christian literature such as the Gospels and the Acts of the Apostles were carnivalesque. 'As in the menippea, rulers, rich men, thieves, beggars, hetaera etc. come together here on equal terms on a single fundamentally dialogized plane.' He goes on to cite 'the scene of crowning and decrowning the "King of the Jews" in the canonical gospels.'[8]

The parodies of Church rituals and idiom which he recognized in medieval popular culture are not therefore, to be read as an atheist rejection of Christian dogma, but on the contrary as a testing, renewal and regeneration of the Christian Gospel, which purifies it from its institutional accretions and returns it to the sphere of everyday existence. 'True ambivalent laughter does not deny seriousness but purifies and completes it.'[9] Of course it is paradoxical to invoke a purification through dirtying, but it is just that psychologically shrewd paradox at which Bakhtin is aiming – one which was already implied by Christ's infringements of the traditional Jewish pollution laws (e.g. Matthew 15.1–2) and by his reputation as 'a man gluttonous, and a winebibber, a friend of publicans and sinners' (Matthew 15.19). That is why Bakhtin stresses the reluctance of carnival laughter to anathematize its objects and its willingness to reincorporate and renew the offender.[10] This is a version of the gospel of forgiveness and reconciliation, contrasted with expulsions and persecutions (II Corinthians 18–19). Those critics such as Stallybrass and White who have criticized Bakhtin for his uncritical populism since festivities in practice often violently abused and demonized weaker social groups[11] have failed to see that in applying his term 'carnival' so comprehensively to biblical, literary, festive and discursive practices, Bakhtin is not offering an empirical description of particular festivals, but on the contrary, as René Girard has since done more explicitly, he is reading the Christian Gospel as laying bare and thus neutralizing the scapegoat mechanisms which are at the roots of all social collectivities.[12]

Bakhtin's subject is, in short, the philosophical and literary development of the idiom of festivity to express a religious outlook which is oriented towards another world or Utopia, the Greek word means no-place, and is consequently at odds with worldly hierarchies which it relativizes. That outlook is also, in Bakhtin's words, 'dialogic' and 'unfinalized'.[13] It does not take a God's eye view, but that of an existing incarnate subject in dialogue with other subjects. Hence it is at odds with all deterministic or teleological systems which picture individuals as the results of prior causes, or the vehicles of a biological or historical teleology. The view in short is Platonic rather than Aristotelian, and Kierkegaardian rather than Hegelian.[14] It is Kierkegaard who provides the key to Bakhtin's serio-comic literary tradition when he writes, in *Concluding Unscientific Postscript*, that humour is 'the incognito of the religious'.[15]

PLATO'S DIALOGUE OF SOULS

We cannot therefore adequately consider any particular writer's relation to festive customs – and this includes Shakespeare – without also considering his relation to writings which had already transformed the logic of feasting and Saturnalias for their own literary or philosophical purposes. For Bakhtin, for Kierkegaard and Erasmus, the first port of call is the Socratic dialogue. In Bakhtin's words: 'The Socratic discovery of the dialogic nature of thought, of truth itself, presumes a carnivalistic familiarization of relations among people who have entered the dialogue, it presumes the abolition of all distance between them.'[16] That 'discovery', and we should weigh the word, is that: 'Truth is not born nor is to be found inside the head of an individual person; it is born between people collectively searching for the truth.' Bakhtin continues: 'Socrates calls himself a "pander": he brought people together and made them collide in a quarrel, and as a result truth was born; with respect to the emerging truth Socrates called himself a midwife since he assisted at the birth.'[17] In that he opposes the dialogic birth of truth to official monologism which claims to possess the ready-made truth, Bakhtin is developing Kierkegaard's point that 'Socrates' infinite merit is to have been an existing thinker, not a speculative philosopher who forgets what it means to exist.'[18] Nor, I think, should we imagine that Bakhtin is forcing Socratic dialogue into a scheme which is alien to it. On the contrary it is remarkable to observe how many of Bakhtin's analytical categories are actually derived from Plato, thus strangely paralleling his brother's attempt, still uncompleted at his death, to base a modern linguistics on *The Cratylus*.[19] For example, Socrates repeatedly contrasts his marketplace dialogues with the rhetorical speeches of the law courts and assembly and with written discourses, presenting the latter as coercive, static, unable to change and spuriously authoritative, concealing by their syntax the gaps in thought and uncertainties which would be exposed in one-to-one dialogue. Of written speeches, Socrates says: 'they seem to talk to you as though they were intelligent, but if you ask them anything, they go on talking to you just the same forever' (*Phaedrus*: 275e). Such sentiments provide Bakhtin with his notion of dialogue, being the natural condition of language which monologic discourse may seek to conceal, but reveals in spite of itself.

Although Bakhtin's brief account of the Socratic dialogue does not single out any particular text, it is in fact in *The Symposium*, the most self-consciously literary of all the dialogues, that Plato forged the connections between dialogue, festivity and serio-comedy which Bakhtin's concept of 'carnival' presupposes. If there is a weakness in Bakhtin's account of ancient serio-comic literature, it is that he sometimes writes as if the literature represents a *reduction* of the polyphony and laughter of festivals: whereas it seems more plausible to think of works like *The Symposium* as extending the philosophical scope and complexity of official festivals by treating them as metaphors for life in relation to death, and for the upside-downness of the dominant values of the Athenian state and its rhetorical institutions. Both Diotima, the female philosopher, and Socrates, the intellectual midwife, by playing symbolically andro-gynous, anomic roles stand on the symbolic threshold between the *polis* and nature, and between life and death, facilitating the rever-sal of normal values which attends the rebirth or re-orientation of the soul – the *psuche*.

In the famous 'midwife' analogy in the *Theaetetus* Socrates explains that he is concerned 'not with the body but with the soul that is in travail of birth' (150c). It is thus impossible to separate Socratic irony and dialogue from what to Athenians must have been the startling conception of personal identity indicated by Socrates' new use of the term *psuche* (soul) which in his hands took on an ethical shape, having previously been used to describe a person's shade or ghost after death rather than his essence while alive.[20] 'Are you not ashamed,' Socrates asked the leading citizens of Athens, 'that you give attention to acquiring as much money as possible, and similarly with reputation and honour, and give no attention to truth and understanding and the perfection of your soul?' (*Apology* 29c). It was this conception of the soul that occa-sioned the unorthodox conception of dialogic education imaged by the parable of the cave in *The Republic*. 'Education', says Socrates, 'is not in reality what some people claim it to be ... what they aver is that they can put true knowledge into a soul that does not possess it' (518c). The new art (dialogue or dialectic) assumes that 'the soul possesses vision but does not properly direct it', and therefore 'turns the soul round' from merely socially acquired 'second-hand' opinions (*doxa*) to 'see' by its own light. This new dialectical educa-tion clearly subverts the hierarchy of one who knows and possesses the truth instructing one who is ignorant of it. Moreover, the insist-ence on the priority of the *psuche*, which Plato conjectures existed before birth and will survive death, over the social role or function, could have levelling consequences. In *The Meno*, for example, Socrates' questioning reveals that a slave-boy is as capable of 'recol-lecting' geometry as an educated aristocrat and, by implication, that he has the same capacity for virtue, the original topic of conversa-tion. Aristotle in *The Politics* would try to refute this revolutionary notion by reiterating the Gorgias-Meno view that there are different types of virtue fitting to different social functions: for example, silence brings credit to a woman but not to a man; and 'the amount of virtue required by a slave will not be very great but only enough to ensure that he does not neglect his work through intemperance or fecklessness.'[21] It is this line of thinking, and not Plato's poetics of the soul, which found its way into Aristotle's reflections on propriety of characterization in *The Poetics*,[22] and thereafter into the mainstream of classical and Renaissance drama with its comic slaves and silent women.

The Socratic–Platonic discovery of the dialogic principle cannot then be disentangled from an unprecedented conception of the individual soul. And indeed this may be the sub-text of Bakhtin's book on Dostoevsky, where the 'Copernican revolution' of the relations between author and character, in which the former surrenders his omniscience, sounds very like a version of Socrates' relation to his interlocutors, in which, 'ignorant himself', he goads them (the gadfly), or cajoles them (the ironist) into discovering and declaring their own truth (the midwife). Consider, for example, Bakhtin's use of the term 'soul' in the following reflection:

> Towards the psychology of his day – as it was expressed in scientific and artistic literature, and as it was practised in the law courts – Dostoyevsky had no sympathy at all. He saw in it a degrading *reification* of a person's soul, a discounting of its freedom and unfinalizability, and of that peculiar indeterminacy and indefiniteness which in Dostoyevsky constitutes the main object of representation: for in fact Dostoyevsky always presents a person *on the threshold* of a final decision, at a moment of *crisis*, at an unfinalizable – and unpredeterminable – turning point for the soul.[23]

To the psyche-dialogue conjuncture of most of the dialogues *The Symposium* added the motifs of festivity and tragi-comedy, the latter being a transgression of orthodox rhetorical and theatrical precepts. And it is this work in particular that the learned comedians of Renaissance Humanism, Erasmus and Rabelais, would cite as a precedent for their own 'festive' works – *The Praise of Folly* and *Gargantua*.[24] *The Symposium* is festive because it is set at the end of the Dionysiac festival, and because it invokes holiday departures from conventional norms, first sounding the theme of holiday reversals when the servants are invited to choose the menu themselves and treat their masters as their guests (175b). Holiday freedom is then transposed into rhetorical terms by Eryximachus'

proposal that the participants should make speeches in praise of
the god *Eros*, a paradoxical undertaking since *Eros* up to this point
had not been a god with a life and character of his own, but was
simply the word for love. It is for this reason that in making his
proposal, Eryximachus refers to the ludic genre of the paradoxical
eulogy, mentioning a book he has read which sang the praises of
salt in extravagant terms (177c). To deify love is thus in keeping
with the Bacchic holiday indecorum. The private party goes further
than the public theatrical festival of which it is the counterpart by
having a tragedian (Agathon) and a comedian (Aristophanes)
speak alongside each other, while on the stage comic and tragic
modes could not be mixed, a point which is underlined by Socrates'
failure to persuade the two dramatic poets that 'the same man
might be capable of writing a tragedy and a comedy' (223d). As
reinvented by Plato, the speeches of Aristophanes and Agathon are
already illustrations of the intrinsic ambiguity of what were conventionally seen as 'pure' genres. Aristophanes' speech is low and
grotesque in style, but allegorizes a high mystery and strikes a note
of longing, while the tragedian's speech is a brilliant parody of the
ornate style of Agathon's teacher, Gorgias of Leontini, which
though uniformly 'high', teeters on the brink of absurdity. The
principle of contradiction between form and content flouts the
rhetorical doctrine of propriety (matching style and subject). It is
memorably summarized in Alcibiades' comparison of Socrates to a
Silenus, a cheap and ugly statue which opens to reveal another
statue of a god within. Socrates resembles such a Silenus because
his physical ugliness is contradicted by his interior beauty, and
because his plain speech which appears to be about 'packasses and
blacksmiths and tanners' has the effect of lyric poetry on its hearer:
'I am smitten', says Alcibiades, 'with a kind of sacred rage and the
tears start in my eyes' (215e). In response to Socrates' doubleness,
Alcibiades' eulogy of him becomes itself ambivalent: he praises him
for his wisdom and virtue but also blames him for his 'arrogant'
refusal to be seduced by the speaker's charms (219c). This simultaneous blessing and cursing illustrate precisely that ambivalence
which Bakhtin claims for the carnival idiom, and it accompanies a
gesture of mock-crowning (the defining carnivalesque ritual): the
drunken Alcibiades takes a few of the ribbons from the garland he
has brought for Agathon, the victorious tragic poet, and places
them on the head of Socrates, the tragi-comic social misfit who will
be publicly tried and condemned, a Dostoyevskian moment (213e).

Alcibiades' drunken 'odi et amo' shows a soul divided between political and 'philosophical' values which are envisaged as opposites, so that to be highest in one realm is to be lowest in the other. 'Socrates', says Alcibiades, 'has turned my whole soul upside down and left me feeling as if I were the lowest of the low' (216a).

We might add that *The Symposium* as a whole has the form of a *Silenus* in that at its symbolic centre is Diotima's account of the lover's initiation into the 'mysteries of love' (210a). It is in keeping with the topsy-turvy logic that narrative authority is invested in a woman who instructs the exclusively male symposiasts. Socrates attributes not only his philosophy of love to her but also his dialogic method, which he claims she taught him (201e). Diotima's comparison of the progress of love to the Eleusinian mysteries reminds us of another structure which is common to many rituals – the progression from noise and revelry to *hiera*, sacred things which are revealed in silence (211c). It is Diotima's narrative, quoted by Socrates, quoted by Aristodemus, quoted by Apollodorus, which provides, for the reader, the formal, literary equivalent of the inner sanctum of the mystery cult. We then return to revelry with Alcibiades' drunken entrance. This literary nest of boxes or whispering gallery, forerunner of Apuleius' tales-within-tales and Shakespeare's plays-within-plays, is perhaps designed to remind the reader of the fact that mimetic art is always at several removes from the immaterial truth. However sparkling the rhetoric, knowledge remains as Socrates says at the outset 'a shadowy thing' (176c).

THE ERASMIAN SYNTHESIS

By far the most important intermediary between the ancient serio-comic tradition and Shakespeare, is Erasmus. His contribution in bringing about a new synthesis might be summarized as follows. (1) As a classical scholar, he rediscovered the Menippean tradition, treating even post-Christian pagan exponents of it such as Lucian and Apuleius with respect.[25] (2) He reconnected this literary tradition with anonymous oral wisdom in the huge collection of classical proverbs the *Adagia*, in which he shows, for example, in 'Scarebeus aquilam quaerit' ('the beetle searches for the eagle') how the people have criticized tyranny by supporting the dung-beetle in his battle with the eagle.[26] (3) He proposed a new Saturnalian

reading of the Gospels which brings the logic of the reversal of high
and low, riches and poverty, wisdom and folly to their centre. This
effectively constituted a new theology of 'folly' which synthesized
the Socrates of the *Phaedrus* who affirms 'the superiority of heaven-
sent madness over man-made sanity' with St Paul's numerous references to the 'foolishness' and 'madness' of Christianity. (1
Corinthians 1: 18; 1: 25; 3: 18; 4: 10; 2 Corinthians 11: 16; 11: 17;
Phaedrus 244d).[27] The fact that Erasmus, in interpreting 2
Corinthians 5: 13 as an expression of 'erotic' ecstasy, was influenced
by the Orthodox tradition of exegesis via the commentary of the
twelfth-century Archbishop of Bulgaria, Theophylact, provides
another suggestive connection with Bakhtin's tradition.[28] (4) Via the
topic of the Sileni of Alcibiades from *The Symposium*, he connected
Socrates and Christ as holy fools, and brought Socrates closer to
being the archetype of the theatrical clown: 'He had a yokel's face,
with a bovine look about it, and a snub nose always running; you
could have thought him some stupid, thick-headed clown.' 'Yet it
was not unjust that in a time when philosophers abounded, this
jester alone should have been declared by the oracle to be wise.'[29]
(5) True to the anachronistic discourse of classical serio-comedy he
used the ancient genres in modern controversies. For example,
he imitated Seneca's *Apolokyntosis*, a satire on Claudius' self-
deification, in his own *Julius Exclusus*, in which the fisherman Peter
excludes the warmongering Pope Julius II from heaven. (6) Along
with his friend Sir Thomas More, he developed the idea of Socratic
irony as a politically strategic mode of discourse. The Humanist
contention that the power of kings should always be moderated by
counsel and that the sign of a virtuous king is his willingness to be
criticized, is complemented by the idea that under tyranny, which
is the historical norm, the philosopher must adopt the mask of a
fool. Folly, having commented that kings 'dislike the truth', goes
on to say that 'the words which cost a wise man his life are surprisingly enjoyable when uttered by a clown',[30] and later quotes
Horace's advice 'to mix folly with counsel'.[31] The topic informs
More's ironical dialogue about royal counsel in *The Utopia*, which
counsels Henry VIII while arguing that it would be foolish to do so,
and is later developed by Sir Thomas Elyot in his indirect defences
of More against Henry's tyranny, *Pasquil the Plain* (1532) and *Of the
Knowledge which Maketh a Wise Man* (1533).

   It also seems likely that the structure of *The Praise of Folly* had a
considerable impact on the way in which the theme of festivity or

holiday, and the traditional opposition between carnival and Lent, would be interpreted by Rabelais in Book IV of *Gargantua and Pantagruel*, by Bruegel, and by Shakespeare, who would have known Erasmus's work in Chaloner's Edwardian translation of 1549. In spite of its appearance of being a seamless improvisation, the structure of *The Praise of Folly* is actually tripartite. Part 1 is comic, and in it Mother Folly identifies herself with nature, pagan wisdom and the attitude of the festive crowd. Part 2 is mirthless and satirical. It is the antithesis of Part 1. Its theme is the unnatural cruelty of civilized man, and the betrayal of the Christian Gospel by nominally Christian institutions and theologians. Monasticism in particular comes under attack for the externality and unnaturalness of its mortifications. 'Others will show off a voice made hoarse by incessant chanting, or the inertia brought on by living alone, or a tongue stiff with disuse under the rule of silence.' Christ, says Folly, who promised his Father's Kingdom for deeds of faith and charity would not acknowledge such ostentatious and competitive displays of abstinence.[32] Thus, in the 'Lenten' section, the scourge of satire is turned against the scourge of cruelty and self-mutilation. Part 3, however, is at once a synthesis and negation of the first two parts. Pagan pleasures and the tortures of Christendom are superceded by a truly Christian joy or ecstasy, no longer vitiated by mortality as in Part 1, nor by worldly vainglory as in Part 2. In this section there is also an explicit synthesis of Christian and pagan wisdom in the proposition that Platonists and Christians 'come very near to agreeing', in according more reality to invisible than to visible things. It is a good joke, however, that even in the Christian era, Folly can borrow Socrates' words from the *Phaedo* in her casual aside to the effect that *most people* don't believe the soul exists because it is invisible to the eye.[33] *Plus ça change.* With a glittering array of quotations from the Bible and Plato, sacred folly or madness is climactically revealed to be different from both the comforting illusions and narcotics which *claimed* the name of folly in the first part, and the pedantic claims to learning and piety which *earned* the name of folly in the second part. Folly now comes to mean the mystical experience of the supernatural, thus completing the triad of nature, anti-nature and the supernatural.

In what is effectively a Platonic ascent like that of the cave parable in *The Republic* or the ladder of love in *The Symposium*, both of which are cited, desire, purified of both its physical attachments and its mental egoism, attains the *summum bonum* ecstasy, which is literally a standing outside oneself: 'when the whole man will be outside himself, he will enjoy some ineffable share of the supreme good which draws everything into itself.' The best image we can have of heavenly bliss, says Folly, is the madness of lovers: 'For anybody who loves intensely lives not in himself but in the object of his love, and the further he can move out of himself and into his love the happier he is.' I have started to quote because the writing takes flight here, but also because the terms are very close to that of Shakespeare's recognition scenes. 'Those who are granted a foretaste of this,' writes Erasmus, 'experience something very like madness ... one moment they are excited, the next depressed, they weep and laugh and sigh by turns, in fact they are truly beside themselves. Then when they come to, they say they don't know where they've been, in the body or outside of it, asleep or awake.'[34]

There is already, then, in Erasmus' *The Praise of Folly* a tripartite, serio-comic structure hiding behind a festive mask. The idea was developed in Bruegel's famous picture of 1559 where the battle of Carnival and Lent which dominates the foreground and is also portrayed as a battle between the tavern and the Church, has been shown by Gaignebet to be an allegory about time, with the battle itself being only one stage in a sequence which can be read like a circular calendar.[35] This subtle undermining of the illusion of materiality, immediacy and disorder is effected by clues such as the fact that the branches on the top left of the picture are bare, while those at the top right are in leaf. The circle is only completed when the eye rests on a white house mid-way between tavern and Church where spring-cleaning is going on. Sitting on the window-sill in the only place in the picture from which it is possible to see the whole scene, sits a white-faced Easter fool. This figure, scarcely noticed at first may be an allegory of what Erasmus provocatively called 'the folly of the cross'.[36] He is at a vantage point from which both the claims of the flesh (Carnival) and of the falsely pious (Lent) look equally worldly. Moreover, as Peter Burke has suggested, the battle which is satirically observed, may be a commentary on the controversies over popular recreations which became increasingly virulent during the Reformation, thus making Lent into a historical rather than merely a calendrical phenomenon.[37] This reading would be supported by the fact that earlier in the same decade, Rabelais' fourth book (1552) had used the imagery of Carnival and Lent to recommend an Aristotelian 'mediocritas' which avoids the extremes of belly worship and the repression of nature. In the same book he had satirized the aggressive extremes of the Papimanes who worship the Pope, and the 'demoniacles Calvins, imposteurs de Genève',[38] implying that, while apparently opposed, both sides in the wars of religion are similar in their betrayal of what Erasmus had characterized as the gospel of peace.

How then does Shakespeare develop what I hope I may have won the right to call the Socratic-Erasmian tradition, in his own theatrical transformations of the idea of festivity? First, as is well known, he develops the paradox of the wise fool and the foolish wiseman in a variety of ways, but what is perhaps more significant is that the nature of the dramatic medium enables him to re-connect this topic with its Socratic origin by making his fools into questioners or catechizers, rather than makers of speeches. A Fool such as Feste always takes the words of his interlocutor as his point of departure, and in this way, to use the Socratic simile, becomes a midwife to the subjectivity of others, their contradictions and aspirations, without appearing to have any point of view, or even life-project or personal relationships himself. 'He must observe their mood on whom he jests,/The quality of persons and the time' (*Twelfth Night* 3.1.62–3). Starting with Feste, this Socratic conception of the language of folly, as a kind of midwifery, is later developed by other protean figures, whose multiplicity of roles is a symptom not of Machiavellianism but of selflessness, such as Edgar who plays fool to sorrow, and Paulina who plays fool to tyranny.

PAULINA'S POLITICS

Paulina is the perfect example of a Socratic 'Silenus', in that she appears in Act 2 of *The Winter's Tale* as a comic anti-body within the tragic movement, a verbal and physical transgressor of the decorous, claustrophobic world of the royal bedchamber. But when she reappears in Act 5, it is first to require absolute obedience to Apollo's oracle against the worldly advice that Leontes should remarry, and then to preside, priestess-like, over the ritualistic statue-scene which Stevie Davies has associated with the Eleusinian mysteries,[39] but is of course also associated with the Christian eucharist – 'an art/Lawful as eating' (5.3.110–11). Thus the comic and garrulous mask, like her name, at first hides and then reveals a sacred identity. Moreover, her first appearance is as a sort of comic midwife, carrying the baby from mother to father in search of godparents and cooing over its resemblance to the father. Leontes bitterly refers to her as 'Lady Margery, your midwife there' (2.3.160). In this capacity, like Erasmus' Folly Part 1, she appeals to 'thou, good goddess nature' (2.3.104). The idea of midwifery is subtly developed in her Act 5 reappearance, under the auspices of Apollo's oracle. Now, like Socrates and Diotima, she is a *spiritual* midwife, whose every word is designed to transform Leontes subjectively prior to the statue moving. This inward journey, on which she leads him, via a series of renunciations, is from a destructive madness which he previously mistook for an empirically grounded reason to a liberating madness when the soul no longer identifies with the senses: 'No settled senses of the world can match/The pleasure of that madness' (5.3.72–3). The transformation from Paulina's advocacy of nature to her advocacy of faith is very close to that of Erasmus' Mother Folly, while Leontes' progression from a destructive to a redemptive madness recalls Socrates' discussion of the sacred manias in the *Phaedrus*, two of which, that of the lover and the poet, Shakespeare refers to in *A Midsummer Night's Dream*. The third sacred madness is the prophetic, associated both with the Delphic oracle and with tragedy, when an ancestral madness besetting certain families, is cured by recourse to 'prayer and worship.' 'Thus', concludes Socrates, 'did madness secure for him that was maddened aright and possessed, deliverance from his trouble' (245a).

Paulina's comic rebellion in Act 2 helps to clarify the vexed question of the politics of festivity in Shakespeare, whether, in the current jargon, the festive mode 'contains' or 'subverts' the dominant ideology. Both descriptions seem inappropriate in this case since Paulina's behaviour is too funny and too directly aimed at persuading the king to be called anti-monarchical, while also falling outside the class of 'licensed' folly since it is unpredictable and unwelcome. As a garrulous woman who defies the ideal of wifely silence, and behaves like a warrior in championing the queen, Paulina is related to a long tradition of unruly theatrical women, acted by men, like Lysistrata, Noah's wife and Maid Marion, and to folk-customs which allowed women temporary rule, such as those of Hock-tide when women tied up their husbands. Her noisy intrusion into Leontes' silent bedchamber which she associates with trumpeting (2.3.34) and he calls 'noise' (3.3.39) recalls in particular the 'rough music' of charivaris which usually took place on Shrove Tuesday (the English Carnival) to mock offenders against the proper government of the wife by the husband, particularly cuckolds and scolds.[40] Shakespeare takes care to plant an image of 'charivari' in the audience's mind before Paulina's first appearance, when Leontes imagines a festive crowd deriding him as a cuckold:

> Thy mother plays, and I
> Play too but so disgrac'd a part, whose issue
> Will hiss me to my grave, contempt and clamour
> Will be my knell.

(1.2.187–9)

But although Paulina's 'clamour' in a sense fulfils this premonition, it does so ironically by making Paulina into a solitary reveller set against the solemn group of male courtiers, and the object of her mockery not a cuckold but a mental delusion of cuckoldry. Where the ritual of charivari identifies a scapegoat, Shakespeare's play identifies and distances the psychological mechanisms which require scapegoats, as Leontes, secretly fearing that he will be the crowd's victim, seeks to divert its rage and laughter towards a series of alternative victims, including the 'scold' or 'witch' Paulina, the impotent 'unroosted' husband, Antigonus, the 'adulteress', Hermione, and the 'bastard', Perdita. The female fool's diversion of this aggression towards herself while she attempts to lead her powerful interlocutor towards self-knowledge is therefore more adequately seen in the context of Socratic and Christian 'folly' than simply of popular tradition or the history of the crowd. And indeed Paulina brings the tragic part of the play towards its conclusion, with an ironical allusion to 'fooling':

> Now, good my liege,
> Sir, royal sir, forgive a foolish woman.
> The love I bore your queen – lo, fool again! –
> I'll speak of her no more, nor of your children …

(3.2.226–9)

The values expressed by Paulina's clowning may not be those of 'democracy' a word which for Elizabethan political theorists usually meant 'plebeian domination' (she is after all an aristocrat), but neither are they absolutist. She becomes as it were the commonwealth's, and *a fortiori* the audience's, representative at court, thus temporarily making the public theatre into something more like a parliament than an extension of monarchical pageantry:

> I'll not call you tyrant;
> But this most cruel usage of your queen
> (Not able to produce more accusation
> Than your own weak-hing'd fancy) something savours
> Of tyranny.

(2.3.116–20)

The audience laughs because she could hardly be ruder, while the apparently judicious disclaimers merely intensify the abuse. There is a continuity here with the ironical Socratic mode of Humanist dialogues with Henry VIII, as he arrogated more power to himself. The emphasis which falls on the understated word 'savours' recalls Plato's encounter with another Sicilian tyrant, Dionysus, as re-told by Thomas Elyot, in *Of the Knowledge which Maketh a Wise Man*, written in response to Henry VIII's dismissal of his chief counsellor, More. On hearing Plato's comparison between the king and a tyrant, Dionysus (to quote Elyot quoting a fictionalized Plato) 'frowned and became angry. And interrupting my words said unto me: This is a tale of old fools/that cannot be otherwise occupied. And I answered again, that these words of his/savoured of tyranny.'[41] The rationale that Paulina offers for her apparently unruly behaviour is that of counsel and, by analogy, medicine:

> Good, my liege, I come –
> And I beseech you hear me, who professes
> Myself your loyal servant, your physician,
> Your most obedient counsellor; yet that dares
> Less appear so, in comforting your evils,
> Than such as most *seem* yours ...

(3.2.53–7)

Paulina's role of 'physician' is seriously articulated here, but it becomes funny at the point when she treats the patient as if he were healthy. An actress should always get a laugh for example when she coos over the baby in the normal way of midwives and god-parents as if she has failed to notice that both her life and the baby's are in immediate danger from a homicidal tyrant:

Behold, my Lords,
Although the print be little, the whole matter
And copy of the father – eye, nose, lip,
The trick of's frown, his forehead, nay the valley,
The pretty dimples of his chin and cheek, his smiles,
The very mould and frame of hand, nail, finger.

(2.3.98–103)

In its feigned normality, or naturalness, such a passage parallels
Petruchio's 'taming of the shrew', where the clown-physician's
strategy is to ignore his patient's actual violence and treat her ironically as if she perfectly embodied the ideal of womanhood:

Say that she rail, why then I'll tell her plain
She sings as sweetly as a nightingale;
Say that she frown, I'll say she looks as clear
As morning roses newly washed with dew;

(*The Taming of the Shrew*, 2.1.170–3)

Although, on one level, the ironist's response is 'madly' inappropriate, it gains depth from the thought that it is directed to the interlocutor's deeper self rather than his or her outward behaviour, thus
implying a division between the part of the psyche which knows
the truth and the part which is trying to enslave the wise part or
shout it down. Hermione will later say to Leontes: 'You my lord,
best know/Who least will seem to do so ...' (3.2.32–3). As Paulina's
physician analogy indicates, such fooling, whether it is aimed to
cure those who are structurally low (the rebellious daughter) or
high (the tyrannical King), is premised on a harmony model of both
the psyche and the state (which are analogues of each other) rather
than on a conflict of interests model. (Leontes' best interests, those
of Hermione and of the commonwealth are the same.) In that
respect the episode conforms to the pattern which Kevin Sharpe
has argued was prevalent in Jacobean political discourse. 'In the
natural body of man,' Sharpe writes, 'health depended on a
harmony of the various humours, on a balanced constitution; and
so again as the physician of the state, it was the duty of the king to
preserve a balanced constitution (the word takes on a political
sense in our period) in the body politic.' Sharpe goes on to say that
ideas of harmony account for the way in which political upheavals

were treated 'not (as we naturally do) as rival contests of power, but rather as temporary imbalances in the body politic'.[42] By professing loyalty and obedience, but also regarding the king, who should be the commonwealth's physician, as sick, and the duty of the counsellor to heal him, Paulina is working with precisely this picture. The ideal of harmony, balance and symbiosis within the state, an ultimately Platonic conception, is not being used to legitimize power, but on the contrary to restrain the king's prerogative.

Paulina's apparent rebellion against the king is thus paradoxically an expression of obedience, because the king is, in Camillo's words 'in rebellion with himself' (1.2.355), a slave to passion, and it is only self-government which distinguishes the king from the tyrant. The distinction between good authority and arbitrary power is lost on many literary critics, who tend to identify the notion of hierarchy with that of coercion, or the ideological suppression of class-conflict. But it must be significant that in Shakespeare's play it is the mad Leontes who describes power in this way, as a sheer subordination, while for Paulina, as for her namesake St Paul, true obedience is the opposite of servility. Moreover, Antigonus and Paulina, the husband and wife counsellors, symbolize the idea of political order as a *marriage* between ruler and ruled which depends as much on love, friendship and unity, as on obedience. Leontes' accusations that Antigonus is hen-pecked and 'unroosted' (2.3.75–6), and that Paulina is a witch and a scold, who cannot rule her tongue, shows such a fear of disorder that it amounts to a proto-Hobbesian ideology of rule or be ruled. Antigonus counters wittily, ambushing a traditional image of rule to suggest that a good rider, like a good husband, and a good king, is one who knows how to work with the subordinate's energies rather than against them. 'When she will take the rein I let her run' (2.3.51), while Paulina insists that her husband can rule her, because he is an honourable man, but would forfeit that right if he commanded her to do something dishonourable (2.3.47–9). For Antigonus, therefore, the idea of rule is qualified by an appeal to nature, and for Paulina by an appeal to ethics. What is most striking is their married solidarity.

To sum up, humour and free speech, are here seen as the tests of legitimate authority, not, except by Leontes, as its enemies. The festive scene extends the idea of counsel since Lady Paulina (her rank is important) is a member of a triad of aristocratic counsellors, two of whom, Camillo and Antigonus, have already failed to persuade Leontes that he is wrong. Aristocratic counsel was often seen in neo-Platonic writings, such as Contarini's as itself providing the harmonic mean between the extremes of the monarch and the people.[43] But the triad of good counsellors in *The Winter's Tale* is symbolic rather than realistic, since a woman could not actually be a member of the Privy Council. The fact that the most effective, and funniest, counsellor is a woman, and that she will eventually become regent of Sicily, expresses a further transformation of counsel into a festive world-upside-down mode. When, as in tyrannies, the human order opposes or inverts the invisible, sacred order, then truth and goodness, both key words in Paulina's discourse, are forced into exile, and have to adopt the mask of folly before balance can be restored. Like *Hamlet* and *King Lear*, where Hamlet and Edgar respectively assume the fool's role, the *Winter's Tale* dramatizes a split between the secular and sacred order to the point where the former has become an inversion of the latter. It is at this point that apparently to turn the world upside down, as fools and festival do, is in fact to remember its forgotten shape. (Hamlet, Paulina and Prospero are, like Socrates, guardians of memory, agents of recollection.)

RITUAL STRUCTURES

Paulina's brief festive intervention in the tragic movement also anticipates the shape of the play as a whole which is schematically tripartite, and which conforms to the pattern tyranny – festivity – sacred harmony, or, translated into the terms of classical genre theory, tragedy – comedy – tragi-comedy. The extremes of formality, tyranny and terror at the Sicilian court, are symbolically corrected by their opposites of masquerade, freedom and laughter in the Bohemian country, before the third movement affirms the principle of proportion or moderation of which music is the fitting symbol.

Taken as a whole the pattern is a particularly schematic version of a tripartite structure which has often been recognized as operating more generally in Shakespearean comedy and romance, and which Northrop Frye characterized as the phase of irrational law, the phase of identity loss and the phase of discovery of identity.[44] One of the beauties of such a description is that it implies that the initial social order is wrong or unnatural, and the final discovery is not predetermined. It is worth remembering, in this context, that

Bakhtin's theory of the two independent 'worlds' of medieval culture, the official and unofficial, was an answer to Lunacharsky's account of carnival as a safety-valve, used by the ruling classes to control the lower orders.[45] Likewise the structuralist theories of ritual in the 1960s were rejections of the same kind of functionalism in anthropology which unfortunately later pervaded 'new historicist' criticism when it claimed that apparent 'subversion' was a means of 'containment'.[46] For Mary Douglas the role-and-category confusions of rituals the world over show a willingness to 'tear away even the veils imposed by the necessities of thought';[47] while for Victor Turner the breaking down of normal codes initiates a mode of 'communitas' which attempts 'to recognize an essential and generic bond without which society would be inconceivable'.[48] These formulations seem to me to be implicitly religious, but it is in Edmund Leach, himself a convinced atheist, that the anti-functionalist view is most forcibly expressed. For him the goal of ritual behaviour is the construction of an alternative sacred world to the profane one, 'where normal time has stopped, sacred time is played in reverse, death is converted into birth.'[49] To this account Leach adds the intriguing suggestion that the recurrent ritual forms of formality and masquerade, or fasting and feasting, are not self-sufficient, but mark out the symbolic exit and entrance into the sacred mode where total symbolic reversal may take place. On these structuralist readings, then, the intensely ambiguous middle rather than the disambiguating conclusion becomes the goal of ritual behaviour – a notion which can easily be transferred to theatrical experience. Just as the third part of Erasmus' *The Praise of Folly* is the madness of ecstasy, when normal categories of identity collapse, so arguably the climax of Shakespearean comedy and romance are the scenes of recognition or conversion where the audience is invited into a new sense of communion with the actor-characters on stage – rather than the often perfunctory or merely conventional return to social norms which then takes place to bring them back to earth, and out of the theatre.

Here are some examples of the discontinuity and incommensurability between the sacred 'middle' and the temporal end. In the case of *The Winter's Tale*, the ritualistic statue-scene over which Paulina presides with Leontes as her initiate is the goal of the theatrical experience, enacting a symbolic cessation of time, while the subsequent return to social order with Leontes in charge again and Paulina married off is just a comic narrative coda. It is not the

'function' of the statue scene to restore Leontes to power. Similarly
the riddling reunion of the twins in *Twelfth Night* has an emotional
intensity and rhythmic solemnity which the subsequent marriages
lack. In both these cases the 'sacred' phase reached via 'masquerade' is not fully incorporated into the conventional conclusion. The
point is made self-consciously in *A Midsummer Night's Dream* where
the dream, whatever its subliminal effects, fades rapidly from the
lovers' consciousness, and Bottom's fleeting resolve to have his
supernatural experience written down and performed before the
duke is not realized in the last act (4.1.215–19). Even in a tragedy a
similar pattern may be observed. In *King Lear*, Lear's recognition of
Cordelia (4.7) is marked out by language and rhythm as a sacred
episode – a meeting of souls – reached after a phase of chaos. And
its significance is not cancelled out, but rather contradicted, or
counterpointed, by the murder of Cordelia which follows, a contradiction which stresses the incommensurability of spiritual values
and temporal events, and not as many recent critics argue, the nonexistence of the former.

The proximity of masquerade and a sacred phase in rituals is
matched linguistically by the similarity between the words 'reversal'
and 'conversion' which share the stem 'vertere', to turn, and are key-
terms in dramatic and religious discourse respectively. Shakespeare
uses the word 'conversion' in the penultimate phase of *As You Like It*
to put a seal on just the sort of modulation from masquerade to
sacredness or from nature to the supernatural which is under discussion. Shortly after the famous wooing scene in which Rosalind
disguised as a boy announces herself to be 'in a holiday humour', a
remarkable shift of tone and mode takes place with the entrance of a
ragged stranger carrying a bloody napkin. He tells the story of the
rescue of a sleeping wild man from the clutches of a snake and a
lioness by a passer-by who turns out to be his brother. We have
momentarily left the world of dramatic comedy for that of visionary
allegorical narrative, like Spenser's. The story is an improbable fairy-
tale and is remarkably pictorial in its sensory detail. At the same
time it can be interpreted allegorically: the ragged sleeper is the soul
trapped by the body, in the wood of moral error; the snake and the
lion are the lustful and irascible passions and the rescuing brother is
redemptive love which, in renouncing revenge, frees the captive
soul. At its climax the story shifts startlingly from the third-person to
first-person narration 'in which hurtling/From miserable slumber I
awaked' (4.3.131–2). This appears to restore dramatic continuity by

identifying the narrator and the protagonist of the story as one and the same, namely a character in the main plot, Oliver, Orlando's elder brother, whom we have already met in Act 1 in a smarter costume. But the shift of pronouns adds another puzzle, never to be resolved, of how the speaker can describe a picture so vividly which includes his own sleeping body. Maybe Oliver is like one of those tasters of heavenly bliss in Erasmus who 'don't know where they've been, whether inside the body or outside of it, asleep or awake'. When asked whether he is Orlando's brother, his language, while on one level being a periphrasis for 'yes', remains paradoxical, as if the word 'conversion' were the answer to the riddle: what is both 'I' and 'not I'?

> 'Twas I, but 'tis not I. I do not shame
> To tell you what I am, since my conversion
> So sweetly tastes, being the thing I am.

> (4.3.135–7)

Oliver's narrative taken as a whole makes the point that the 'conversion' experience resists assimilation into the linear narrative of dramatic plots and tale-telling: ungrammaticality whether in the verbal system or the role system, is often a sign of the sacred.

On the basis of what I have said about tripartite structures, we might expect those plays which allude to the battle of Christmas and Lent to show the claims of both parties to be found wanting with respect to a third viewpoint associated with Plato's sacred madness or St Paul's folly of the cross. In *Twelfth Night*, where the title refers to Christmas revelling, this is indeed the case. The Christmas lord of misrule, Toby Belch, is opposed to the prim Lenten puppet Malvolio, but the pattern is only completed by the pairing of Feste and Viola who can be identified with Socratic and Christian folly respectively. Although Belch at first wins the audience's approval in his verbal combat with the Lenten figure, Malvolio, 'Dost thou think because thou art virtuous there shall be no more cakes and ale?' (2.3.114–16), the context of the combat is the waning of Toby's power in his niece's household, which may suggest the same seasonal theme as Bruegel's painting. 'After Christmas comes Lent' was proverbial. Moreover, Toby's drunken illusion of defeating time is a poor substitute for immortality: 'But I will never die,' sings Toby. 'Ah Toby there you lie,' replies Feste (2.3.106–7). His claims of festive fellowship also prove to be deceitful, since he is exploiting his friend Sir Andrew for his purse, much as Iago does to Roderigo. He ends up not laughing but angry, having been physically trounced for his material fixations like the drunken clowns in *The Tempest*. Lent, on the other hand, who claims to respect 'place, persons, time', and has impressed his mistress as being 'sad and civil' (3.4.5) is in fact only a 'time-pleaser' (2.3.148), and when time untangles the plot, he has a more limited jurisdiction than he thought. Dressed in yellow stockings and smiling, he is tricked into revealing the sexual nature which he has hitherto dissembled, and thus to yield to the power of Time by providing an example of 'midsummer madness' (3.4.56) in a scene which also affords 'more matter for a May morning' (3.4.142). The contest between Christmas and Lent, however, has only taken us towards the end of Act 3, leaving the remaining two acts to develop a serious or sacred phase. Viola initiates it by hoping that 'Tempests are kind and salt waves fresh in love' (3.4.384). The Fool, dressed as a priest, subjects Lent to a more subtle form of therapy for his spiritual pride than the Christmas team could manage (4.2), Sebastian experiences the rapture of love as a Platonic madness (4.3.1–21), and finally the rhythmic recognition scene brings with it the themes of *ek-stasis*, 'Do I stand there?' (5.1.226) and of resurrection: 'Thrice welcome, drownèd Viola!' (5.1.241).[50]

PURITANS AND CHRISTIANS: *MEASURE FOR MEASURE*

In *Twelfth Night* and *Measure for Measure*, the Lenten position in the old triad is no longer taken by the monastries and the papacy as it was for Erasmus but by some version of Puritanism. This is not I think a matter of Shakespeare propagandizing for an aristocratic order against the radical threat of middle-class nonconformism, as many critics suppose. After all, though Maria calls Malvolio 'a kind of puritan', she immediately makes it clear that this is a matter of him thinking it socially advantageous to appear to be 'godly': 'The dev'l a puritan that he is, or any thing constantly but a time-pleaser' (2.3.147–8). And Angelo who is the real thing, a legally trained and theologically literate member of the Puritan movement, is a Lord – a court Puritan. If Shakespeare's idea is really to propagandize for the aristocracy, against the jumped-up, then it is odd to exclude the titled praisers of holiday, Sir John Falstaff (in *Henry IV*), and Sir Toby Belch, the latter a lover of country sports, from the new society symbolized by the coronation and the recognitions.

The truth is that the kind of social order which the plays assume is one in which those with either a Puritan style or 'precisian' convictions are wielding considerable power, and do not see their loyalty to the aristocratic household, or the monarchical state, as in any way incompatible with their 'singularity' of bearing and their contempt for 'the lighter people' (*Twelfth Night*, 3.4.71, 5.1.339) or 'levity' (*Measure for Measure*, 5.1.222).

It is a world like that envisaged by the leading historian of English Puritanism, Patrick Collinson, when he argues against those who represent Calvinism as a revolutionary force, that 'wherever we look in the world of late Elizabethan and Jacobean magistracy we are likely to find a similar spectacle of Calvinist paternalism, on its own terms as factious and subversive as the homily on obedience.'[51] The case against both the fake Puritan Malvolio, and the 'precisian' Angelo, is made by these festive plays in almost identical terms to those in which Erasmus had attacked pre-Reformation clerics, namely that (1) they have disowned the common nature which they share with mankind, particularly their sexuality; (2) their concern with the letter rather than the spirit, their outward displays of piety, and their lack of charity, make them more like the Pharisees than Christ. (3) That as holders of office they forget the temporary nature of that power, the fact that 'power' is not a Christian word. Erasmus had said this explicitly quoting Matthew 20. 25–6, 'The princes of the gentiles hold sway over them, and those that have power exercise it over them, but it shall not be so among you.'[52] It is a Christian conception of authority as opposed to a pagan conception of power which Shakespeare is affirming by making Malvolio a 'steward', and Angelo a 'deputy', designations which traditionally imply the subservience of all magistrates to God. As reluctant deputies or substitutes they become types of 'proud man/Dressed in a little brief authority/ Most ignorant of what he's most assur'd/(His glassy essence …)' (2.3.117–20). Plato's thought that it is the tyrant who is most ignorant of his own soul ('glassy essence') becomes particularly ironical when applied to someone who is theologically erudite.

In Shakespeare, the Erasmian outlook comes, as it did in Rabelais, into conflict with Calvinism. In *Measure for Measure* two aspects of Calvinism are on trial: the theological division into the elect and the reprobate, and what has been called Calvin's 'nomocracy', his attempt to make the law of the land an instrument of moral reform, and in doing so his reliance on the Old Testament decalogue rather than the New Testament Sermon on the Mount. The way in which Angelo describes the revival of the capital law against fornication has a prophetic, apocalyptic ring to it: 'The law hath not been dead, though it hath slept ... Now 'tis awake ...' (2.2.91–94), and the programme itself is paralleled both by 'Puritan' proposals to make adultery a capital crime, and by the extreme severity of actual punishments administered to fornicators and other sexual offenders by disciplinarian Calvinist magistrates from the 1570s onwards in contrast to the 'toyish censures' traditionally imposed by Church Courts.[53] More generally, Protestant conceptions of civil administration militated against the separation of secular and sacred spheres of action which had for example allowed the knight and the monk to follow different codes of conduct. One of the casualties of the new drive towards unification was the temporal alternation of periods of festive licence with periods of formality and worship which characterized the medieval calendar. May-days and church-ales came to be seen particularly by the 'hotter sort of Protestant' as unacceptable concessions to paganism and sinful appetites, rather than as integral parts of a dialectical system which, in Victor Turner's terms, alternates the principle of 'communitas' with that of 'hierarchy'. The idea of different codes of conduct for different times and places came to be seen as hypocrisy (even when one of those places was the theatre) by men who sought to follow the Bible in the minutiae of their daily lives. If, as Turner argues, the ritual process recognizes a common bond of nature, then this must be one reason why ritualism became particularly unacceptable to men who were guided by a theology of predestination which saw salvation and damnation as causes of differences between men, albeit inscrutable ones, rather than potentials within each person. It has been argued by Louis Dumont that Calvin's attempt to unify the field of civil government and religion created the conditions of a new kind of individual who no longer accepts the alterity and provisionality of this world in relation to the soul's pilgrimage towards another, better one, but instead sees himself as an instrument of God's will in purifying this one.[54] If we are to look for this new inworldly individualism, i.e. an individualism which faces the world as a rational instrument of divine will, then surely we find it in Angelo rather than Hamlet who is the usual quarry for hunters of the 'modern' individual.

Angelo's attempts to unify the secular and sacred fields by spiritualizing society, while, like a surgeon, sealing himself off from contagion, leads paradoxically to an internal splitting of the psyche, revealed in soliloquies which alternate between self-exaltation and self-disgust. The Calvinist self-examination is however, carnivalized and dialogized by being uttered in a public theatre, 'Let no man hear me …' (2.4.10). Like Calvin himself, Angelo betrays an anxiety about boundaries, identifies sin and pollution, and regards sexual desire as evil. 'The boundaries dividing the reprobate from the elect can never be crossed,' Calvin had written in a commentary on Luke, and in a commentary on the psalms that 'sins resemble filth or uncleanness.' In the *Institutes* he maintains that 'all human desires are evil, and we charge them with sin not as they are natural but as they are disordered.'[55] All these emphases are present in Angelo's agonized reflection: 'Having waste ground enough/Shall we desire to raze the sanctuary/And pitch our evils there?' (2.2.169–71). Here sex, evil and excrement are identified in the word 'evils' as Angelo pictures himself as both a transgressor of the mentally hygienic division between virtuous women and prostitutes, and as an excremental desecrator of an altar. Unable to accept that sexual desire can be anything but evil, he sees no choice but to be either the elect self or the reprobate other, finally opting for the latter: 'Let's write "good angel" on he devil's horn' (2.4.16). Thus the sexual love which could regenerate him, and in the Platonic tradition is seen as the foundation of sacred love, is experienced as a catastrophe. The clown Elbow's verbal Saturnalia identifies the problem exactly: 'But precise villains they are, that I am sure of, and void of all profanation in the world that good Christians ought to have' (2.1.54–6).

These 'foolish' words adumbrate a Christian defence of holiday and Sunday recreations against Puritan attack. An elaboration of that defence might include Christ's defence of his disciples profanation of the Sabbath in Matthew 12, 5–7, which anticipates Elbow by revaluing the word 'profane': 'Or have ye not read in the law that on the sabbath days the priests in the temple profane the sabbath and are blameless? But I say unto you, That in this place is one greater than the temple' (Matthew 12. 5–7).

In fact no play could illustrate Bakhtin's serio-comic conception of carnival more fully than *Measure for Measure*. The festive topic of the world upside down provides a unifying motif as befits the liminal occasion of its court performance – effectively the first Christmas of a new reign, on 26 December 1604, following James I's royal entry in March, and cementing the bond between the King and the King's Men after their first full year of service.[56] The topic is used against popular 'liberty' by the Duke:

> And liberty plucks justice by the nose;
> The baby beats the nurse and quite athwart
> Goes all decorum

> (1.3.29–31)

and, tit-for-tat, against corrupt power by Pompey Bum: ''Twas never merry world since of the two usuries [copulation and money-lending], the merriest was put down, and the worser allow'd by order of law' (3.2.5–7). The logic of reversal invades both language, in Elbow's unintentional 'misplacings' such as 'benefactors' for 'malefactors', and plot, in the chain of substitutions, starting with Angelo for the duke and leading downwards inexorably through the exchange of bodies in bed to the exchange of heads in prison. This plot parodies the verbal usage which regarded both rulers and whores as stand-ins, 'pro-stare' meaning to stand for (a wife), and monarchs being 'substitutes', for God on earth, inferior magistrates their 'substitutes' and so on. The system is reduced to absurdity when to preserve justice the duke becomes a kind of pimp, while to escape justice the pimp becomes an executioner.

Even the duke's gloomy homily, 'Be absolute for death ...' is a modulation of the same motif, portraying death as a kind of jester who levels the distinctions between nobility and baseness, riches and poverty, wisdom and foolishness on which the pride of man depends:

> Merely thou art death's fool,
> For him thou labour'st by thy flight to shun,
> And yet run'st towards him still.

> (3.1.11–13)

> If thou art rich, thou'rt poor
> For like an ass, whose back with beavy ingots bows,
> Thou bear'st thy heavy riches but a journey,
> And death unloads thee.

> (3.1.25–8)

The image of a man who follows death in a circle while imagining he is fleeing him, or of the rich man behaving like a donkey by carrying Death's gold for him, are comic and pictorial: they might have come straight out of a popular chapbook. The speech is a series of pictures: like its theme, mortal folly, it gets nowhere.

Elsewhere grotesque pictures are not spoken but enacted. The hybrid images which Bakhtin recognized as typical of popular grotesque art are exemplified by the mock-execution scene where the proposed victim is a drunken wild man (mankind) held up on either side by a pimp-clown possibly in motley (sex) and an axe-wielding executioner in a black mask (Death) (4.3). Refusing the last rites offered by the disguised duke, the wild man, Barnardine, speaks as if he himself were duke and exits, 'If you have any thing to say to me, come to my ward!' (4.3.62–3), thus simultaneously undermining the authority of Church, State and playwright by refusing to be a mere cog in the comic plot. Interrupting the series of substitutions, he obliges the plot to declare its absurdity by conjuring up an unlikely pirate to provide the head that he has refused to relinquish (4.3.69–81).

Barnardine becomes the Christmas play's lord of misrule only because, as the basest of the base, he is an unexpected step below Pompey Bum who has performed the office hitherto. The latter's name, itself a hybrid of high and low, makes fun of the 'body politic', and even turns it upside down in the riotous court scene where it is difficult to tell Bum from Elbow: 'Which is the wiser here,' asks Escalus, 'Justice or Iniquity?' (2.1.172). It is Pompey, named 'Clown' in the cast list, who speaks up for nature against law (2.1.230–1), while Lucio's detraction of Angelo as 'begot between two stock-fishes' (3.2.108) and his unwelcome praise of the duke for 'eating mutton on Fridays' (3.2.181–2), a sexual innuendo, shows the idiom of meaty carnival or Christmas versus fishy Lent still thriving in the taverns and brothels.

But do all these very material preoccupations jeopardize the thesis of this essay that in Humanist serio-comedy, carnival borders on the sacred? Not if it is remembered that Bakhtin's sub-text is that carnival regenerates or purifies the Christian Gospel by subjecting it to the test of laughter. Neither allegorical versions of the play, which equate the duke with Providence nor 'new historicist' accounts which see the play as royal propaganda, are adequate,[57] since the duke is no more exempted from the test than Angelo. In Act 3 he is comically discountenanced by the clown, Pompey, and the wit, Lucio, in confrontations which suggest that he is sexually self-ignorant (3.2), while as we have seen, Barnadine in Act 4 objects to him playing at God, a false god who requires scapegoats, with the result that the Arden edition finds it necessary to transfer one of the duke's lines to the Provost on the grounds that it is too undignified to pass royal lips! It is perhaps as much a mistake to look for consistency of character in the duke as in say Erasmus' Folly, since what 'character' he has changes with the generic shifts dictated by Shakespeare's tragi-comic design. If the farcical aspect of the role comes to the fore in Acts 3 and 4, after the serious beginning, in Act 5 the duke's role shifts again to become that of ironist. If in the first act he was the duke, and in the second to fourth, played the friar, thus experiencing unaccustomed humiliations, in the last act he returns to play the duke, to test the other characters. The focus shifts from him to them in what is effectively a play within a play.

This metatheatrical conception is announced by two tiny scenes in which the duke tells Friar Peter that 'The Provost knows our purpose and our plot' (4.5.2) and Isabella reveals that Friar Lodowick (the duke) has instructed her to 'speak indirectly' in order to 'veil full purpose' while Mariana's 'part' is 'to accuse him' – Angelo (4.6.1–4). Hence one of the pleasures for the audience throughout the long scene which takes up the whole final act is to try to distinguish between speeches which have been 'scripted' by the duke in advance (the duke, the Provost), those which have been partly scripted (Isabella, Mariana) and those which are improvised by speakers who do not know that they are in a play at all (Escalus, Lucio, Angelo). In this context, the exuberance with which the duke plays an ignorant version of himself who ironically praises Angelo and accuses Isabella of lying, is delightful, and when he complicates his performance by re-entering as the friar, it is reminiscent of Feste playing both Sir Topas, the curate, and 'himself', in quick succession (*Twelfth Night*, 4.2). As if to underline the high-spiritedness of the duke as performer, the Friar Lodowick that he now plays is quite different from the former Friar Lodowick, seeming almost as mad as Sir Topas as he rants like a hell-fire preacher against his would-be judges: 'Respect to your great place! and let the devil /Be sometime honour'd for his burning throne!' (5.1.292–3). The doubling of these two very different roles of duke and friar by the same actor, the one inviting flattery, the other aggression, conveys the idea that judgements are usually distorted by prestige. Even the benevolent liberal magistrate Escalus fails the test by being unable to distinguish between appearance and reality. Provoked by the foreign friar's criticisms of Viennese morals, he turns momentarily savage in condemning the Friar to torture and imprisonment for 'slander to the state' (5.1.323), his patriotism leading him to side against the outsider with a coarse slanderer (Lucio) and a hypocritical fanatic (Angelo). This may be Shakespeare's comment on English anti-Catholic paranoia. We might say that the duke's role in the last act is compounded of God (Angelo famously likens his omniscience to 'power divine', [5.1.369]) and a self-consciously theatrical fool. The compound is by now a familiar one; it is that of the Socratic midwife who rather than judging others provokes them into revealing and judging themselves. As the duke himself has put it, according to Isabella: "'tis a physic/That's bitter to sweet end' (4.6.7–8).

The scene over which this serio-comic figure presides confirms the pattern we have been noticing by being the third of three trial scenes: a 'carnivalesque' one in which iniquity gets the better of justice and the penalty is 'to continue' (2.1.191); a 'Lenten' or wholly serious one in which Angelo upholds the letter of the Mosaic law in refusing to grant clemency to Claudio (2.2), and, finally, this tragi-comic one which, announced by trumpets (4.6.12) can be seen as a prefiguration of the Day of Judgement when all souls stand naked, divested of the 'seeming' (2.4.15) which goes with 'a furr'd gown' (3.2.7) and 'brief authority' (2.2.118). The imagery of clothing and nakedness had also been central to Plato's rewriting of the myth of Hades in the *Gorgias*. Pluto complains to Zeus that the wrong people are going to the Isles of the Blessed and to Tartarus. Zeus explains that, 'Cases are judged badly ... because those who are tried come to judgement with their clothes on, for they are still alive when judged; and therefore, many, said he, who possessed evil souls are invested with fine bodies and lineage and wealth, and when the trial takes place many witnesses come forward to testify that they have lived righteous lives.' Henceforth, he decrees, 'souls must be stripped naked' and 'the judge must be naked too scanning with his soul itself the souls of all immediately after death' (523^{c-e}).

If a single moment of sacredness can be isolated from this strange web of royal entry and day of reckoning, it is when Isabella kneels to beg forgiveness for Angelo, believing him responsible for her brother's death. Peter Brook recognized the centrality of this gesture when he instructed the actress playing Isabella to wait in silence for as long as she possibly could before going down on her knees.[58] It is a ritualistic moment comparable to that when the statue moves in *The Winter's Tale*. It is also a psychological turning point since Isabella is beset by two conflicting voices like that of a good and bad angel in a morality play, Mariana pleading for her husband's life – 'Sweet Isabel, take my part!' (5.1.430) – and the duke urging vengeance:

> Should she kneel down in mercy of the fact
> Her brother's ghost his paved bed would break
> And take her hence in horror.

> (5.1.434–436)

In this way the duke tests Isabella's capacity to make her own decision at the risk of making himself seem unsympathetically harsh. His secret wish, which we infer from the fact that he knows Claudio is alive, is that Isabella should ignore his prestigious advice because of her sisterly love for Mariana. The structure, which is exactly paralleled in Prospero's treatment of Miranda and Ferdinand in *The Tempest* is the opposite to what many critics think that they see in such scenes, ruthless power disguising itself as mercy.[59] The idea is sublime and replicates the relation between God and the human soul as a renunciation of power on God's part which leaves the soul free. On her part Isabella's plea for mercy images the internal victory of a supernatural love over natural inclination of which Angelo's self-repression was a travesty and the restraints followed by the votaries of St Clare a symbol only.

NOTES

All quotations from Plato are from *The Collected Dialogues of Plato* ed. E. Hamilton and H. Cairns, (Bollingen Series LXXI, Princeton University Press), 1961. All quotations from Shakespeare are from *The Riverside Shakespeare* (Boston, Houghton Mifflin Company), 1974.

1. Mikhail Bakhtin, *Rabelais and His World*, trans. H. Iswolsky (Cambridge, Mass.: MIT Press, 1968).
2. K. Clark and M. Holquist, *Mikhail Bakhtin* (Cambridge, Mass.: Harvard University Press, 1984), pp. 120–45.
3. *Ibid.*, pp. 322–5.

4. *Rabelais*, p. 19.
5. J.A.T. Robinson, *The Body, A Study in Pauline Theology* (London: SCM Press, 1952), p. 9.
6. *Rabelais*, pp. 20, 83.
7. *Ibid.*, pp. 21, 198.
8. Mikhail Bakhtin, *Problems of Dostoevsky's Poetics*, trans. Caryl Emerson (Minneapolis and London: University of Minnesota Press, 1984), p. 135.
9. *Rabelais*, pp. 122–3.
10. *Ibid.*, pp. 12, 28.
11. Peter Stallybrass and Allon White, *The Politics and Poetics of Transgression* (London: Methuen 1986), p. 19.
12. René Girard, *The Scapegoat*, trans. Y. Freccero (London: Athlone Press, 1986).
13. Bakhtin, *Problems of Dostoevsky's Poetics*, particularly ch. 2, pp. 47–77.
14. Bakhtin criticizes idealistic philosophy for replacing the unity of exis- tence by the unity of consciousness, by employing such concepts as 'the absolute spirit'. *Problems of Dostoyevsky's Poetics*, pp. 80–1; Kierkegaard's adversary throughout *Concluding Unscientific Postscript* is Hegelian idealism.
15. Søren Kierkegaard, *Concluding Unscientific Postscript*, trans. P.F. Swenson (Princeton, NJ: Princeton University Press, 1968), p. 386.
16. Bahktin, *Problems of Dostoevsky's Poetics*, p. 132.
17. *Ibid.*, p. 110.
18. Kierkegaard, *Concluding Unscientific Postscript*, p. 184.
19. Clark and Holquist, *Mikhail Bakhtin*, p. 20.
20. J. Burnet, 'The Socratic Doctrine of the Soul', *Proceedings of the British Academy*, 7 (1915–16), pp. 235–59.
21. Aristotle, *The Politics*, trans. T.A. Sinclair (Harmondsworth: Penguin), pp. 95–6 (260a14) and 182 (1277b16).
22. 'the portrayal should be appropriate. For example, a character may possess manly qualities, but it is not appropriate that a female char- acter should be given manliness or cleverness' (Aristotle). 'If the speaker's words are out of key with his fortunes, a Roman audience will cackle and jeer to a man' (Horace) (in *Aristotle, Horace, Longinus, Classical Literary Criticism*, trans. T.S. Dorsch [Harmondsworth: Penguin, 1965], p. 15 and p. 83).
23. Bakhtin, *Problems of Dostoevsky's Poetics*, p. 61.
24. Erasmus cites 'the figures of Silenus described by Alcibiades' to intro- duce a multiply ironical passage on illusion and reality in 'Praise of Folly', trans. Betty Radice, in *Collected Works of Erasmus*, V. 27 ed. A.H.T. Levi (Toronto, Buffalo, London: University of Toronto Press, 1986), p. 102. Rabelais begins the preface to *Gargantua*: 'Most noble boozers, and you my very esteemed and poxy friends – for to you alone are my writings dedicated – when Alcibiades, in that dialogue of Plato's entitled *The Symposium* praises his master Socrates, beyond all doubt the prince of philosophers, he compares him, amongst other things to a Silenus', going on to compare his own book to such a Silenus. François Rabelais, *The Histories of Gargantua and Pantgruel*, trans. J.M. Cohen (Harmondsworth: Penguin,1955), p. 37.

25. See the literary genealogy in the preface to 'Praise of Folly' addressed to Thomas More, *Collected Works* V.27, p. 83. More and Erasmus translated Lucian together in 1505–6. Generically, Lucian's satires mixed Socratic dialogue with Aristophanic farce. Erasmus salutes Apuleius, the middle Platonist, for his abundant style, and as a master of the Lucianic lying tale in 'De Copia Verborum,' in *Collected Works of Erasmus* V.24, ed. Craig R. Thompson (Toronto, Buffalo, London: University of Toronto Press, 1978), pp. 303 and 634.

26. Desiderius Erasmus, *The Adages of Erasmus*, trans. M.M. Phillips (Cambridge: Cambridge University Press, 1964), pp. 229–63.

27. 'The Praise of Folly', *Collected Works*, V.27, pp. 147 and 152–3 develops points which are seriously made in *The Paraphrases of the New Testament*.

28. M.A. Screech, *Ecstasy and the Praise of Folly* (London: Duckworth, 1980), pp. 140–51.

29. Erasmus, *Adages*, p. 27.

30. Erasmus, *Collected Works*, V.27, p. 110.

31. *Ibid.*, p. 142.

32. *Ibid.*, pp. 131–2.

33. *Ibid.*, p. 150.

34. *Ibid.*, p. 153.

35. Claude Gaignebet, 'Le combat de Carnaval et de Carême', *Annales. E.S.C.* (V.27 May–April, 1972), pp. 313–45.

36. Erasmus, *Collected Works*, V.13, p. 148.

37. Peter Burke, *Popular Culture in Early Modern Europe* (London: Harper and Row, 1978), p. 207.

38. Quoted in M.A. Screech, *Rabelais* (London: Duckworth, 1979), p. 371.

39. Stevie Davies, *The Idea of Woman in Renaissance Literature: The Feminine Reclaimed* (Brighton: Harvester Press, 1986), pp. 172–4.

40. See E.P. Thompson, 'Rough, Music: le charivari anglais', *Annales, E.S.C.* (Vol. 27, May–April 1972), pp. 285–312, and David Underdown, 'The Taming of the Scold', in *Order and Disorder in Early Modern England*, ed. Fletcher and Stevenson (Cambridge, 1985). Lisa Jardine draws attention to similarities between 'Lady Skimmington' and Paulina in *Still Harping on Daughters* (Brighton: Harvester Press, 1983), pp. 115–19.

41. Thomas Elyot, *Of the Knowledge which Maketh a Wise Man* (Oxford, Ohio: The Anchor Press, 1946), p. 22.

42. Kevin Sharpe, *Politics and Ideas in Early Stuart England* (London and New York: Pinter Publishers, 1989), p. 14.

43. Quentin Skinner, *The Foundations of Modern Political Thought* V.1 (Cambridge: Cambridge University Press, 1978), pp. 141–2.

44. Northrop Frye, *A Natural Perspective, The Development of Shakespearean Comedy and Romance* (New York: Columbia University Press, 1965), pp. 72–8.

45. Clark and Holquist, *Mikhail Bakhtin*, p. 313.

46. e.g. Stephen Greenblatt in *Political Shakespeare*, ed. J. Dollimore and A. Sinfield (Manchester: Manchester University Press), pp. 18–47.

47. Mary Douglas, *Purity and Danger* (London, Boston, Henley: Routledge and Kegan Paul), p. 171.

48. Victor Turner, *The Ritual Process* (Harmondsworth: Pelican, 1969), p. 83. Turner takes the term 'communitas' from Martin Buber's *I and Thou* (1922).

49. Edmund Leach, 'Two Essays Concerning the Symbolic Representation of Time', in *Rethinking Anthropology* (London: Athlone Press, 1961).

50. For a fuller discussion of *Twelfth Night* in these terms, see A. Gash, 'Shakespeare's Comedies of Shadow and Substance: Word and Image in *Henry IV* and *Twelfth Night*', *Word and Image* (V.4, Nos. 3 and 4, July–December 1988), pp. 626–62.

51. Patrick Collinson, *The Religion of Protestants: The Church in English Society* (Oxford: Clarendon Press, 1982), p. 177.

52. Erasmus, 'The Education of a Christian Prince', trans. N.M. Cheshire and M. J. Heath, in *Collected Works* V. 27, pp. 233 and 228.

53. Donald McGinn, 'The Precise Angelo', in James G. McManaway, Giles E. Dawson and Edwin E. Willoughby (eds.), *Joseph Quincy Adams Memorial Studies* (Washington, 1948), pp. 129–39; Collinson, *The Religion of Protestants*, p. 159.

54. Louis Dumont, 'A Modified View of our Origins: the Christian beginnings of modern individualism', in *The Person*, ed. M. Carrithers, S. Collins, S. Lukes (Cambridge: Cambridge University Press, 1985), pp. 113–19.

55. W.J. Bouwsma, *John Calvin* (New York, Oxford: Oxford University Press, 1988), p. 36.

56. 'Mesur for Mesur' by 'Shaxberd' is listed in the Revels Accounts as having been performed at the Whitehall banqueting hall on St Stephen's Day, 1604.

57. An example of an allegorical reading is G. Wilson Knight, *The Wheel of Fire* (London: Methuen, 1960), pp. 33–97; an example of an explicitly anti-carnivalesque Foucauldian reading is Jonathan Dollimore 'Transgression and Surveillance in *Measure for Measure*', in *Political Shakespeare*, ed. Dollimore and Sinfield, pp. 72–87.

58. Peter Brook, *The Empty Space* (London: MacGibbon and Kee, 1968), p. 89.

59. e.g. Stephen Greenblatt, 'Martial Law in the Land of Cockaigne', *Shakespearean Negotiations* (Oxford: Clarendon, 1990), pp. 129–63.

10

'Swimming on bladders': the Dialogics of Reformation in Shakespeare & Fletcher's *Henry VIII*

Gordon McMullan

Henry VIII was, as is generally known, responsible for burning down the Globe. This is the report of a young merchant called Henry Bluett, writing in early July 1613 to his friend Richard Weeks:

> On Tuesday last there was acted at the Globe a new play called *All is Triewe*, which had been acted not passing 2 or 3 times before. There came many people to see it insomuch that the house was very full, and as the play was almost ended the house was fired with shooting off a chamber which was stopped with towe which was blown up into the thatch of the house and so burned down to the ground. But the people escaped all without hurt except one man who was scalded with the fire by adventuring in to save a child which otherwise had been burnt.[1]

All is True, or *Henry VIII* as it is better known to us, was Shakespeare's penultimate stageplay and the second of his three collaborations with Fletcher; it is also that rare bird, a play for which we can give an exact date of first performance, simply because of its peculiar status as the play that destroyed the Globe. The theatre itself, of course, rose like another rare, mythical bird (to invoke one of the play's dominant images) from its own ashes; but

211

the fate of the play which caused the trouble – or at least the details
of whose production caused the trouble – has been less clear-cut,
highly popular in the nineteenth century, less so in the twentieth,
despite some successful modern productions.[2] Yet *Henry VIII* is a
play whose critical neglect has been the cause of a range of inaccu-
rate assertions both about Shakespearean history and about
Shakespearean romance; and it is in those inflammatory *details* that
the trouble resides.

This essay is in truth as much a reading of a letter as it is of a play
– not Henry Bluett's letter (though that serves as valuable contrast),
but that of the diplomat Sir Henry Wotton, perhaps best known for
his grandiose and optimistic scheme to convert the state of Venice
to the Protestant cause. He writes to Sir Edmund Bacon, prefacing
his letter with a few political observations before moving on to the
week's sensation:

> Now, to let matters of state sleep, I will entertain you at the
> present with what hath happened this week at the Bank's side.
> The King's players had a new play, called *All is True,* represent-
> ing some principal pieces of the reign of Henry VIII, which was
> set forth with many extraordinary circumstances of pomp and
> majesty, even to the matting of the stage; the Knights of the
> Order, with their Georges and garters, the Guards with their em-
> broidered coats, and the like: sufficient in truth within a while to
> make greatness very familiar, if not ridiculous. Now, King Henry
> making a masque at the Cardinal Wolsey's house, and certain
> chambers being shot off at his entry, some of the paper, or other
> stuff, wherewith one of them was stopped, did light on the
> thatch, where being thought at first but an idle smoke, and their
> eyes more attentive to the show, it kindled inwardly, and ran
> round like a train, consuming within less than an hour the whole
> house to the very grounds.
>
> This was the fatal period of that virtuous fabric; wherein yet
> nothing did perish but wood and straw, and a few forsaken
> cloaks; only one man had his breeches set on fire, that would
> perhaps have broiled him, if he had not by the benefit of a provi-
> dent wit put it out with bottle ale.[3]

Examination of this letter (especially by contrast with Bluett's),
reveals it to be both an acute and subtle reading of the play and a

central text for any attempt to construct a dialogics of Renaissance theatre.

It is (it should immediately be stated) impossible to say if Wotton's comments are an eyewitness assessment or an elaboration of a report: he does not *say* he was there, at least not for the fateful performance in question, but he *does* offer both description and opinion of the production, and he is very clear both about the order of events and the relationship of the details of staging to the outbreak of fire. He gives the title – *All is True* – that we can only assume is the original one for the play when first acted, altered to complete the sequence of history plays for publication in the First Folio and now embedded as *Henry VIII* in cultural memory. He notes the *selectivity* of the play, its episodic nature as 'representing some principal pieces' of Henry VIII's reign. And he emphasizes the material detail of the production, the play's unique status as spectacle, the 'many extraordinary circumstances of Pomp and Majesty,' 'even', as he says, 'to the matting of the stage'. But where Bluett sets out simply to describe the week's exciting events, Wotton provides a *moral* narrative, noting both the hubris of the representation and the destruction of the theatre as a result of that representation, and concluding with a carnivalesque dénouement which curiously implies that 'nothing did perish' after all. In other words, he describes not simply the accidental burning-down of a public building, but a *comoedia apocalyptica*, adapting a specifically Reformation genre to act as commentary on the play and on the theatre.

Wotton's attitude to the event of the play – both the production and the ensuing conflagration – is inescapably ambivalent, at once gleeful and unsettled. He claims he will 'let matters of state sleep' in order to report events on the Bankside, yet the scene he describes is itself quite clearly a representation of 'matters of state' – 'some principal pieces of the reign of Henry VIII … set forth with many extraordinary circumstances of pomp and majesty.' More to the point, this representation of 'matters of state', he assures us indignantly, was 'sufficient in truth within a while to make greatness very familiar, if not ridiculous'. This notorious observation has frequently been read out of context, and it remains remarkably difficult to interpret. It may imply that all political plays, no matter how serious in intent, are inevitably trivializing; it may suggest a specific satirical or allegorical intent for the play; it may simply be an acknowledgement of the necessity of mythologised distance for the maintenance of power. But two words, in the context of the play, bear closer attention: 'truth' and 'familiar'. The play *All is True* is, after all, as Lee Bliss and others have shown, obsessed with truth and the varieties of truth and testimony; here, because of the vagaries of Jacobean punctuation, it is not clear (as it would be if we could be sure that 'in truth' is a subordinate phrase) whether it is the accuracy of the play or of Wotton's report of the play that is at issue.[4] And in a play which focuses on the family – on marriage, infidelity, divorce, remarriage, childbirth and, above all, inheritance – the function of the word 'familiar' is equally unclear, signifying either simply ordinariness and comprehensibility or, more danger-ously, that it is the play's representation of the arbitrary process of royal reproduction which provokes ridicule. Either way, it is the material detail of the production which irritates Wotton, and he rel-ishes pinpointing the exact moment (the firing of the cannon to mark Henry's arrival at Wolsey's masque) at which the blaze began. He offers a fascinating account of the processes of distrac-tion and destruction which it is hard not to read politically – a fire begins which is ignored by the people as an 'idle smoke', but which turns out rapidly to burn 'the whole house to the very grounds'.

Yet in the last section of his letter Wotton stands this apocalyptic narrative on its head in a moment of carnival bathos which con-trasts noticeably with Bluett's account and which offers a new and unexpected mode of interpretation for the play. He presents an impossible paradox, a 'fatal period' in which 'nothing did perish', and the paradox is resolved by way of a carnivalesque dialectic – 'only one man had his breeches set on fire, that would perhaps have broiled him, if he had not by the benefit of a provident wit put it out with bottle ale.'[5] Suddenly, then, after his unease over the proximity of 'greatness' and 'ridicule', Wotton, even as he hints at the role of providence in this comic apocalypse, gleefully invokes the 'lower bodily principle', so christened in Mikhail Bakhtin's ground-breaking work on the writings of Rabelais.[6] The irony of Wotton's presentation of events here is that he notes and condemns the essentially subversive nature of theatre – that the nearer the players come to exact verisimilitude, the more dangerous their rep-resentations – and he embraces an event which marks a reflexive act of judgement upon them (judgement which is precisely a result of the dangerously accurate detail of their production) only to cele-brate their evasion of that judgement by way of the return of the subversive principle itself. It is the dialogical impetus of theatre – its desire to imitate, and therefore inevitably to parody, to reproduce exactly the details of the authority it aims to undermine – that brings about the destruction of the theatre; yet the narrative of the destruction of the theatre, in its insistence upon survival exemplified in the 'lower bodily principle', reproduces that dialogical impetus once again. The moral apocalypse is both complete and wholly undercut by the return of the carnival impulse that provoked that apocalypse in the first place.

It could be argued that *Henry VIII* is, in practical terms at least, the most dialogical play in the Shakespearean canon, being the collaborative product of two playwrights (Shakespeare and Fletcher) whose words reach us in the First Folio text via the efforts of two compositors, an intimate collaboration in which the playwrights exhibit interactive knowledge of a principal source (Holinshed's *Chronicles*) which was itself the product of complex collaborative construction and of a secondary source (Foxe's *Acts and Monuments*) which was subject to collaborative accretion, in one instance at the hands of Fletcher's own grandfather.[7] Yet *Henry VIII* is not, by and large, the first play critics turn to when they want to demonstrate the relationship between Bakhtinian dialogic and Shakespearean drama. This is in part due to the play's own ostensible rejection of the 'popular' – the Prologue states immediately that anyone who has 'come to hear a merry bawdy play,/A noise of targets, or to see a fellow/In a long motley coat guarded with yellow,/Will be deceiv'd'[8] – but in part also due to a critical tendency to provide oversimplified Bakhtinian analyses which gloss over the distinctions between the specifics of carnival as an embodiment of the dialogic and the at least double definition of the dialogic noted by Ken Hirschkop as 'both the natural state of being of language as such and a valorized category of certain discourses'.[9]

Critics have been unsurprisingly inclined either to focus on the overtly carnivalesque elements within certain plays in order to set up a dialectic between authority and subversion and celebrate the latter or else to posit drama as an intrinsically carnivalesque form, despite Bakhtin's habit of emphasizing the 'novel' (idiosyncratically defined) rather than the stageplay as the key dialogic genre. For Graham Pechey,

> carnival covers the whole nexus linking discourse with spectacle and with gesture and with the signifying possibilities of bodies in

space; carnival is (in short) the theatre of history: broadly popular in its content, if exceptional in its occasions.[10]

This is a noticeably dramatic definition: carnival as 'the theatre of history,' the performative expression of the dialogical nature of communication, yet this cannot imply that theatre, even Renaissance theatre, is *uniformly* carnivalesque. There is an distinct space between, say, Racine and Rowley on the spectrum from monologic to dialogic, the notional polarities of discourse in Bakhtin's writings. And since carnival is defined in its relation to the official (and vice versa), the same King's company play by Shakespeare, for instance, will have a different status *vis-à-vis* the carnivalesque if it is performed at court or at the Globe. Since vast swathes of a text's polyphony may remain unheard or unattended to (or be produced or created afresh) by each of its audiences, the performative function of drama must be determined in relation to the audience, who respond immediately, without the reflection-time available to the reader of written texts. Moreover, if Sir Henry Wotton is to be believed, carnival is in no way contained within the walls of the theatre; in his narrative, the carnivalesque is released, in the Bakhtinian tradition of 'no footlights', at the precise moment of the theatre's destruction.

To observe of *Henry VIII* both that it offers grotesque characterization and carnivalesque expression and that its structural principle is a dialogue between the official and the unofficial, between state spectacle and popular unease, would in many ways be to oversimplify the play's conscious engagement with the state of the Reformation in 1612–13 and thus the vast question of the constitution of subjectivity in Jacobean England. The Reformation is an undeniable watershed in the affairs of the subject, social, cultural, sexual and political, and here is a play (the penultimate play, and the last history play, in the Shakespeare canon) which broaches (however equivocally) the origins of that Reformation. It plays with epochs, simultaneously differentiating between and identifying the Henrician and Jacobean periods, in order to outline a complex underlying politics of optimism and regret, of patriotism and irony. Its version of regret, though, offers little opportunity for the kind of nostalgia associated with the myth of the Bakhtinian Renaissance (which is, after all, a facilitating postulation, not a documented history), little sense of some earlier time in which social life was coherent, political life open, sexual life untrammelled. Life before the Henrician schism, according to this play, was subject to all the modern inconveniences – uncertainty, surveillance, silencing, betrayal, divorce, execution. And life in 1613, far from redeeming that time, is presumed (quietly, unfussily, for how else would the audience recognize them?) to exhibit all of these features, thereby questioning profoundly the assumptions of stability and clarity at the core of state ideology under James. The very interpenetration of stage-play and political event explicated in detail in R.A. Foakes's Arden edition – the close though complex relationship between the language and form of the play and the events and texts of the death of Prince Henry and the marriage of Princess Elizabeth in late 1612 and early 1613 – makes inescapable the deliberate equation of the reigns of Henry and James. And it is this interpenetration, I would argue, that makes a dialogic analysis of this play so productive.

Dialogism is perhaps most succinctly defined in Bakhtin's notes as the process of 'bringing distant things closer without indicating the intermediate links' (Pechey, p. 39), of breaking down borders by placing ostensibly discrete concepts or time-periods into productive exchange. This definition is crucial both chronologically and politically for a reading of *Henry VIII*, a play which compresses time, asking its audience to imagine they 'see/The very persons' of this 'noble story/As they were living' (Prologue, 25–7) and which is described huffily by Wotton as making 'greatness very familiar, if not ridiculous'. 'Bringing distant things closer' could be said to be the guiding principle of this play, both to familiarize and to defamiliarize, aligning in order to unsettle, giving the play its peculiar quality as a complex commentary on Reformation England. This is, of course, achieved in part by way of the social irruption of the particular embodiment of the dialogical principle that is known as carnival, but there is also evidence of a more sustained and subtle dialogue between playwright and audience throughout the play, creating a productive ambivalence in each scene by latching onto certain habitually submerged possibilities within words which might otherwise go unheard. And I would argue that in *Henry VIII* we see the conscious deployment of the dialogical principle by both playwrights across the range of its manifestations, from the quiet, uneasy provocation of the dialogue inherent within the individual word all the way to the blatant juxtapositional workings of the overt carnivalesque. The result is a play which appears much more engaged, much more complex, much more political, than has generally been acknowledged.

There is a curious crux in Wolsey's farewell to political life speech in 3.2 which neatly demonstrates both the interaction of playwright and audience and the operations of the dialogic within the palimpsest of the single word. The character of Wolsey is curiously drawn. In many ways, he is the embodiment of the carnival grotesque: he invokes the physical language of carnival ('no man's pie', we gather, 'is freed/From his ambitious finger', 1.1.52–3); he is overweight and plebeian (a 'butcher's cur', a 'keech' who 'can with his very bulk/Take up the rays o'th' beneficial sun,/And keep it from the earth', 1.1.120, 55–7); and he embodies social inversion ('A beggar's book', complains Buckingham, 'Outworths a noble's blood', 1.1.122–3). His origins mean that he is no Falstaff: neither gentleman nor buffoon, he is in many ways the personification of intolerant authority. At the same time, as the 'beggar's book' makes clear, he can also claim the status of underdog, enraging the arrogant aristocrats simply by being of what they would call 'low' or 'no' birth. For them, 'being not propp'd by ancestry', Wolsey is 'spider-like' (1.1.59, 62), less than human because lacking either rank or respect. This might well evoke in the audience a degree of sympathy, yet we know the cardinal is violent, cruel and arbitrary, orchestrating Buckingham's betrayal and effectively acknowledging Campeius's allegation that he was responsible for the death of Gardiner's predecessor as King's Secretary.

By the time of Wolsey's downfall, in other words, we have seen him in a bewildering variety of guises, and it is not clear how we are expected to respond to his farewell speech. Do we empathize? Or mock? Are we, like the earls, pleased to see him destroyed? Or are we happy that he at least appears to claim the grace of repentance? This ambivalence is exemplified in the phrase I incorporated in the title of this paper. 'I have ventur'd', he says, 'Like little wanton boys that swim on bladders,/This many summers in a sea of glory,/But far beyond my depth' (3.2.358–61). On the face of it, this is an acknowledgement that he was not suited, or born, to the power he achieved; and there is something touching about the analogy, a kind of childhood summer innocence destined for tragedy. Yet close inspection of the adaptation of source-material for this scene suggests a second current of thought behind the apparently sympathetic analogy. Act 3.2 is the only scene in the play in which it is quite clear that both playwrights have a hand; Fletcher takes over roughly half-way through, depending at times very closely on the same idiosyncratically selected sections of

Holinshed as his senior collaborator, but characteristically also turning to the most up-to-date of chronicle histories, Speed's *Theatre of the Empire of Great Britain*.[11] And a glance at Speed's account of Wolsey's demise casts an entirely new light on the use of the word 'bladder': far from a touching analogy, the lines Wolsey is given become a tasteless joke on his corpulence and on the manner of his death. 'Formerly,' recounts Speed, 'wee haue spoken of the rising of this man, who now being swolne so bigge by the blasts of promotion, as the bladder not able to conteine more greatnesse, suddenly burst, and vented foorthe the winde of all former fauours ... whose death himselfe had hastened by taking an ouermuch quantity of a confection to breake winde from off his stomacke.'[12] We may well recall Holinshed's introduction of the cardinal as 'a proud popeling; as led with the like spirit of swelling ambition, wherwith the rable of popes haue beene bladder like puffed and blowne vp'; and we realize that, for any in the audience acquainted with these sources, and particularly with Speed, a fashionable history published only eighteen months earlier, the word 'bladder' would simultaneously evoke not only the apparent child-like innocence of the analogy but at the same time the harshest of carnival humour.[13]

This kind of *double entendre* is central to the playwrights' strategy, a conscious dialogizing sustained by both writers throughout the play which quite deliberately sets out to unsettle the audience, making truth and certainty impossible. The effect is to locate the English Reformation within a dialogic framework which insists upon incompletion and which blurs presumed boundaries, between individuals, between events. We see this process enacted upon the language of Reformation – conscience, conversion, faith, Reformation itself: each of these words is detached from its ostensibly higher meaning and degraded to the level of the material. At 1.3, for instance, Sands, Lovell, and the Lord Chamberlain light-heartedly discuss the king's proclamation intended to wean those young courtiers who accompanied him to France away from the French habits they brought home with them. Lovell explains that the proclamation is for 'The *reformation* of our travell'd gallants', forcing them into '*renouncing* clean/The faith they have in tennis and tall stockings', and Sands is convinced that 'there's no *converting* of 'em' (1.3.19, 29–30, 43). Thus Reformation is equated with passing fashion, and a model of history is implied which is a far cry from the linear hopes of reformers. Suddenly, Reformation

ceases to be the goal of history, becoming instead at best a temporary reorientation awaiting a further turn of the wheel.

It is the *conscience* which bears the full weight of this process of
dialogic degradation, the bedrock of individual spirituality thoroughly ironized. We first hear of Henry's conscience a few scenes
after he has met Anne Bullen at the masque. Henry has been sitting,
'reading pensively' (2.2.62SD), and he bursts into rage at the intrusion of Norfolk and Suffolk, a rage only abated (to the indignation of
the dukes) by the arrival of Wolsey, whom the king, broaching the
subject of his marriage, calls 'The quiet of my wounded conscience'
(2.2.74). And he returns to this theme in conversation with Wolsey
at the close of the scene, by which point the sexual and spiritual
aspects of his internal struggle over the question of the marriage
seem to have become somewhat blurred. 'O my lord', he sighs,
'Would it not grieve an able man to leave/So sweet a bedfellow?
But conscience, conscience; O 'tis a tender place, and I must leave
her' (2.2.140–3). As Judith Anderson has noted, 'conscience' here has
begun to take on a decidedly physical form: in the context of the
word 'bedfellow' and the potency implications of 'able', the 'tender
place' appears more genital than spiritual (Anderson, p. 130). And if
we needed confirmation of this, the scene instantly changes to the
dialogue between Anne Bullen and the Old Lady, in which a clear
dialectic is developed between Anne's ostensible purity and the Old
Lady's courtly pragmatism. 'By my troth and maidenhead', claims
Anne, 'I would not be a queen' (2.3.23–4), and the Old Lady's
response underlines the equation of conscience and vagina:

> Beshrew me, I would,
> And venture maidenhead for't, and so would you,
> For all this spice of your hypocrisy:
> You that have so fair parts of woman on you,
> Have too a woman's heart, which ever yet
> Affected eminence, wealth, sovereignty;
> Which, to say sooth, are blessings; and which gifts
> (Saving your mincing) the capacity
> Of your soft cheveril conscience would receive,
> If you might please to stretch it.

> (2.3.24–33)

We are left in little doubt about the nature of motivation at the
Henrician court, as conscience is represented here as grotesquely

material ('cheveril' is a soft, malleable leather: 'kid-gloves'), and the Reformation finds its true roots in a sexual transaction.

It is clear, too, that those observing royal spectacle, those inter-pellated by official ceremony, are just as frankly aware of these motivations as those in power. As the two Gentlemen provide their commentary on Anne's coronation procession, we hear the Second Gentleman in particular respond both spontaneously and know-ingly to the queen's undoubted sexual charisma: 'Heaven bless thee!' he cries out as he sees Anne,

> Thou hast the sweetest face I ever look'd on.
> Sir, as I have a soul, she is an angel;
> Our king has all the Indies in his arms,
> And more, and richer, when he strains that lady,

and he adds, crucially: 'I cannot blame his conscience' (4.1.42–7). This, of course, opens up the whole question of the transition from Katherine to Anne (and, by implication, the continuing list of Henry's wives), an issue broached as the Third Gentleman appears, 'stifled' (4.1.58), from the packed Abbey, to draw a carnivalesque picture of the general response to Anne's beauty (a passage, inci-dentally, apparently without direct source, inserted into a scene otherwise very closely dependent upon the wording in Holinshed):

> Hats, cloaks
> (Doublets, I think) flew up, and had their faces
> Been loose, this day they had been lost. Such joy
> I never saw before. Great-bellied women,
> That had not half a week to go, like rams
> In the old time of war, would shake the press
> And make 'em reel before 'em. No man living
> Could say 'This is my wife' there, all were woven
> So strangely in one piece.

> (4.1.73–81)

This procreative festivity, with its curious blend of violence and fecundity, embodies the hopes of Henry and his people for a male heir through Anne, but it is the Gentleman's last sentence which arguably offers the most radical reading of English Reformation history in the course of the play, a reading which is both the logical corollary of the degradation of 'conscience' and a crushing repudiation of the assumption that the individual subject was the product of Reformation. In the moment of Anne's coronation – the first of the series of remarriages, opening the floodgates to a futile quest for a healthy heir – wives become indistinguishable, 'all ... woven/So strangely in one piece', and this is seen to be especially true of royal wives.

Rather than differentiating between them, the play seems perversely and deliberately to blur the differences between Katherine and Anne, and thus to make the transition from Roman Catholicism to Protestantism, as both symbolized in and provoked by Henry's divorce and remarriage, a much more problematic and unresolved process than might at first appear. On the one hand, we see Katherine as the embodiment of the old, Roman Catholic England and Anne as the embodiment of the new, Reformation England. On the other hand, we see Katherine as the embodiment of a certain stability which is in many ways comfortable, comprehensible, and credible, and we see Anne as the embodiment of divorce and schism, uncertainty and unpredictability. Moreover, where Anne is portrayed as a Bathsheba figure (though one for whom a wife rather than a husband must be destroyed), Katherine is depicted as a strong, dignified, faithful woman. At the same time, remarkably, source-study again reveals that the climactic death-bed vision which effectively apotheosizes Katherine is in fact an amalgam of dreams dreamed by *Protestant* women; by, of all people, Anne Boleyn herself – whom Wolsey describes as a 'spleeny Lutheran' (3.2.99) – and by her ostensible mentor in the Lutheran faith, Margaret of Angoulême, one of whose books was well-known to have been translated by none other than the young Elizabeth I.[14]

As the play proceeds, the queens seem to lose their distinct symbolic significance, and as all become 'woven/So strangely in one piece', we begin to see the essential futility of the Henrician Reformation. The sequence of Henry's wives foreshadows the sequence of post- and counter-Reformation reigns, the apparently cyclical movement from Henry to Edward to Mary to Elizabeth – and now, under James, from the viewpoint of 1613, to what? The restless displacement of queens, each change both conclusive and inconclusive, embodies the long-term process of Reformation: England moves from reign to reign in the hope of a religious resolution just as Henry moves from queen to queen in the hope of a son and heir. The play ignores Edward VI, presumably because it would not have been appropriate, in the immediate wake of the death of Prince Henry, to focus (as had Rowley in *When You See Me You Know Me*) on a prince who died young, but at least survived long enough to be king. Instead, it leapfrogs directly to the birth of Elizabeth, notably failing to offer that much-desired son (a failure reported by, of all people, the bawd-like Old Lady), presenting Elizabeth – even in Cranmer's prophetic recuperation – as a splendid but nevertheless equivocal (because female) resolution.

As the play draws to a close, the brief but potent carnival scene at 5.3 serves both to question the ostensible calm and control of the final, prophetic scene and to underline the actual confusion and uncertainty behind the ceremonial. The blurring of distinctions, the difficulty of controlling popular energy, the contradictory effects of celebration, and the mockery of the transience of fashion all act to tie this scene closely to the rest of the play, demonstrating the short-sightedness in the theatrical tradition of cutting this scene in production for the sake of 'pace' and 'coherence'.[15] As with the description of the coronation, the ostensible logic of the chaos is celebration of a royal event, in this case the christening of Elizabeth, but right from the start the topography of order is confused: 'do you take the court for Parish-Garden?' (5.3.1–2) demands the Porter of the crowd. And motivations become uncertain as the Porter asks a double question: 'you must be seeing christenings? Do you look for ale and cakes here?' (5.3.9–10). The crowd that besieges the court bears the familiar characteristics of carnival: the quest for 'ale and cakes'; the phallic humour in the reference to the 'strange Indian with the great tool' (5.3.33) and in the sad few remaining inches of the Porter's Man's once-proud four-foot cudgel; the personification of consumption as an anonymous voice in the crowd claims to 'belong to th' larder' (5.3.4); the grotesque figures of the red-faced man and the haberdasher's wife in the Porter's Man's narrative. The intransigence of this crowd and the violence required to contain them vividly demonstrate the ease with which carnival can turn to unrest and violence: the Porter's Man points out that the only way to move the crowd would be to 'sweep 'em from the door with cannons,' adding that they 'may as well push against Paul's as stir 'em' (5.3.12, 15). Celebration has become siege, and the Porter's Man provides a graphic account of the manoeuvrings of the opposing forces in a carnivalesque battlefield:

> that fire-drake did I hit three times on the head, and three times was his nose discharg'd against me; he stands there like a mortar-

piece to blow us. There was a haberdasher's wife of small wit near him, that rail'd upon me till her pink'd porringer fell off her head, for kindling such a combustion in the state. I miss'd the meteor once, and hit that woman, who cried out 'Clubs,' when I might see from far some forty truncheoners draw to her succour, which were the hope o'th' Strand where she was quarter'd; they fell on, I made good my place; at length they came to th' broom-staff to me, I defied 'em still, when suddenly a file of boys behind 'em, loose shot, deliver'd such a shower of pebbles, that I was fain to draw mine honour in and let 'em win the work.

(5.3.42–57)

This comically violent scene is perfectly believable as Henrician festivity; yet its details ensure it also expresses the audience's London, the London of 1613. For one thing, the Porter and his Man are anachronistically aware of the place of the Jacobean stage on the boundary between civic order and chaos, most apparent in the confusion of court and Parish-garden, but also in the Porter's identification of the 'file of boys' with slings with the riotous 'youths that thunder at a playhouse, and fight for bitten apples' (5.3.59–60). And a number of details of dress – linked to the earlier equation of Reformation and the cycle of changing fashion – locate the scene firmly (and humorously) in 1613, most notably the 'pink'd porringer' lost by the haberdasher's wife (a particu-larly self-conscious example of the latest Jacobean fashion, appro-priate enough for the wife of a hatter) and the person 'i' th' chamblet' addressed by the Porter at the end of the scene (cham-blet is, again, a material freshly in fashion in 1613, and, as a partic-ularly costly cloth, a hint either that the crowd is made up of people from a broad social spectrum or else that the siege has come unexpectedly out of a gathering of people in their Sunday best).[16] Either way, of course, the point is simultaneously to equate and to distinguish between Henrician and Jacobean London. In the crowd's response, the official equation of James's daughter Elizabeth with Henry's daughter Elizabeth is given popular validation by a mob for all seasons. This is an example of the containment process of which commentators on the festive are particularly wary; at the same time, the effect is both to equate the uncertainties of Henrician England with those of Jacobean England and to imply that, now as then, the Reformation has yet to take place.

Perhaps the condition of Reformation, in the end, is its ongoing-ness; perhaps it is better represented in the travelling than in the arriving. The Reformation of this play is inescapably a material Reformation and a transient event. Theological and ecclesiological debate is drawn into the material realm, subject to the lower bodily principle, as conscience becomes vagina, the Lutheran faith spleen, and sacrament riot. This Reformation reflects Bakhtin's grotesque body, in which (in the words of one recent commentator)

> becoming rather than completion is evident, a body whose open-ness to the world and the future is emphatically symbolised by the consuming maws, pregnant stomachs, evident phalluses and gargantuan evacuations that make it up.[17]

The Reformation in *Henry VIII* is an incomplete and ongoing process best expressed not in official ritual and pronouncement but in the corpulence of Wolsey, the lust of Henry, the pregnancy of Anne, the birth of Elizabeth and the sexual energy of the crowds ('Bless me, what a fry of fornication is at the door!' exclaims the Porter, 'On my Christian conscience this one christening will beget a thousand', 5.3.34–6), yet it is also expressed in the anxieties of pregnancy, the cruelties of divorce, and the violence of crowd control.

If carnival is 'the theatre of history', connecting discourse and spectacle, juxtaposing epochs and dialogizing ideologies, then *Henry VIII* is in many ways the most truly carnivalesque play in the Shakespearean canon. To focus solely on fools and buffoons – as the bulk of 'Bakhtinian' analyses of Shakespeare tend to do – is to diminish the potential of dialogic criticism. To perform a dialogical reading of *Henry VIII* – in its very dismissal of 'fool and fight' – is to deploy Bakhtin's insights in a way which necessarily goes beyond the inappropriately limited 'carnivalesque' readings that have been undertaken for, say, *1 Henry IV,* and to argue that the value of Bakhtin's writings for the interpretation of early modern texts in general is greater than might be implied by his rather schematic overview of the 'Renaissance' as an epoch. Reading *Henry VIII* in light of Bakhtin's analysis of the nature of communication, we find a play which offers a far more complex vision than either criticism or performance has yet been able to suggest both of the relation-ship of politics and drama and of the state of the Reformation in James I's England.

NOTES

1. Letter of Henry Bluett to Richard Weeks, 4 July 1613, in Maija Jansson Cole, 'A New Account of the Burning of the Globe', *Shakespeare Quarterly* 32 (1981), p. 352. I am grateful to David Richards, my first-year tutor at Birmingham in 1981, for sparking an early fascination with Bakhtin's writings.

2. Successful recent productions of the play include Howard Davis's Brechtian RSC production in 1983, Ian Judge's ceremonial staging for the 1991 Chichester Festival, and Greg Doran's powerful production at the Swan, Stratford, in 1996.

3. See Logan Pearsall Smith, *The Life and Letters of Sir Henry Wotton*, 2 vols (Oxford: Clarendon Press, 1907), II, pp. 32–3.

4. Lee Bliss, 'The Wheel of Fortune and the Maiden Phoenix of Shakespeare's *King Henry the Eighth*', *ELH* 42 (1975), pp. 1–25; Judith H. Anderson, *Biographical Truth: The Representation of Historical Persons in Tudor–Stuart Writing* (New Haven and London: Yale University Press, 1984); Gordon McMullan, 'Shakespeare and the End of History', *Essays and Studies* 48 (1995), pp. 16–37.

5. The burning of a 'wooden O' is, at least in one Jacobean signification, the destruction of a kind of 'nothing'.

6. Mikhail Bakhtin, *Rabelais and his World*, trans. Hélène Iswolsky (Bloomington: Indiana University Press, 1984).

7. On Holinshed, see Annabel Patterson, *Reading Holinshed's 'Chronicle'* (Chicago: University of Chicago Press, 1994); on Foxe and Richard Fletcher senior, see Gordon McMullan, *The Politics of Unease in the Plays of John Fletcher* (Amherst: University of Massachusetts Press, 1994), ch. 1.

8. William Shakespeare [and John Fletcher], *King Henry VIII*, ed. R.A. Foakes (London: Methuen, 1957), Prologue ll.14–17. All subsequent quotations will refer to this edition.

9. Ken Hirschkop, 'A Response to the Forum on Mikhail Bakhtin', in Gary Saul Morson (ed.), *Bakhtin: Essays and Dialogues on His Work* (Chicago: University of Chicago Press, 1986), p. 75 [first published in *Critical Inquiry* 11 (June, 1985)]. On the concept of the dialogic, see especially Bakhtin, *The Dialogic Imagination: Four Essays*, ed. Michael Holquist, trans. Caryl Emerson and Michael Holquist (Austin: University of Texas Press, 1981); see also Michael Gardiner, *The Dialogics of Critique: M.M. Bakhtin and the Theory of Ideology* (London: Routledge, 1992); and Tzvetan Todorov, *Mikhail Bakhtin: The Dialogical Principle*, trans. Wlad Godzich (Minneapolis: University of Minnesota Press, 1984).

10. Graham Pechey, 'On the Borders of Bakhtin: Dialogisation, Decolonisation', 51, in Ken Hirschkop and David Shepherd (eds), *Bakhtin and Cultural Theory* (Manchester: Manchester University Press, 1989), pp. 39–67. All subsequent references will be given parenthetically in the text.

11. For authorship attribution, see Cyrus Hoy, 'The Shares of Fletcher and his Collaborators in the Beaumont and Fletcher Canon (I–VII)',

Studies in Bibliography 8–15 (1956–62); for a more linguistically sophisticated intervention, see Jonathan Hope, *The Authorship of Shakespeare's Plays: A Socio-linguistic Study* (Cambridge: Cambridge University Press, 1994). Scene-by-scene attribution can, though, never be more than tentative. For a view which is to some extent at odds with my assumptions in this essay, see Gordon McMullan, '"Our Whole Life is Like a Play": Collaboration and the Problem of Editing', *Textus* 9 (1996), pp. 437–60; which in turn draws from *inter alia* Jeffrey Masten, 'Beaumont and/or Fletcher: Collaboration and the Interpretation of Renaissance Drama', *English Literary History* 59 (1992), pp. 337–56.

12. John Speed, *The Theatre of the Empire of Great Britain* (London, 1611), 2.769.

13. Raphael Holinshed, *The Third volume of Chronicles, beginning at duke William the Norman* (London, 1587), 837b.

14. E.E. Duncan-Jones, in 'Queen Katherine's Vision and Queen Margaret's Dream', *N & Q* 8 (1961), cites Charles de Sainte Marthe, *Oraison funèbre de la mort de l'incomparable Marguerite Royne de Navarre et duchesse d'Alençon* (Paris, 1550), p. 105. In 1545, the young Elizabeth translated an early work of Margaret's, 'Le Miroir de l'âme pécheresse', as a New Year present for her Protestant stepmother, Queen Katherine Parr. John Margeson suggests that the description of the vision may also have been influenced by Holinshed's report of a dream of Anne Boleyn shortly before her death (Holinshed, 940b); see Margeson (ed.), *King Henry VIII*, The New Cambridge Shakespeare (Cambridge: Cambridge University Press, 1990), p. 19.

15. The classic case is Kean's heavily cut version of the play. See Charles Kean, *Shakespeare's Historical Play of King Henry the Eighth; Arranged for Representation at the Princess's Theatre* (London, 1855).

16. Marie Channing Linthicum, *Costume in the Drama of Shakespeare and His Contemporaries* (Oxford: Oxford University Press, 1936), pp. 218–19.

17. Simon Dentith, *Bakhtinian Thought* (London: Routledge, 1995), p. 68.

Index